Shemsu Heru Mentchu-Hotep
— and the —
Spirit of the
Medjay

Mfundishi Jhutyms Ka en Heru
Hassan Kamau Salim

Cover: Logo and design by Mfundishi Jhutyms Ka en Heru Hassan Kamau Salim

Inquiries and Book Orders should be addressed to:

Great Writers Media
Email: info@greatwritersmedia.com
Phone: 877-556-0487

ISBN: 979-8-89175-035-7 (sc)
ISBN: 979-8-89175-036-4 (ebk)

Rev 11/18/2020

Shemsu Heru Mentchu-Hotep

and the

Spirit of the Medjay

Book Two

To my father, who connects me to Afraka and a bloodline of spiritual warriors. To my mother, who taught me leadership and responsibility. To my sister and brothers, who continue to give me unconditional love, respect, and support. To my children, Zuwena and Hassan Iman Salim, who taught me how to be a loving and supporting parent. To my children's mother, Cynthia, thank you for allowing me to be a cocreator. To my wife, Ifasewa, who teaches me good character and love for the Elliott family. To the shrine of Jhuty Heru Neb-Hu and to my spiritual family and all my blood family, thank you for your love, respect, and support. To my Ghana family, Nana Yaw Obesey and his father, Baba Obesey. And last but not the least, to all my teachers, *Dua Ntchr!* To all the spiritual warriors, past and present, may this work inspire you to greatness and to complete the great works of our Afrakan ancestors. May Afrakans at home in the diaspora learn the lessons of sovereignty and Ma'at, pan-Afrakanism, or parish!

SHEMSU HERU MENTCHU-HOTEP AND THE SPIRIT OF THE MEDJAY

Book Two

FOREWORD

There has been a lot of debate among Egyptologists as to the origin of the Egyptians (Kemetyu). A clear majority of white scholars see the ancient Kemetyu people as anything other than black Africans. Indeed, there has been more ink flowing in books, doctoral theses, and professional journals on the state of Egypt (more accurately known as Kemet) and world history. Even in standard textbooks that are used worldwide, Egyptians are portrayed as a white population and Kemet itself is placed in the Mediterranean area, not in Africa. Very recently, even Hollywood yet again depicted Egyptians as white in the film *Gods of Egypt*.

This is a major problem since these myths go beyond academia and have been stated by ambassadors and foreign affairs experts as facts to be used and stated repeatedly. In truth, they are lies that have been perpetuated to miseducate the people of the world as to the importance of African civilization and the achievements of African people. It is imperative that we have scholars that can set the record straight as to the importance of Africa in world affairs and the peopling of the world.

In Mfundishi Jhutyms Hassan Salim's second volume of his book, *Mentchu-hotep and the Spirit of the Medjay*, he has put forth the truth about Kemet and its place in history, as well as the place of the Egyptian people (Kemetyu). Salim unequivocally and unapologetically demonstrates the African blackness of the ancient Kemetyu, and he properly takes those facts for granted. This book is a true depiction of Kemetyu life. Salim goes further when he brings in the symptomatic approach that occurs when the Egyptians acted out in a nonsymbolic way.

Salim's latest book demonstrates his ability to be a great storyteller. The book's beautiful illustration brings to light the great grandeur of the Kemety civilization. What Salim really does, which is of prime importance, is to give his reader the opportunity to experience existentially the beauty, power, and ambience of Kemet. His book stands alone as one of the most important books written about Kemet in the twenty-first century. Salim's depiction of ancient Kemet is a display of his great and unique scholarship.

What is important about Salim's work is that he realizes that the symbolism of ancient Kemet is vast and must be understood properly if one is to accurately interpret the lives of the ancient Kemetyu. Salim realizes that the Kemetyu were destroyed by their symbolic behavior, which produced decisions that were based on superstitions and myths. Scholars understand the effect that superstitions had on the behavior of ancient Kemetyu, who struggled to solve the problems of civilization, including Kemet, where conflict drove symbolic thought and behavior. As noted in Salim's wonderful storytelling, the hero Mentchu-hotep railed on a platform of symptomatic thought and behavior in a way that would return Kemet to its former greatness.

The great scholars Chancellor Williams and Cheikh Anta Diop both emphasized the need to know the *whys* of the destruction of black civilization. Diop, in his book *Civilization or Barbarism*, talked about the superstitions of the ancient Kemetyu, but it is unclear whether he saw that as the main cause for their destruction. Williams, in his book *The Destruction of Black Civilization,* saw as a crucial element in the destruction of African civilization the colonization of the minds of the Africans. Indeed, what we have to understand is that this colonization of the mind is how symbolism presents itself in the neurological processes of the brain.

The scholar Sir James George Frazer, in his book *The Golden Bough,* placed his entire platform on the superstitious behavior of not only Africans but also humanity. That superstitious behavior that Frazer talked about not only colonized African civilization but also colonized the minds and behavior of all humanity. That is why it is imperative that humanity change from a symbolic behavior pattern to a symptomatic one.

Mfundishi Jhutyms Hassan Salim is a great scholar and narrator. In *Shemsu Heru: Mentchu-hotep and the Spirit of the Medjay,* his main emphasis is to demonstrate redemptive symptomatic thought. Symptomatic thinking must be the guide to all humanity if there is to be peace and justice in all civilizations.

Edgar J. Ridley
Chairman, Edgar J. Ridley & Associates
Author, *The Golden Apple: Changing the Structure of Civilization,* Volumes 1 and 2
September 2017

CHAPTER 1

THE UNIFICATION
OF SEMA TAWY

Shemsu Heru Nswt Bety Sa Ra Mentchu-hotep, the mighty
Medjay warrior chief of Kemet, sat in silent meditation with
the rest of the Medjay *medju* as he recited silently to himself
one of his favorite affirmations:

> I have always existed.
> I am the Divine Spirit.
> Heru consciousness.
> I am my people.
> And we have the power.
> We have always had the power.

1

We are *Ntchr*.
The Ntchr is all.
We were born to be reborn.
Our rebirth is an unending act of love.
Life is eternal and an interwoven, continuous miracle on a journey toward the light, which is the Divine Spirit.
Heru consciousness, the internal power that brings Ma'at.
Our purpose is to bring forth healing, balance, truth, justice, righteousness, and eternal harmony while we are in this body.
But I am not this body.
This body is my temporary temple, a vehicle to facilitate my mission.
I have always existed.
I am my people, the sum total of everything that has ever happened.
I am everything that has been and the potential to be.
Your heru consciousness, I am an eternal spirit . . .

Shemsu Heru Sa Ra Mentchu-hotep sat in silence for a long while, gathering his thoughts through his breath. He had been taught by his great Medjay teachers that within you, there is a stillness and a sanctuary to which you can retreat at any time and be your divine self. The power of affirmations can change your thinking, your attitude, and finally, your behavior. Affirmations help to change what happens in your life by strengthening and changing your thoughts, attitudes, and habits to support the goal you wish to achieve. Any worthwhile accomplishment requires an investment of time and effort. He had to shift his mind from a state of war to peace, love, and healing. His breathing was full and long, as only his stomach expanded and retracted.

*****

Shemsu Heru Sa Ra Mentchu-hotep's royal messenger falcon flew onto the arm of Hmt Nswt Wrt Neferu (great royal wife Neferu) while she was in prayer in the sacred temple of Het Heru in Waset, the capital city of Kemet. Excitement rushed through her heart. It was their favorite falcon. She and Mentchu-hotep had raised it together from a chick. She stroked it gently on its head and back as she took the message wrapped around a beautiful gemstone, which she had never seen before, very carefully from the mighty falcon's legs. She would place this stone with her many stones that she had collected from her husband's many journeys. She then gave the mighty falcon some water and its favorite food. She knew it flew all the way nonstop from the Hapy Delta to Waset over four hundred miles to her. Neferu quickly called to her family so they could all hear the news together.

As they all gathered around, with the look of suspense on their faces, she began to read, "*Yem tchnu hotep* [I offer you satisfaction], royal family and friends. The war is over, and we were victorious. We fought like the most powerful warrior, Ntchru, as we crushed our enemies on land and water. But now, the real battle begins."

"I knew father would whip them," said the teenage prince Mentchu-hotep as he stood up and threw a few kicks and punches in the air.

Neferu continued, "Mentchu, Sekhmet, Sebek, Heru, and Set all fought on our side. And our enemy never had a chance! Even the Ta-Sety bowmen fought couragiously with us as we were surrounded with the power of *Mentchu hna Khnum* [the Ntchr of war and the Ntchr of divine creation, the Divine Moulder]. We must now clean away the horrors of war. Now we must heal our great nation. Tell all our people and friends of our mighty victory but that we will need all their help to repair our great nation, Kemet! We shall return home in thirty days. Nothing but *Mrrr* [love] to you, my beloved Neferu. Give mrr to my beloved mother, Nswt Mwt Ntchru Iah, whom I owe my life to and to Hemt Nswt Tem and, of course, to my son of the sun, Prince Mentchu-hotep! *Ankh, Udja, Sneb-Neb, Amen-Ra em Ma'at* [All life, all prosperity, and good health from the unseen and seen manifestation of the Creator in harmonious balance]."

*****

The Medjay medju unit walked along the Hapy Eteru coast in harmonious silence as we watched the after-war cleanup. All the foreign dead bodies were burned, and prisoners were gathered and placed on a large vessel for deportation. All their weapons were gathered to be sent back to Waset to be refashioned and reused for Kemet warriors. The priest from the temple of Het-ka-Ptah had gathered many of the townspeople together to aid in the cleanup and the healing of the wounded. Any dead Medjay or Kemety soldiers were placed seperately so they could be shipped back to Waset for a royal funeral and special burial. We were back together again as one family after over 140 years of division.

I was so proud to walk with the Medjay medju, these giants among men, as one of their equal. They all wore the three Golden Fly-Bee necklaces around their necks, the medals of the highest honor of bravery in battle, meaning you repeatedly stung your enemy in victorious battle. How could I reward them? They were all wealthy men at the head of their private stations in life. I must think of some way to give them special honor when I return to Waset. I would ask my Hmt Nswt Wrt Neferu. She would know.

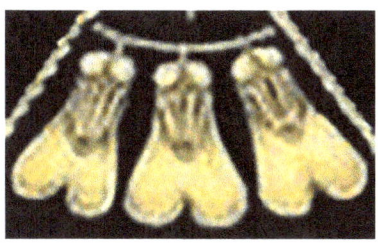

The Golden Fly-Bee, the highest medal for battle in Kemet and Kash

I could hear the subtle cries of the trees and the forest as they, with a gentle power, unfold and struggle to proclaim their right to make a contribution to the harmony, health, beauty, and peace of our reunification, Sema Tawy—the united two lands. I watched the instinctive movements and sounds of all the animals that walked, crawled, and flew in our beloved land called Kemet, as they tried their best to harmonize and respond to the laws of nature, Ma'at. I could see and hear the rhythmic motion and intelligent communications of all the life forms that swam the waters of the Hapy Eteru, proclaiming the majesty and beauty of being. All these forms, infused with life and purpose, were expressing a magnificent spirit, power, and force that I had only dreamed about. But we all could feel it happening all around us as we walked in silence.

As Kheper-Ra rose the next morning, Chief Medjay Jhutyms Ka-en-Heru came to my quarters. I stood up to greet him, and he grabbed my right arm in the Medjay falcon grip. "Success woke me up, motivation made me breakfast, and destiny gave me my agenda as Amen-Ra smiled on my face. Life has just confirmed that the way of the Medjay warrior is real," explained the great *Djedi*. "Those who are skilled in combat do not become angered. Those who are skilled at winning do not become afraid. So, Shemsu Heru Sa Ra Mentchu-hotep, the wise win before the fight, while the ignorant fight to win."

"Tiw, I can see all those points in our battle yesterday, Grand Master."

"*Nefer,* I shall see you in two weeks, Shemsu Heru. I have consulted the Djedi council, and you are officially Sa Ra Mentchu-hotep, Nswt Bety Neb Khrw-Ra, Nb Tawy, Bik Nebu, Nebty, Nb Khau, Kha Nakht, and Nb Ma'at. Remember, you are in *nefer aa* [great] hands because Jhuty will guide you and Heru has your back. We did not win this mighty war by knowing what we know. We, the mighty Medjay, won by doing what we know. You have grown tall and strong, like your mighty warrior ancestors. The Asians tried to bury your family in the south. They didn't know you were their seeds," he said as he walked away, smiling.

The great chief Djedi Jhutyms Ka-en-Heru led over three thousand warriors down the Hapy Eteru into the delta and escorted the foreign troops out of Kemet and cleared our borders of Asiatics and undesirables with the help of the Ta-Sety bowmen. Then he led an army to the west against the Tjemehu and Tehnenu Libyans and into the Sinai Peninsula against the Mentjiu nomads, defeating them with ease, as he reclaimed the Kemet borders from foreign settlers. Kemet must be returned to the Remtch, the original people. Ma'at must be restored. Just as the desire for ethnic or spiritual peace became a desire for harmony among all groups, the desire for national peace must become a desire for the two lands of Kemet in order to live in harmony.

There was a gathering of all the townspeople, along with our warriors. I had the local priest pour libation, and one of the priestesses sang a hymn to Khnum, Ptah, Mentchu, Ra, and Amen as one divine spiritual force.

"Let the healing begin!" I shouted. "We have the capacity to spread love and peace through our contacts. Our thoughts and hearts must carry the causative agents of harmony, peace, healing, and love. The love in our thoughts and minds are contagious. Our thoughts, feelings, and beliefs are vibratory agents and are also contagious. The love in our thoughts, feelings, and motives are not only contagious. They are infectious. We must infect all of Kemet with Ma'at! This is how we will rise again to an exceptional greatness."

The warriors, along with the townspeople, all yelled, "Dua Ntchr mrr en Ma'at!" (All praises to divinity, love, and harmonious balance!)

"If we desire to have peace in our lives, in our homes, and in our villages and cities—peace in our country, Kemet—we must begin this complex yet simple process by developing peace within ourselves. Deep down in my heart, I knew that peace would not be accomplished if there were no forgiveness. Forgiveness is about you completely freeing yourself from what happened to you. We must eliminate doubt and disharmony from our daily lives and from within our minds, hearts, and thoughts. Remtch, Kemetyu, Kashites, warriors, and Medjay, we are entering our second great golden age since the last great flood. Let's leave a legacy of Ma'at behind for our children and their children's children. The people of Kemet will never live in peace until the people of Kemet have inner peace.

"Spirituality with the innerstanding of forgiveness and gratitude will give us inner peace, my people. With spirituality comes morality. Morality is doing what is right, regardless of what you are told. The foreigners and your former leaders were dictators who were not surrounded by Ma'at. Their way is doing what you are told, regardless of what is right. Spiritual people are not disobedient. We just happen to honor the Ntchr in all of us. Forgiveness is the nature of the heart. That is the only quality that will make it as light as a feather. And finally, gratitude is the ability to be thankful for our divinity—the divinity that exists in you as it does in me. Amen-Ra."

As our warrior ships set sail for the old northern capital, Hut-Nen-nesu, I told the Medjay medju that even though we were victorious in battle and suffered very little casualties, I felt something was still missing. Medjay Priest-Scientist Ka-en-Jhutyms, one of Kemet and Kash's greatest warrior, put his hand on my shoulder as he spoke, "No matter what you imagine that you have accomplished in any lifetime, there will always be a part of you that feels like something is missing, and it's because in your illusions of this illusionary world, something is missing."

A light went off in my head. *Honor and respect are missing,* I thought. "Stop the ships!" I yelled. I took a deep breath before speaking. "We cannot leave these sacred grounds of Sokar without visiting the Mer Khut and sacred tombs of Shemsu Heru Netchrikhet, Sa Ra Djoser [divine of his body—the Holy One], Sekhemkhet [powerful in his body], Khaba [the soul appears], Huni [the smiter], Unas, and Teti, who gave us the *Mer Khut Sabayet* [*Pyramid Texts*]. And also Pepy Mery-Ra [beloved of Ra], Mer-en-Ra, and Pepy Nefer-ka-Ra [the beautiful spirit of Ra]."

All the Medjay agreed, and for the next three hours, we walked the sacred burial grounds of the great and glorious ancestors, the *Akhu* of the first golden age in the sacred land of Sokar.

The Medjay of Kash as elite Kemetic warriors

We gathered together as we entered the Step Pyramid complex, which stood majestically in front of us, as six-stepped layers standing 204 feet (62 meters) high. And it took our breath away. Our beloved Shemsu Heru Netchrikhet's (divine of body) pyramid was surrounded by an enclosure wall more than 30 feet (10 meters) high and 5,250 feet (1,600 meters) long. Once we were inside the courtyard, we marveled at temples and chapels containing thirteen false doors, as well as one real entrance in the southeast. The entrance corridor was made of stone, but the ceiling was carved to look as if it was made of wood. A three-ton piece of granite sealed the entrance, covering nearly 40 acres (16 hectares)—the size of a small village.

As in earlier tombs, the Step Pyramid's burial chambers were underground, hidden in a maze of tunnels, probably to discourage grave robbers. Invaders looking for wealth during the First Intermediate Period, nevertheless, plundered the tomb.

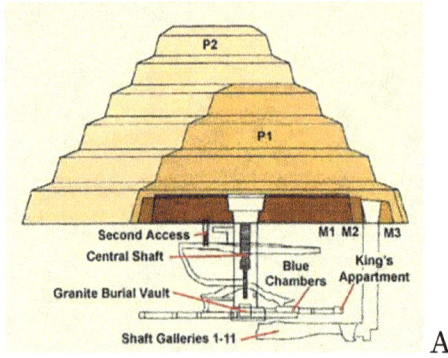

A

B

C

D

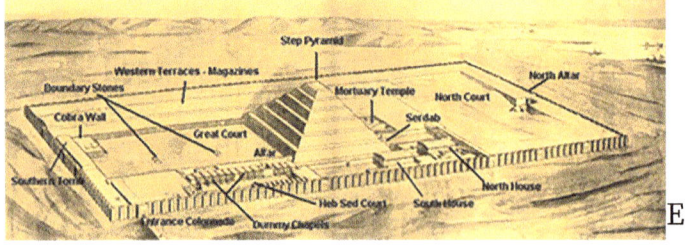

E

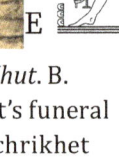

F

A. A side-cut view of Netchrikhet's Step *Mer Khut*. B. Netchrikhet Djoser. C. A front view of Netchrikhet's funeral complex. E. A view of the whole complex. F. Netchrikhet Djoser wearing the *Hdjet* (white crown from the south).

"We shall take this limestone *Wdj* [stela] back to Waset and place it in the Holy of Holies in the sacred temple of Amen as a gift of Shemsu Heru Netchrikhet's greatness."

Djoser's limestone stela

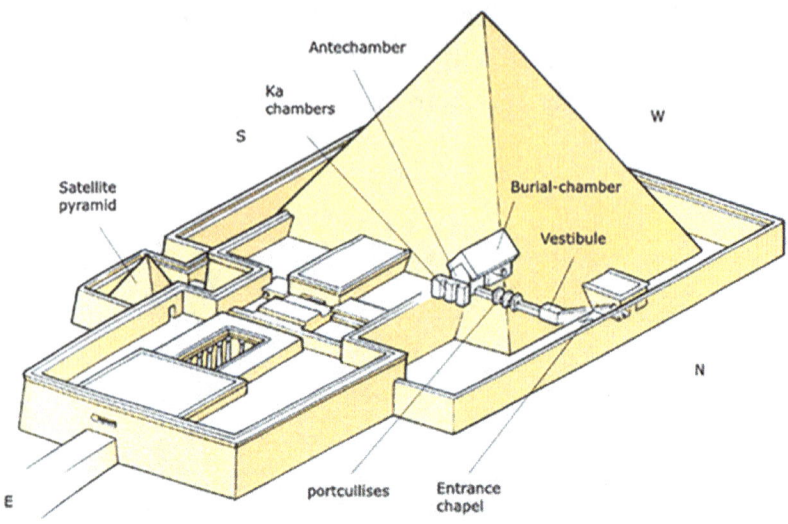

The Mer Khut of Unis

After leaving Heru Netchrikhet Nswt Djoser's burial complex, we visited the Mer Khut of Unis at the southwestern corner of Heru Djoser's enclosure. It was almost diagonally opposite to the Mer Khut of Nswt Userkaf (ca. 2487–2480 BCE), the founder of the so-called Fifth Dynasty. The causeway to the Mer Khut of Unis was 750 meters long and was equal to Nswt Bety Khufu's. In its roof, a slit was left open so a shaft of light could illuminate the gallery of brightly painted reliefs of which only fragments survived. A wide array of scenes once covered the wall—boats transporting granite palm columns, craftsmen working on gold and copper, harvesting scenes (grain, figs, and honey), offering bearers, battles with enemies, bearded Asiatics. Two boat graves (each 45 meters long) lay side by side south of it.

The antechamber of the pyramid tomb lay directly under the center axis of the pyramid. In the east, a doorway opened to the uninscribed *ka* chamber with three recesses. The middle recess of this ka chapel (intended for sitting statues of the Nswt Unis) lay exactly behind the spirit door of the mortuary temple.

The sitting statue was attested in the funerary domain from the first golden age onward. It was the three-dimensional realization of the picture of the slab stela, representing the enthroned tomb owner in front of an offering table to which he was stretching out one hand. The stretched (mostly right) hand was shown resting on the thigh and the left hand often on the breast. During the Mer Khut, the Great Pyramid builders during the first golden age, the sitting statue was a formal part of Giza's sacred burial grounds. It was placed in a closed tomb. In this inner cult place dedicated to the provision cult for the deceased, the ka statue was the *double* of the tomb owner, representing the latter as corporally intact, provided and able to receive provisions by way of the *sahu* enshrined in the karst sarcophagus and by way of the ka and/or *Ba* visiting the tomb and recognizing its own image in the Ka statue.

The *Unis Sbayt (texts)* formed the oldest extant corpus of spiritual texts written in old Mdw Ntchr. They were Nswt Bety Unis's literary testament. Together with those in the tombs of his successors—Nswt Bety Teti, Pepy Mery-Ra (beloved of Ra), Mer-en-Ra, and Pepy Nefer-ka-Ra (the beautiful spirit of Ra)— they constituted the oldest corpus of ancient Kemet's spiritual, funerary, and theological literature, in particular, that of Iwnu, called the *Mer Khut Sbayt* (*Pyramid Texts*). Iwnu was situated on the northeast of the Nswt Bety and spiritual capital of the first golden age—namely, Men-nefer—and on the east bank of Eteru er Hapy. Both antechamber and burial chamber had as a central theme the resurrection of the Nswt Bety and his ascent to heaven.

Offering rituals, one of the instruments of resurrection, accompanied the presentation of offerings. But on the eastern table of the burial chamber, the Nswt Bety established his independence of food supply. These were the deified elements of Kemety antirational epistemology: Sia (understanding), Hu (authoritive speech), and Heka (efficient words of power). These natural types of cognition in a Kemety mode form the core of the mental spirituality of the Kemetyu. The hidden, dark potential of Mdw Ntchr was evidenced by the sacrificial rituals found in mortuary literature. The Ba (soul) of the deceased read the words and manifested their meaning. The direction of the texts was thus identical with the soul's path through the tomb, moving from the innermost parts of the burial chamber (the *Duat* in the west) through the antechamber (the eastern horizon or *Akhet*) to the outside of the Mer Khut (pyramid) via the second northern tunnel, flying to the northern stars, reaching the Field of Offerings.

- *The Duat (burial chamber).* Though a part of the world, but neither earth or sky, the underworld is inaccessible to the living and outside normal human experience. It is separate from the sky and is reached prior to it. This Field of Reeds is the realm of the deceased and the deities and the mystery of Asr. The Nswt Bety has perpetuated offerings and has stood at the door of the horizon to emerge from the Duat and start his spiritualization.

- *The horizon (antechamber).* Akhet, translated as "horizon," is both the junction of the sky and earth and a place in the sky underneath this point (before eastern dawn and after western dusk), a secret interstitial zone reached and crossed by boat. It is a zone of transition and a "radiant place," or the "land of the honored souls." The horizon is the place of becoming effective, the focus of the becoming (*akh*), an effective spirit that the *Mer Khut Sbayt.*

14

- *The imperishable sky (northern tunnels).* With the process of transfiguration (ultimate spiritualization) being completed, the akh spirit leaves the tomb and ascends to the northern stars.

Highest, Subtlest, Eternal Realm of the Deities	*akh* (spirit)	The essence is luminous and divine and abides in the soul and body as it pleases.
	khaba (spirit and body)	The light of the stars is perpetual and is the house of the essence of the Nswt Bety.
Higher, Subtle, Transitional Realm of the Beatified Souls	*ba* (soul)	This is the witness at judgment, beautified by Asar, freely existing in its own body, gratified by the offerings to the Ka.
	sah (soul and body)	It is liberated as the result of sahu and funerary rituals

Lower, Gross, Temporal Magical Cycles of the Netherworld and the Unity of the Two Lands	ib (heart or ego)	Restored and weighed, only the truth is light enough to balance the feather.
	ka (vitality, ego, and body)	It is free to move the double remains near the sah fed by offerings.
	Khat (corpse)	The sah does not decay; the sah and tomb are a symbolization of eternal existence.

Last but not the least, we read the work of Hotep-Ptah (Ptah-hotep), who was a vizier (first minister) under the reign of Djedkare Isesi of the first golden age, the *Teachings of Hotep-Ptah*, the earliest and surviving literature of moral philosophy. The teachings take the form of advice and instructions from a father to his son. Hotep-Ptah's thirty-seven teachings or instructions were the only ones to come down to us in its totality. His maxim had been rightly called "the oldest book in the world" and was published on papyri over two thousand years before me, Nswt Bety Neb Khrw-Ra Sa Ra Mentchu-hotep. However, after I read this work, I knew I had to preserve and resurrect copies during my leadership of the second golden age.

These passages were according to Hotep-Ptah:

Do not be proud and arrogant with your knowledge. Consult and converse with the ignorant and the wise, for the limits of art are not reached. No artist ever possesses that perfection of which he should aspire. Good speech is more hidden than emeralds, yet it may be found among maids at the grindstones.

Do not scheme against people. The divine Ntchr will punish accordingly. If a man says "I shall live by scheming," he will lack bread for his mouth . . . People's schemes do not prevail. The Ntchru command is what prevails; therefore, live in the midst of peace. What the Ntchr gives comes by itself.

Follow your heart as long as you live . . .

*****

The Medjay medju were all together again as they sat in a circle in front of their large warship en route to the northern capital. He already knew he would change its name back to its original name of Hut-Nen-nesu, "the mansion of the royal child." Its ancient principal Ntchr was Herishef, originally a ram; this went back to the time of Shemsu Heru Narmer (the striking catfish), the first Nswt Bety and uniter of the two great nations.

Nswt Bety Neb Khrw-Ra Sa Ra Mentchu-hotep left a dozen scribes behind to copy these important documents so they could be remembered and used during his rule of Kemet. Once all the warriors were back on their ship heading for the northern capital, Nswt Bety Neb Khrw-Ra Sa Ra Mentchu-hotep looked at his Medjay medju unit. *What power,* he thought. *Nine of the most powerful warriors in the world, only now, I am not just Medjay Sa Ra Mentchu-hotep but I am Shemsu Heru, the Nswt Bety Neb Khrw-Ra Sa Ra Mentchu-hotep, the supreme commander of all of Kemet.* He looked at his fleet of warriors with so much gratitude and pride. He knew that without the might, wisdom, and strength from his southern neighbors Kash, Ta-Sety, and specifically, the Medjay, this would not be possible. His eyes swelled with tears of love and gratitude as he knelt on one knee and spoke, "*Dua* to our Medjay medju unit. I know that only two out of the ten of us are naturally born from Kemet in our Medjay medju unit, and I want to thank you all personally for making Kemet your home. I will be forever in your debt, and Kemet will be forever in your debt! Your names will be recorded and forever remembered! But I need you even more now to strenghten and unify our great nation-state, Sema Tawy. We must learn to use these new natural and cultural resources that will revive the traditional policies of the great rulers of the first golden age."

"May I speak, Nswt Bety Neb Khrw-Ra Sa Ra Mentchu-hotep?"

"Of course, Meday Priest-Scientist Ka-en-Jhutyms. I might be the ruler, the Nswt Bety, but you are still my *neb seba* [master teacher]."

"Where we were born is irrevelant. We are Medjay. We are the greatest warriors on earth. We know that our first allegiance is to the divine Ntchr represented as Amen-Ra, expressed through Khnum-Ra and Mentchu, with the divine guidance of Jhuty, Seshat, and Ma'at, which is inside each of us. Our second allegiance is to Chief Medjay Jhutyms Ka-en-Heru and the grand council of Djedi, who represent the soul of our exsitence on this planet. And our chief has made it crystal clear that our third and final allegiance is to you, Shemsu Heru Nswt Bety Neb Khrwu-Ra Sa Ra Mentchu-hotep and the resurrection and rebirth of Kemet!

"This Medjay medju was strategically put together to help you on your mission. Your mission is and has always been our mission! Tiw, Sa Ra Mentchu-hotep, this is on our Jhuty list also. We have the skills and experiences to lead expeditions to the mines and quarries, as well as to foreign ports for trade—import and export. We have the skills for the restoration of temples and construction of huge funerary monuments. We have the agricultural skills to expand food production and build irrigation canals. We know the language and culture of our people as far south until it reaches the mighty, great waters at the end of our continent. We are all divine *seshu*, scribes, teachers. We understand and innerstand the latest science and technology, and some of us are priest-scientists, herbalists, and divine healers. But we are all here for you, for Kemet!"

All the Medjay dropped on one knee with their right hand in the center, forming a perfect circle, and shouted in one voice, "Dua Ntchr, the resurrection of Kemet under divine governance! Seven, five, three!" Seven virtues of a warrior—rectitude, courage, benevolence, politeness/propriety, honesty/sincerity, honor, and loyalty. Five keys to health—holistic nutrition, sensible exersise, efficient rest, proper hygiene, and positive attitude. Three states of mind—alertness/awareness, clear mind, and emotional balance.

Medjay Kemety warship headed by Sa Ra Mentchu-hotep

We sailed in silence for the next few hours, following the light from the Mer Khut of Khufu (protected by Khnum), and then finally, we could see Heru-em-Akhety (Heru protector in the horizon from Ra up to Ra down). Oh, how I longed to travel these magical waters (*Mw*) of Eteru er Hapy, past Heru-em-Akhety, and to take in its majesty. I could hear my heart pounding extra loud as I drank in this divine view. I wanted to touch its pawse and lay in its bosom and sleep inside its strength. I had wanted to do this before I was born!

Heru-em-Akhety sitting in front of the three great Mer Khut of Khufu, KhafRa, and MenkauRa. Heru-em-Akhety was built before the last great Ice Age, over eight thousand years ago, before Mentchu-hotep was born.

Below, Ra setting in the west

*****

The Mer Khut of Khufu, the great pyramids, completely encased in beautiful, smoothly polished limestone could be seen shining across the desert from over a hundred miles away.

Shemsu Heru Nswt Bety Neb Khrw-Ra Sa Ra Mentchu-hotep was now the protector of these sacred monuments, tombs, and divine temples, with their huge libraries that contained millions of documents, which included most of the sum intelligence and known story of the human race on planet earth. He somehow knew that this work of rebuilding, uniting, and protecting was going to be much harder than defeating and expelling the foreigners from Kemet. *What lies behind us and what lies before us are tiny matters compared to what lies within us,* he thought. Those were the words that Chief Medjay Jhutyms Ka-en-Heru had drilled into his head since his youth. He knew he was going to have to rely on that inner strength in order to rebuild Kemet. His thoughts went back to his childhood, and he could hear the chief Medjay say to him, "Life is about moments. Don't wait for them. Create them!"

Shemsu Heru Sa Ra Mentchu-hotep looked at Medjay Priest-Scientist Ka-en-Jhutyms, who stood beside him, as he spoke, "I hope I can recharge the people and change this nation back to greatness. Look at these buildings and temples. This is a monumental, colossal responsibility."

Medjay Priest-Scientist Ka-en-Jhutyms just smiled. "If you want to change this nation, first change your thinking to deep thought. Think like Heru, the mighty spiritual warrior with higher consciouness, then begin by changing your words. Start speaking the words of your dreams, your aspirations of an independent and powerful nation-state. Speak of who you want to become, and speak of what you want this nation-state to become, not the words *I hope* or *maybe*. As a Medjay, those words don't exist!

"Let me share a few words my father, the great Djedi Jhutyms Ka-en-Heru, has taught me and which I agree with. Our enemy, the Asiatics from the east and west, have taught us [1] that the only way to defeat your enemies' culture is by practicing your own; [2] that you should always promote your women as the standard of beauty; [3] that you should view everything from your perspective first; [4] that if you have a problem with your own kind, make a truce so that all your attention is on the enemy or your problem; [5] that you can end up at the top from any inferior position; and [6] that if you are attacked by an enemy, don't forgive and don't forget. A snake is a snake is a snake, and a log can stay in water for *renpt medju* [ten years] and never become a crocodile."

"Thank you. Dua Ntchr. I will remember these things and pass this wisdom down to my son."

Diorite statue of Nswt Bety KhafRa, showing Heru consciousness

That evening, Sa Ra Mentchu-hotep stood in front of a life-size diorite statue of KhafRa, with Heru the great falcon attached to the back of its head. If you looked at the statue straight ahead, you could not see the falcon; you could only see it from the side or back view. Heru, the symbol of the falcon, represented a symptomatic symbol of controlled strength of the Ntchru on earth as higher consciousness, which the Nswt Bety was. The symbolism of Heru was the protection and the projection of Shemsu Heru. Now this awesome responsibility was his, Shemsu Heru Sa Ra Mentchu-hotep's. He ran his fingers across the hard, smooth, brilliantly carved diorite stone, belonging to another unknown and unnamed ancient Kemety genius craftsman. He smiled, thinking that his chief architect, Hem Sem Tepy Kha-ef-Ptah, probably knew his name. And like Imhotep was the chief craftsman of Heru

Netchrikhet, he would make sure everyone knew the great minds that surrounded him, for he would etch their names in stone for all eternity.

As Sa Ra Mentchu-hotep Nswt Bety Neb Khrw-Ra surveyed his new northern capital, along with the Medjay medju, he was filled with a sense of excitement, even though there was a tremendous amount of work to be done. He already saw the greatness in his head and how he wanted it to be. As soon as you honor the present moment, all unhappiness and struggle dissolves and life begins to flow with joy and ease. When you act out the present moment of awareness, whatever you do becomes imbued with a sense of quality, care, and love— even the simplest action. He knew he would rebuild this city and his nation-state one stone at a time. He would select his thoughts, just like the Nswt selected his clothes each morning meticulously.

Again, he could hear the words of Djedi Grand Master Jhutyms Ka-en-Heru saying, "Your mind must arrive at your destination before your life does. Great minds have purpose. Others have wishes." *Tiw, we rise by lifting others,* he thought. He would use his imagination to create a great Ma'atian reality in Kemet.

CHAPTER 2

THE RETURN TO THE
WAY—MA'AT

A procession of the Kemety priest and Sa Ra Mentchu-hotep

The Shemsu Heru Nswt Bety Neb Khrw-Ra Sa Ra Mentchu-hotep led a victory procession after uniting Upper and Lower Kemet into one nation-state—Sema Tawy, the united two lands.

Sa Ra Mentchu-hotep had dreamed of this moment a thousand times, and now it was a reality. He tried to look into the eyes of everyone in his path as his warriors carried him through the streets. He wanted every person to feel like they were a part of his historical victory over his Northern and Asiatic foes. Every Remtch wanted to get a look at the invincible Medjay ruler from the south. Mothers and fathers held up their babies and little ones for a closer look at the mighty falcon ruler as he waved back and gave them a closed-fist salute. Every once in a while, he winked at someone, making them feel extra special.

Thousands of people gathered around as the Nswt Bety Neb Khrw-Ra Sa Ra Mentchu-hotep, the Medjay medju, and the Kemet/Kash warriors marched through the streets in the northern royal capital at Hut-Nen-nesu. He wanted to show the people that they were safe and that they were united again. Free food and beer were given to the multitude. Several dance and drum groups representing Upper and Lower Kemet, even Kash and Ta Ntchr, performed for three days well into the night. But the highlight was a Medjay Mentchu combat demonstration on the second day.

Seven Medjay from Kash put on a show that would stay in their hearts forever and get passed down to their children's children. The first Medjay leaped into the air, like a giant black crane, swirling and pecking with his hands like a real crane. Then he doubled-flipped backward in the air, caught a wooden staff thrown at him by another Medjay upside down, stuck the pole in the ground, and landed on one end with one leg seven feet in the air in perfect balance. The crowd went wild with excitement.

The second Medjay gave off a loud lion's roar that scared half the crowd to death before he went into his lion dance. Some people swore he metamorphosed into a lion a few times during the dance. He then took a boomerang from his shirt and threw it almost a quarter of a mile before it made a perfect circle, coming back to the Medjay. And like a giant lion, the Medjay leaped nine feet in the air, caught the boomerang in his mouth, flipping backward, and landed at the feet of the wooden pole like a cat, with the first Medjay still on one leg.

The third Medjay slid into a snake dance along the ground. It was incredible. It was like two snakes fighting each other. Finally, he leaped over the Medjay lion onto the pole and slid up the wooden pole with the crane Medjay still on it with one leg. The Medjay snake struck at the crane stylist a few times, but they were all blocked by the Medjay's hands that acted like a crane's beak. Half the crowd had their mouths hanging open. The Medjay crane, still on one leg, looked down at the Medjay snake looking up at him while he was wrapped around the pole, with the Medjay lion watching both of them at the base of the seven-foot wooden pole.

The fourth Medjay fought like a crocodile. He twirled in circles like a crocodile, pulling and drowning its prey underwater. Every move of the Medjay looked like it would break a bone. Another Medjay swung a sword at him, and the crocodile Medjay broke the sword in half.

The fifth Medjay fought like a baboon, jumping and flipping in the air, making baboon sounds. A warrior threw two coconuts at the baboon, and he smashed them both with his bare hands.

The sixth Medjay leaped like a falcon, and his hands and feet turned into mighty talons, ripping, clawing, and catching an iron spear and arrows with his feet and hands in the air.

The seventh Medjay was a black panther and, like the lion, was very strong and agile but was much quicker in his movements as he demonstrated a black panther dance. The black panther, while flipping in the air, caught an iron spear that was thrown at him. Then he took the spear and threw it straight up in the sky. It looked like it vanished in the clouds. He drew a circle on the ground and placed a dot in the center, like the symbol of Ra. Then the Medjay began to count backward from ten, and he had the children and the crowd count with him. "Medju, peseju, khemenu, sefekhu, sesu, diu, fedu, shmut, senu, wa, nefer." At *nefer*, the spear stuck in the center of the circle on the black dot of Ra. The crowd screamed with excitement. Once the crowd calmed down from the excitement, three warriors came at the black panther. With one leap in the air, he kicked two of the warriors in the head, knocking them unconscious, as he blocked and grabbed the third warrior by the arm, flipping him to the ground, placing his opponent in a choke hold and arm bar at the same time. After the black panther, each of the other six Medjay animals also fought three new opponents each, defeating their opponents with ease. No match lasted more than a minute. Every little boy in the crowd and a few girls said, "I want to be a Medjay." Several of them gave poor imitations of animals as they made unrecognizable sounds!

*****

Shemsu Heru Nswt Bety Neb Khrw-Ra Sa Ra Mentchu-hotep summoned one-third of his royal court from the capital city, Waset, to meet with trusted and newly appointed officials from the north together in the northern capital city of Hut-Nen-nesu. "We must return to the way of Ma'at. Ma'at must mean the same for every man, woman, and child of Kemet, north or south. The reward of Ma'at, which is heaven, must be open to everyone who lives a life of Ma'at. You see, a person without direction and purpose is like a ship without a rudder or a captain. It's estimated that about 90 percent of Remtch here in the north can be compared to ships without rudders or ships without captains. Subject to every shift of wind and tide, they're helplessly adrift. And while they fondly hope that they'll one day drift into a rich and successful port, you and I know that for every narrow harbor entrance, there are a thousand miles of rocky coastline. The chances against them drifting into a rich and beautiful successful port are a thousand to one, and if they reached this rich port, many of them don't have the skills or knowledge to take advantage of its vast richness.

"But the 9 percent who have taken the time and exercised the discipline to decide on a destination and to chart a course and learn the skills to be the captain of their own ship sail straight and far across the deep Wedjy Wr [great green ocean or sea] of life, reaching one port after another and accomplishing more in just a few years than the rest have accomplished in a lifetime."

Sa Ra Mentchu-hotep walked around the grand table in front of his royal court as he recollected his thoughts. "I believe everyone needs a *Jegna*—someone to help guide you and coach you and to believe in your success. I was taught to surround myself with the dreamers and the doers, the believers and the thinkers, but most of all, to surround myself with those who see greatness within me, even when I can't see it in myself, for only a fool counsels himself. There are a few of you in this room who have been my Jegna. And my greatest Jegna has been Chief Medjay Grand Master Djedi Jhutyms Ka-en-Heru and Vizier Dagi, along with my loving parents. I can also say with great pride that I am a Medjay warrior! However, the Medjay medju under the guidance of Medjay Priest-Scientist Ka-en-Jhutyms has also been and still are my Jegnas. They have taught me how to navigate my ship and how to be a strong and wise captain.

"I want to encourage each of us to remember that our treasure and our hearts are inseparably linked to our consciouness. Take a good look at those two issues and see where adjustments may need to be made. We need to live in a nation where our personal and family dreams and aspirations are in alignment or in harmony with the dreams and aspirations of the nation. Kemet, Sema Tawy, and Kash are those nations! We will not only be better off mentally, spiritually, and physically but wealthier because of our connection to the process. We will also experience more peace in our heart as both of us grow and mature in each area of our nation's development.

"There is no freedom without struggle, no power without resistance, and no glory without the possibility of defeat! Our great ancestors have taught us 'sovereignty or death'! My sole purpose for bringing you all here for the next few weeks is to figure out how we become the Jegna for a nation. My great priests and priestesses, elders, and wise council, how do we make this happen?"

Vizier Dagi asked permission to speak, "May I speak, my *Neb aa?*"

"Tiw."

"Only you, the Nswt Bety [ruler of Upper and Lower Kemet], the *Sa Ra* [son of the sun], can do this! You are the voice of Amen-Ra, and we all are your servants. Let me explain that during the first golden age, the Nswt Bety is the follower of Heru [Shemsu Heru]—an early title of the ruler of Upper and Lower Kemet as an incarnation of Heru. Heru acts as the

Nswt Bety who provides for everybody, and the Nswt Bety determines the proper protocol. The Sa Ra, the victorious Heru [the son of Ntchr Asar], cares for his people and provides their needs. To the Remtch of Kemet, the Nswt Bety's presence is what allows everything to grow. You are the divine Heru, and your power, along with the Ntchru, causes great change. You are the son of Ra and, hence, Ntchr. You could not change this even if you wrote it in stone!"

"But you know, this is all symbolic thought. It is not real, only mythology, and we must bring the people into the real world," said Sa Ra Mentchu-hotep.

"Let me be perfectly clear regarding the powers of the Nswt Bety. This protorational structure emerged and still exists," said Vizier Dagi.

1. *Manifestation of Heru.* Nswt Bety is an exceptional witnessing power as his *serekh* (or proclaimer) is constantly overshadowed by the divine power of Heru, who is above all and oversees all (as the great eye).

2. *Incarnation of the divine.* Nswt Bety is a Ntchr, a divine principle incarnate, a principle of transcendence, the uniter of the two lands, and an apex of an absolute, ceremonial theocracy.

3. *Son of Ra.* Nswt Bety is the *Sa Ra*, the preexistent creative principle of eternal repetition (*neheh*) and, hence, a participator in his father's work.

4. *Asar.* Nswt Bety, before taking off to the sky, resurrected, as did Asar.

5. *Heru, son of Asar.* The throne of Heru is the throne of Nswt Bety, which justifies the Nswt Bety.

"As differential and dynamic principles of existence [part of creation], they can also be compared with concrete concepts or stable mental symbolizations of specific natural processes observed over a very long period of time," he added.

1. *The creative principle.* The world was created by light, a metaphor of conscious awareness.

2. *The verbal principle.* Through speech, all things emerged out of the primordial waters.

3. *The tenacity (or continuity) principle.* All things are sustained thanks to the ritual activity of the Nswt Bety and his representatives, which are the Ntchru.

4. *The material (or magical) principle.* All creative intent solidifies, gains a concrete material shape, and is inherently protected against corruption, inertia, and counterforces. Being an architecture, the universe makes sense.

"*Unis pa sekhem ur sekhem em sekhemu.* For the Nswt Bety's great power overpowers the powers. The Nswt Bety is a sacred image, the most sacred image of the sacred images of the great one." Vizier Dagi sat down after making all points clear about the power of Nswt Bety Neb Khrw-Ra Sa Ra Mentchu-hotep.

"My new chancellor, Medjay Akhtoy Ba-Heru, please speak."

"Vizier Dagi is correct. You have to empower us, your royal cabinet, in front of everyone. Because to the Remtch of Kemet, you are the living Ntchr. Look outside the largest monument in the world, the Akhet en Khufu, standing as a symbol of the Nswt Bety's awesome power. Heru-em-Akhety, the powerful lion with the Nswt Bety's head, standing guard over your great monuments—which was built before the Remtch came into being as a nation-state—again represents a power beyond their wildest imagination. Now add that to what you did four days ago. You defeated the greatest army in the world, almost without a fight. You crushed a frightening foreign army in hours, and people are still talking about you controlling the weather. They think they saw lightning coming from your sword, like a Djedi warrior. They say you cut all three heads of their leaders off with one swing of your mighty sword. And remember, thousands of warriors saw you transform into a mighty black panther. To them, only a Ntchr could do this!"

"But you know all of that was not true!" said Mentchu-hotep.

"It does not matter to the Remtch of Kemet or Kash or what we believe in this room. They would kill anyone of us or all of us in this room if we stood against Nswt Bety Neb Khrw-Ra Sa Ra Mentchu-hotep!"

"Viceroy of Kash, Medjay Priest-Scientist Ka-en-Jhutyms, help make this clear."

He stood up. "Don't wait for the perfect moment. Take the moment and make it perfect! We must seize the moment to bring forth Ma'at, like Nswt Bety Neb Khrw-Ra Sa Ra Mentchu-hotep wants. You, the Sa Ra, the son of the Creator, will charge and instruct us to be excellent and command excellence from the Remtch of Kemet. This will be the theme in every temple in Kemet. And this excellence is Ma'at. Excellence is never an accident. It is the result of high intention, sincere effort, intelligent direction, skillful execution, and vision to see obstacles as opportunities. We can't focus on the confusion around us as the results of symbolic thinking. We have to focus on the Ma'at in us, symptomatic thinking. Let's plot the correct symptoms that will lead to the success we want, and let the power in our hearts shift the atmosphere."

Sa Ra Mentchu-hotep stood up quickly with his fist in the air. "Now we are getting somewhere. The world is a magical place. Once we close our physical eyes and view it through our first eye, our Heru eye, we look beyond the illusions, the mythology, and the superstitions and pierce the veil to the true reality. The world is full of magical things, patiently waiting for our senses to grow sharper so our consciousness can expand. This is symptomatic thinking." Sa Ra Mentchu-hotep was in full command; he had grown into the throne. He was embodying the spirit of all the great rulers of Kemet. As he stood, all eyes were on him. "We will heal this nation-state called Kemet together. Healing doesn't mean the damage never existed. It means the damage no longer controls our lives."

His whole congregation stood up, for he had really moved them. "Dua Ntchr," they chanted.

"Freedom and sovereignty is not overcoming what you think stands in your way. Freedom is innerstanding that what is in your way is part of the way."

"Dua Ntchr," they chanted again.

"We must find the place inside of us where nothing is impossible. We shall place the victorious Behdet sign, the winged solar disk of Heru, over every temple door and official building in Kemet. The victorious Heru stands for excellence! It is a symbol that represents the defeat of Set and *esfet*. It is a symbol that says, 'I know myself.' We will teach the people that if they are searching for the laws of harmony called Ma'at, they will find knowledge. If they are searching for Ntchr, observe nature! Exuberance is a great stimulus toward action, but the inner light grows in silence and concentration.

"However, this silence and concentration called meditation must be taught also in all the temples and in every village and in every home. We will call this meditation system *Ma'at Akhu Ba Ankh*—the harmonious balance of the spirit and soul for life. We will exult the status of the priests and priestesses. We will make the scribe so important that it will be every father's dream to have a son or daughter who is a scribe. We must teach that true teaching is not an accumulation of knowledge. It is an awakening of consciousness, which goes through successive stages of mental, physical, and spiritual development. At that point, every Remtch will know that their body is a house of Ntchr. When they innerstand their own power, they will know the meaning of 'know yourself.'"

*****

A new and powerful energy was spreading all over Kemet and Kash. Many Kashites from Ta-Sety, Napata, and Khartoum, even from Punt, came to Kemet to help in the rebuilding of the world's most powerful nation-state. This was surely the second most powerful example of pan-Afrakanism and operational unity since the mighty warrior Shemsu Heru Narmer. New farmlands were plotted and plowed. Old temples were repaired, and many new temples were under construction. These new temples were like universities, teaching the power of nature and the Ntchru.

Know the world in yourself. Never look for yourself in the world, for this would be to project your illusion. To teach, one must know the nature of those whom one is teaching and the subject of what is being taught. In every vital activity, it is the path that matters. The way of knowledge is narrow. Each truth you learn will be, for you, as new as if it had never been written. The first thing necessary in teaching is wisdom from profound information based on Ma'at. The second thing is a master or masters that innerstands this profound wisdom from a Ma'atian symptomatic thought process in all five Djedi domains—mineral domain, plant domain, animal domain, human domain, and spiritual domain. Third, you need pupils or students capable of carrying on the tradition. Your body is the temple that houses the consciouness of this knowledge. Symptomatic thinking will help you experience this information, and your intuition will show you how to apply it! So is above, so is below! Even the greatest master can only point the way. "Dare to be the captain of your own ship!"

But as dynamic as the north was—with its great pyramids, Heru-em-Akhety, and vast farmlands—the capital was still in Waset. And Ipet Asut was the most beautiful of all their temples.

Shemsu Heru Nswt Bety Neb Khrw-Ra Sa Ra Mentchu-hotep also restored Kemety hegemony over the Sinai region, which had been lost to Kemet during the reign of the Nswt Bety Peppy NeferkaRa, since the end of the first golden age.

Nswt Bety Neb Khrw-Ra Sa Ra Mentchu-hotep sent renewed expeditions down north to Phoenicia to obtain cedarwood and up south to Mount Mwenzori and Kilimanjaro for materials for new building projects. Phoenicia was an ancient black civilization centered in the north of ancient Canaan, which, by Mentchu-hotep's time, had become mixed from northern invasions from the Caucasus Mountains with its heartland along the coastal plains of what is now Lebanon. Mount Mwenzori and Kilimanjaro were the Mountains of the Moon from which their ancestors came and a major source of Eteru er Hapy (the Nile River).

*****

Sa Ra Mentchu-hotep sent his viceroy of Kash, Medjay Priest-Scientist Ka-en-Jhutyms, to Waset to create a chapel tomb in proximity to the Waset royal tombs and to bury all their soldiers who were killed in their battle for national liberation and unification. "All their shrouds should bear my name, Nswt Bety Neb Khrw-Ra Sa Ra Mentchu-hotep, in the royal *shenwy*. This will be the famous tomb of the warriors who are true heroes and who died during the conflict between the south and our foes to the north. Seek out their families and make sure they are cared for and that they know we share in their grief but that we honor their contribution to our victory. This Ma'atian action is reciprocity."

*****

Shemsu Heru Nswt Bety Neb Khrw-Ra Sa Ra Mentchu-hotep held the hand of his great royal wife, Neferu, as he spoke, "Hmt Nswt Wrt Neferu [the beauty], I know you were named after our great-grandmother, Nswt Mwt Wrt Neferu, our first royal mother of our second golden age, who was a wife of the first Nswt of Waset, Shemsu Heru Mentchu-hotep. And her sons were Heru Sehertawy Intef and Heru Wahankh Intef, and she was a grandmother of our father, Heru Sankhibtawy [S-ankh-(ib-Tawy)] Intef, and our mother, Nswt Hemet Wrt Iah, his wife. Mother and I know you are a divine seer. And that is why, Neferu, I need your expertise now. I need you to choose a Northern wife from the royal family or from among the Northern nobility.

"Love is a bridge between you and everything. We already have the trust and loyalty of the masses of the common people.

But the nobility and former royal family feel they have been conquered and displaced. It will take more time and planning to win them over, if we can. Their royal family is angry. Think about it. I have killed their king, cut his head off, ripped his heart out, and seized their family's land and private property. If I go among them, there is still fear and anger in their hearts. I need you, Neferu, the Nswt Hmt Wrt, the great royal wife, to comfort them in a time of their loss. Anger clouds the mind, hatred blurs the vision, but peace clears the mind, and love restores the vision. Help them restore their vision, my divine priestess of Het Heru and my great royal wife."

Neferu went into deep thought. There was silence on the outside, but inside her mind, it was racing like a mighty horse from Yam. "It is a new sense of courage that you want me to plant like seeds in their minds. I can see your wisdom, my great Nswt. Courage is not the absence of fear but, rather, the judgment that something else is more important than fear. I must convince them that their participation in rebuilding a unified nation-state of Kemet—Sema Tawy—is of utmost importance. Tiw, my lord. I must convince the nobility that this is an opportunity to begin again but much more intelligently. We have broader markets with almost unlimited trade potential with the corporation of the Medjay warriors and Ta-Sety bowmen from the south, the land of gold, and unimaginable wealth!"

He knew his great royal wife, Neferu, knew exactly what to do as he leaned back in his new royal chair and smiled. "Now existed one more problem: the elders on the council has advised that the former king had one older son, Kaneferre, who has not been found. It is believed that he is in Siwa Oasis with a regiment of one hundred or more Northern soldiers waiting for instructions. I must send a team of Medjay to bring him back or destroy him in order to put an end to this important chapter in ourstory."

Hmt Nswt Wrt Neferu cruising Eteru er Hapy with the royal family. Her beauty and wisdom were legendary.

*****

Hmt Nswt Wrt Neferu had the royal family and some of the wealthiest nobles in northern Kemet eating out of her hands. She had their undivided attention as they cruised down the Eteru er Hapy (the river of Hapy) in her magnificent royal boat. They were served with Kemet's best wine (*irep*) and beer (*hnqt*), along with many exotic and local fruits (*deqaru*) as she spoke to them. "We are family," she explained to her quests, "and it is important for the family to be at peace. Peace does not mean to be in a place where there is no noise, no struggle, no trouble, or no hard work. Peace means to be in the midst of those things and still be calm in your heart and have an inner joy. I'm not asking you to forget what has happened to your royal family. I am here to help you heal from what has happened. Getting over a painful experience is much like climbing a rope. You have to let go at some point in order to move forward."

They, the northerners, were amazed at her elegance, as well as her beauty, while her golden-brown skin glistened in the light of Ra. One of the wealthy nobles spoke, "Great mistress of the two lands, you speak so well for a woman. Where did you learn?"

"At the great temples of Het Heru and Amen-Ra in Waset. In the south, we have many great women who are *seshut* [scribes], business owners, priestesses, officials, and landowners. The Shemsu Heru Nswt Bety Neb Khrw-Ra Sa Ra Mentchu-hotep teaches that all who seek knowledge can find it, regardless of their sex. Growth in consciousness doesn't depend on the sex of the intellect or its possibilities but on the intensity of the inner urge to expand their consciousness. Every Remtch must act in the rhythm of their time. Such is wisdom.

"Shemsu Heru Sa Ra Mentchu-hotep is not only a Remtch, a Medjay warrior, a great husband, and a father but he has transformed into a multidimensional being of great character. This new energy in Kemet is calling for us, all of us, to raise our vibration. He is introducing us to Kemet's second golden age. It's time to step up, noblemen and noblewomen, to the next level of spiritual consciouness." She looked around her ship into their faces, making eye contact with as many as possible. "Do you have the courage to move forward? Courage isn't having the strength to go on. It is going on even when you don't have strength. The war is over, and some of us are still stuck in the mud! But like a lotus flower, we, too, have the ability to rise from the mud, bloom out of the darkness, and radiate into the world."

The mayor asked, "What kind of wine is this in the red vase?"

"It is pomegranate wine from Wast," Hmt Nswt Wrt Neferu said. "Do you like it? Our friends and allies from Kash have taught us how to make it." As she raised her royal glass in the air, she said, "Smau." (Unity.)

Many of the noblemen and noblewomen raised their glasses, also shouting, "Smau!" (Unity!)

"Doesn't your husband work magic?" yelled one of the elderly noblemen.

"There is no such thing as magic. What you call magic is symbolic thinking." Neferu smiled. "What you call magic is a darkness to which you do not innerstand based on false mythologies and superstitions and false rituals. My *Nswt Hee* [royal husband] is not your demon. To face your real demon, you must first look inward and conquer your own darkness. Stop following false mythologies and superstitions. You either get bitter or you get better. It's that simple. You either take and understand what has happened to you and allow it to make you a better person or you allow it to tear you down. The choice does not belong to fate. It belongs to you!

"Like light and darkness, they both exist. You must have a true innerstanding of what is real and what is not! One cannot exist without the other. There is no true master without the power of balance, knowing what is real, which is symptomatic, versus what is not real, symbolic. And my Nswt Hee, Nswt Bety Neb Khrw-Ra Sa Ra Mentchu-hotep, is a true leader and master of symptomatic thinking. Even his new throne name Neb Khrw-Ra means 'the master of the voice of Ra.'"

Neferu stood up and peered into their eyes once again as she walked among them. "True leaders are not looking to build more followers. True leaders, like my husband, Sa

Ra Mentchu-hotep, are looking to build more leaders. The governing class of nobility isn't chosen for quality but is chosen for material wealth. This always means decadence, the lowest stage a society can reach, and this is not what we want, my Northern family. One foot isn't enough to walk with. Wealth alone is not enough, my nobility. Our senses serve to affirm, not to know. We mustn't confuse mastery with mimicry, knowledge with superstitious ignorance.

"Symptomatic thinking using mental, physical, and spiritual consciouness is indispensable for the achievement of knowledge. This is what Shemsu Heru Nswt Bety Neb Khru-Ra Sa Ra Mentchu-hotep offers you. But most of all, my Northern family, we offer you Mrr [love]. Symbolic thinking angers and clouds the mind, hatred blurs the vision, but peace clears the mind and love restores the vision. My husband, the Nswt Bety, asks you for your forgiveness. Forgiveness is not about you completely freeing yourself from what happened to you. Life is not happening to you, my beautiful family. Life is responding to you. What seems to be the right thing to do could also be the hardest thing you ever have to do in your life. Nswt Bety Neb Khrw-Ra Sa Ra Mentchu-hotep believes that one cannot think symbolically and symptomatically at the same time. That is craziness, and it leads to an insane person or a confused, insane nation. Once we change our thinking, then we can change our lives and even our nation."

Nswt Hemt Neferu Wrt walked among the nobles, recollecting her thoughts. "Gratitude is where freedom and destiny meet because gratitude is a divine doorway to the fulfillment of destiny. When you consciously choose to express thanksgiving, causation is set into motion to manifest your destiny of wholeness. Today, enthusiastically leap into gratitude. Join us in this moment of greatness, if for no other reason than that you are alive. Celebrate your great existence as we take control of ourstory as an emanation of Ntchr. Let me say this in closing. You begin to awaken the very moment you realize one fact. You are creating your reality through the energy of your consciouness."

*****

Two soldiers on horseback moving at full speed charged into Siwa Oasis. "General!" one of the horsemen shouted. "I have just received word from Heracleopolis. Our troops have been defeated by the south. Mentchu-hotep has declared himself Nswt Bety Neb Khrw-Ra, ruler of Upper and Lower Kemet, lord of the voice of Ra, Neb Tawy, master of the two lands!"

"How about my father, King Mery Ka-Ra?"

"He was beheaded by the Medjay warrior Mentchu-hotep himself in battle."

The young prince Kaneferre looked at the general. "I must avenge my father! What do we do now?"

The second horseman spoke, "A group of Medjay are on their way here now, and we are no match for them, my lord!"

The general spoke, "How many Medjay?"

"Maybe a dozen or so," said the soldier.

"But general," said the prince, "we are a hundred strong! Surely we can defeat a dozen Medjay."

"I am sure that is just what your father thought before he lost his head! You don't know the Medjay like I do. I have seen them fight. They are like warriors from another world. Their skills in combat are far superior than ours. I have seen them fight—three hundred Northern warriors to thirty Medjay. They fight in units of ten. They created a spinning pyramid on the battlefield and destroyed them all in less than an hour."

"I will stand and fight," said the prince.

"Then you will lose your head, like your father. That is foolish, young prince, if you want revenge. I know the tremendous pain in a son when he loses his father. I have been there. Mentchu-hotep is a Medjay but not his son who is close to your age. Your energy should be on destroying Mentchu-hotep's son, but you must live to do that. And fighting the Medjay is not going to accomplish that. You must escape to Libya and then to the north, across the Wedjy Wr, to the land of the Hittites. There, among these Northern barbarians, you will be protected. There, you can plot a new course on how to kill the prince Mentchu-hotep. We will hold them off while you escape with two of my best soldiers."

Kaneferre and two of their best soldiers mounted their fastest horses and fled toward Libya, with a note from the general to the Libyan king, asking for aid and help from the land of the Hittites.

Not long after Kaneferre's escape, the Medjay warriors were at their doorstep. Invisible in the sand, a voice shouted out, "We are Medjay warriors from Kash. We are part of the Kemet military acting on behalf of Nswt Bety Neb Khrw-Ra Sa Ra Mentchu-hotep. We do not want to kill or harm anyone. The war is over, and you have lost. There is no need to die here in Siwa Oasis. Surrender, and we will escort you back to Hut-Nen-nesu."

"We will never surrender, you black cowards. Come out and fight like men!" shouted the general. The general's men surrounded the house and the stable at the oasis, but they saw no one, heard no one. It was like silence after a lion's roar, as if death dropped on the oasis, as the nervous soldiers waited for an attack from the Medjay warriors.

There were about twenty soldiers in the house with the general. The rest were outside, waiting for the Medjay. After about twenty minutes of total silence, the general commanded one of his officers to look out the window to see what was going on. At that very moment, an arrow struck the soldier directly between the eyes. He died instantly without knowing what killed him. The general said attack, but the soldiers did not see any Medjay. They just started shooting arrows in the air in complete fear. Two by two, soldiers begain to fall from arrows of the unseen Medjay. A group of ten soldiers rushed up a hill. They all died in seconds and never saw their enemies.

Several flaming arrows set the barn and house on fire. After a few mintues, the general and his troops came out, coughing from the smoke. They were surrouned by Medjay warriors. One of the Medjay spoke, "No one else needs to die. This battle is over."

But with the fury of anger in his heart, the general shouted, "Attack!" He was knocked out immediately with one swift strike from a Medjay warrior. The rest were tied up and taken back to Hut-Nen-nesu.

*****

The next morning, a beautiful young lady came to the new royal palace to see Hmt Nswt Wrt Neferu. The royal guard answered the door, "Tiw, may I help you, young lady?"

"Tiw, may I please speak to the great royal mistress of the two lands, please?"

"What is the nature of your business?"

"It is quite urgent. I am the daughter of the mayor."

"Please wait here. I will see if she is available. And your name, please?"

"I am noblewoman Ashait."

A few moments later, Ashait was escorted into the waiting room by the royal guard. "Please sit here. The Hmt Nswt Wrt Neferu will be with you shortly."

Ashait sat nervously in her seat, wondering what she was going to say. She was so moved by the presence of Hmt Nswt Wrt Neferu as she sat on the royal boat. She hung on her every word. If only she could speak like that. She knew that the way Hmt Nswt Wrt Neferu spoke was what her father called Mdw Nefer (excellent speech). She had always wanted to learn Mdw Ntchr (the divine words and writing system), but women were not allowed in her village. She decided she would just fall on her hands and knees and beg Hmt Nswt Wrt Neferu to please teach her. But when the Hmt Nswt Wrt Neferu entered the room, she couldn't say a word. She just fell on the floor and fainted.

The daughter of a wealthy nobleman and mayor,
a member of the royal family, Ashait

*****

"I will travel tomorrow back home to Waset, my Neb aa. My mission here is complete," said Hmt Nswt Wrt Neferu.

"I seem to be missing something," said Nswt Bety Neb Khrw-Ra Sa Ra Mentchu-hotep.

"*Nen,* you are not missing anything. I have found you two royal wives—one from the royal family and the other from a wealthy nobleman. I am taking them with me to start their training. And you shall have no problems from the noblemen or royal family. They think you are the living Ntchr in flesh. They also want to talk about import, export, and trade among the Kashites as soon as possible. Oh, I almost forgot. The noblemen and royal family are sending five hundred heads of cattle to Waset to be split among the temples of Amen-Ra and Het Heru in exchange for teaching their youth, and they also want fifty jugs of pomegranate wine immediately!"

"Pomegranate wine," the Nswt repeated.

"They sit at your feet as they await your instructions, my Neb aa, Sa Ra Mentchu-hotep."

Nswt Bety Neb Khrw-Ra Sa Ra Mentchu-hotep and Hmt Nswt Wrt Neferu

A knock came from the front door of the Nswt Bety's palace. It was Vizier Ipi. "Enter," said Hmt Nswt Wrt Neferu.

"Shemsu Heru Nswt Bety Neb-Khrw-Ra Sa Ra Mentchu-hotep and Hmt Nswt Aa Neferu, I sit at your feet. I don't know what you have done or said, my Neb aa, but the Northern priest and noblemen would like fifty priests and priestesses and scribes from the south to be sent as soon as possible to teach the Mdw Ntchr and the way of Ma'at," said Vizier Ipi, standing in amazement. "The whole town is talking about Ma'at—the principles and laws of building good character. Everyone wants to be a scribe and learn Mdw Ntchr. They are lining up their sons and daughters at our sacred temples for instructions. Trade with Kash has become the new buzzword.

A week ago, Kash was their enemy. Today, everyone wants to go to Abu and trade for Kashite goods and drink pomegranate wine. Do you believe that? Pomegranate wine! Our Medjay, Kemet, and Kash warriors have already started the teachings of the Mentchu combat arts to the Northern soldiers. You have truly worked magic, my Nswt Bety!"

"Not yet. Do we have the king's son, Kaneferre?" said Sa Ra Mentchu-hotep.

"No, he has fled the country, my Neb aa. But we have someone on his trail, and we have a few prisoners we are still questioning."

Seventeen of the one hundred soldiers were captured and held. They were all separated and questioned one by one. Eight of the soldiers were Remtch (indigenous of Kemet), four were Libyan, and four were foreign mercenaries. The general was a northerner from the wilderness beyond the land of the Hittites. They were all offered their freedom if they told where the prince Kaneferre had escaped to. They knew if they told, the general would have them killed. One of the Libyan soldiers spit in the Medjay's face and cursed him. He died instantly before he could finish his foul words. The four foreign mercenaries said nothing and were escorted out of the country to never return. The other three Libyans said, "He is free in our country." They, too, were escorted to Libya, never to return.

The eight Remtch who had families in Kemet were told to tell the truth if they want to return to their families and live a long prosperous life. "We already know he fled to Libya. What else can you tell us?" they were asked.

They explained that the general wrote a note to the Libyan king, but they do not know what it said. But it had something to do about traveling across the Wedjy Wr and the Hittites. They were all released to join their families and that they would be protected from the general.

The general was held in solitary confinement for three days before he was questioned. Vizier Ipi said he would handle this personally. When Medjay Priest-Scientist Vizier Ipi came into the room, he told the guard to untie the general.

"But he is very dangerous, my lord," said the head guard.

"Untie him I said, and leave us alone."

The guard untied the general and left quickly, closing and locking the door behind him. Only two chairs were in the room. The general sat in one, and Medjay Ipi pulled the second chair in front of him and sat calmly and quietly. He placed a sack near the general's feet. "I think you want to look in it before you act or speak."

The general kept his eyes on Medjay Ipi, looking for the right moment to attack. The general picked up the sack and untied it slowly and looked inside. He saw his officer's head, but he was unmoved. *I will get my revenge,* the general thought.

"First, I must tell you that I am the royal servant of Sa Ra Mentchu-hotep Nswt Bety Neb Khrw-Ra. My name is Vizier Ipi. If you would like to live and go free like fifteen of the sixteen soldiers who were captured with you, just answer my questions honestly or you will die like the one disrespectful Libyan in that sack."

"I will tell you nothing, you Kashite dog!" shouted the general.

Medjay Ipi was unmoved by the general's anger. "First, let me tell you what we already know. Prince Kaneferre has escaped to Libya with two of your best soldiers. We also know you wrote him a note to give to the Libyan king to ask for help so that the young prince could escape across the Wedjy Wr. We are already following him. Just tell us the destination so we can bring him back safely without harming anyone else."

The general tried to rush Medjay Ipi, and with just one quick blow under the chin, which the general never saw, he was knocked out cold.

The head guard rushed back in. "Is he dead?"

"No, just tie him back up and bury this sack," replied Medjay Priest-Scientist Vizier Ipi.

The next day, Medjay Ipi returned to the general's holding room with his teacher, Djedi Ma'at Nefert, from Punt, the legendary country down south in the land of the Ntchr—Ta Ntchr. When the general saw that they had brought a woman to cross-examine him, he laughed out loud, "Ha-ha-ha!"

The Djedi ignored him and did not waste any time with small talk. Just one look in his green eyes and red hair, she knew what she was dealing with—a barbaric, paleface savage from the extreme northern lands. She waved her hand in front of his face, and he was out without her touching him or saying a word. They untied him. She placed her hands on his forehead and probed his mind with her mind.

Djedi Ma'at Nefert began to talk with her eyes closed, "Prince Kaneferre is on his way to the land of the barbarian Hittite kingdom in the north, but there is more. He wants revenge by killing King Mentchu-hotep's son, Prince Mentchu-hotep. And also, the four Libyans were commissioned to assassinate the prince, along with the two guards sent with the prince. I can see all their faces very clearly. I will deal with all of them." She opened her eyes. "This man is a danger to society. His heart is full of anger, and his soul is vibrating on a very low level—death and revenge. He is like a mad dog with rabies. He should be eliminated in order to save the lives of many innocent people." The Djedi stood up and walked out of the room, expressing no emotions, leaving Vizier Ipi and the head guard behind.

"Give me your sword and bring me some water," Vizier Ipi said to the guard. The guard gave him his sword and returned quickly with a bowl of water. "Throw it in his face and leave us," said Medjay Priest-Scientist Vizier Ipi. The guard threw the water in the general's face, waking him up, then the head guard left quickly, locking the door behind him as fast as he could.

The general stood up quickly, giving a little space between him and the Medjay. He touched his chin, still remembering their last encounter.

"Every man deserves a fighting chance even if he is guilty of many crimes against the people." Vizier Ipi threw the general a sword. He stood in front of the general, empty-handed. The general smiled as he pointed the sword at Vizier Ipi.

"I want you to enter the land of the dead knowing you had a fighting chance," said Vizier Ipi.

"Too much talk," said the general as he swung his sword toward Medjay Vizier Ipi's head, who sidestepped, blocking the sword with his bare hand and kicking the general in his throat.

The general fell back, coughing for air as he tried to regain his composure. He circled the Medjay. By now, there were four guards watching at the door. The general swung his sword again at Medjay Vizier Ipi, who evaded the sword, kicking the general in the groin, trapping his sword hand as he struck the general in his face with the base of his palm, breaking his long nose. Blood gushed out all over the general's face. The general swung again with fury at the Medjay. Only this time, the Medjay stepped in close, blocking the sword hand with his left hand and stripping it from the general's hand, catching it in his other hand while turning quickly, cutting the general's head off in one circular swing of the sword. The four guards' mouths opened in shock while blood splashed in there faces as the general's head rolled by their feet.

*****

Nswt Bety Neb Khrw-Ra Sa Ra Mentchu-hotep knew his son was in danger, and he had to prepare him without telling him of the extreme danger he was in. Sa Ra Mentchu-hotep talked to his son at great length about the importance of the forty-two ideals of Ma'at. "But there are bad people in the world, especially from the north, who, like Setsh, violate most of the laws of Ma'at and want Kemet to fall. And these northerners want to destroy us, my son—you and me—because we represent Ma'at, so we must be prepared."

"No one can kill you, Father, not even the wild, wretched Tamahu [uncivilized cavemen from the Caucasus Mountains]. You are really like the Ntchru. You are Sa Ra [the son of the sun]!"

Crown Prince Mentchu-hotep SankhkaRa

"Son, you must know the natural order of the universe and the natural order of Kemet. The natural order [Ma'at] emerged out of blackness [Nun] of the primordial ocean of precreation before anything came into existence. This ever-emergent order was established on the risen land, the primordial hill [mount], composed of elements that coexist in a state of constant interaction and over which a radiant sun poured itself—begotten light [Ra as the final manifestation of Atum when the Ennead is completed].

"The life force animating these elements could be strong or weak. Strong elements reigned with an extraordinary power at their disposal. Such a powerful law or principle was called a Ntchr or Ntchru. The more powerful an energy or deity was, the more universal its powerful field of action, and the more exalted the rank of its name and soul. The stages of this process of Nswt Bety deification can be summarized," Sa Ra Mentchu-hotep continued.

1. Nswt Bety realizes he possesses "power" and attributes this to his sacred (feminine) origin and the overseeing, witnessing capacities of the male sky—Ntchr Heru.

2. Nswt Bety affirms that he is a natural principle in his own right, incarnating continuity, tenacity, and sole rulership on earth as "follower of Heru."

3. Nswt Bety is worshipped as the unique "son of Ra."

4. In the afterlife, Nswt Bety's divine meal is composed of the souls, spirits, magic, and power of the Ntchru or deities.

5. Because Nswt Bety had his divine meal (knowledge of the sacred ancestors), he becomes a superpower knowing, except for the hidden dimension of divinity, no equal.

"All these things you must learn and master, my son, as the next Nswt Bety."

The crown prince Mentchu-hotep just smiled at his father, thinking, *There is no way I can remember all this.*

"I heard that, son, and you will learn it."

Wow, thought the crown prince, *my thoughts are not even my own! I must watch what I'm thinking around all the Medjay. They can read minds.*

42 Ideals of Ma'at

1. I honor virtue
2. I benefit with gratitude
3. I am peaceful
4. I respect the property of others
5. I affirm that all life is sacred
6. I give offerings that are genuine
7. I live in truth
8. I regard all altars with respect
9. I speak with sincerity
10. I consume only my fair share
11. I offer words of good intent
12. I relate in peace
13. I honor animals with reverence
14. I can be trusted
15. I care for the earth
16. I keep my own council
17. I speak positively of others
18. I remain in balance with my emotions
19. I am trustful in my relationships
20. I hold purity in high esteem
21. I spread joy
22. I do the best I can
23. I communicate with compassion
24. I listen to opposing opinions
25. I create harmony
26. I invoke laughter
27. I am open to love in various forms
28. I am forgiving
29. I am kind
30. I act respectfully of others
31. I am accepting
32. I follow my inner guidance
33. I converse with awareness
34. I do good
35. I give blessings
36. I keep the waters pure
37. I speak with good intent
38. I praise the Goddess and the God
39. I am humble
40. I achieve with integrity
41. I advance through my own abilities
42. I embrace the All

"Son, you must learn to calm the mind."

"But how do I do that with all the noise around us, Father?"

"Come sit next to me. First, close your eyes. Your mouth is closed, and your tongue is rolled upward so that the tip of your tongue touches the roof of the insides of your mouth. Now breath through your nose. As you inhale, your stomach should expand, and as you exhale, your stomach should retract."

"How come?"

"Just watch, son."

"But you told me to close my eyes."

"OK, open your eyes, son, and feel the sensation of your breath as it flows in and out of your nostrils at the tip of your nose. So we are focusing our attention on two things—the expansion and retraction of the stomach with the inhaling and exhaling of the breath. Feel the beginning, the middle, and the end of every inbreathing and the beginning, the middle, and the end of every outbreathing. We will inhale to the count of five, and we will exhale to the count of five. The most important thing is not the count. You are only counting in your mind, but focus on the awareness of the breath as it goes in and out of the nostrils at the tip of the nose. Remember, feel the beginning, the middle, and the end of every inhale and the beginning, the middle, and the end of every outbreathing. After a while, you will not need to count. It will be automatic. Let the breath breathe itself."

"But, Father—"

"Don't talk. Just close your eyes and breathe, son. Every time your attention moves away from the breath and shifts to a different object of awareness, such as a physical sensation or a thought, gently but firmly draw your attention back to the touch of sensation of your breath. We will continue practicing until all the sand has left our timer. No, no, don't talk. Just breathe. I will let you know when our time is up."

*****

Nswt Bety Neb Khrw-Ra Sa Ra Mentchu-hotep looked in on his two new Northern wives, Ashait and Henhenit. "I see you are studying. Hmt Nswt Wrt Neferu has fixed up your rooms really nice. They are beautiful."

"We are very pleased," said Hemet Ashait. "Neb Aa, Neb Tawy, Nswt Bety Neb Khrw-Ra Sa Ra Mentchu-hotep, please explain to us how come it takes so long to preserve the body after death. Is it to travel to heaven?"

Shemsu Heru took a deep breath, then he thought that he must have sounded just like this when he was a youth. His two new Northern wives—Henhenit and Ashait—were beautiful, with fully developed women's bodies but with minds like twelve-year-old children. "The *jet* [body] must be turned into a *sah* [a physical body prepared for the journey of eternity]. The physical body will decay and return to earth. So our priest-scientist of Enpu, the jackal-headed Ntchr of embalming, prepares the body for eternity. This process takes seventy days.

"All the soft organs are taken out. The liver, stomach, intestines, and lungs are carefully cleaned, preserved, and sealed in special Mesu-Heru [sons of Heru] jars carved to look like the Ntchru who guards these organs. The heart, however, is considered crucial for the eternal journey, so it's placed back into the body, sometimes with a scarab [*Kheper*] for renewal. The brain is also removed through the noise. The body cavity is packed with natron that soaks up all the body's moisture, and the body [*jet*] is left to dry for forty days. Finally, the natron is removed, and the *jet* is filled with spices to maintain its original shape. The *jet* is now wrapped in layers of linen, giving it the finished bandaged look. Finally, the Enpu priests tuck special amulets into the wrappings to help protect the *sah* on its eternal journey. This is why it takes so long, my beloved *Hemet* [wives]."

They both giggled like little girls.

"The Kemetyu and Kashites do not burn their dead, like Asiatics and northerners. What we do is create for immortality the karst, and the mortuary temples are in fact time capsules. We built them with the intentions that they would preserve our culture for thousands of years into the future. Your culture is your immune system. There is only one way to freedom, and that is by practicing your own culture. Slavery is when you practice someone else's culture. A person cannot be a slave when he or she is truly devoted to practicing his or her own natural culture, along with symptomatic thought.

"I must explain that at the center of our culture is Ma'at, and Ma'at clearly states that the body cannot join the Ntchr in heaven, only minds in the form of the soul. This is why the ego doesn't want you to focus on the mind. It wants you to focus only on the body as your reality. Happily, the Divine Spirit has a script, and you can switch over to it anytime you want. But the mind has to be trained to recognize the Divine Spirit or truth. I am so glad Hmt Nswt Neferu has inspired you to expand your consciousness. The word *inspired* means 'in spirit.' By joining with the Divine Spirit, you have been given the answer. Answers come to your mind in the form of guidance, inspired ideas, or dynamic action."

His two young wives started giggling again. Hmt Ashait spoke again, "We are so glad we have the best *Seba* in all of Kemet! Is it time now for dynamic action, my Neb aa?" They both jumped on the Nswt, laughing, giggling, and kissing him all over.

Above, we see southern tribute bearers. Two aspects of this wall painting are worthy of special note: (1) the cattle with stylized horns shaped like humans and (2) the black and reddish-brown pigmentation of the tribute bearers. The latter color is identical to that used in depicting the Remtch of Kemet. The garments, equipment and animals identify the people shown here as being from a nation south of Kemet.

*****

Kemet was truly entering its second golden age. This was a time for growth, but it was also a time for internal healing. Kemet was undergoing a cultural revolution. Kemet's northern borders to Asia were closed to all foreigners; the Namou, Tamahu, and Tjemehu (Libyans) and the only Asiatics who could enter were traders and foreign diplomats. Kemet also put down a rebellion in Libya, led by Djedi Ma'at Nefert, destroying all of Kemet's enemies and would-be assassins. The Tjemehu (Libyans) occupied the lands to the northwest of the Hapy Valley. Even before the time of Narmer, temple reliefs frequently showed them as a defeated enemy, and there were records from the reigns of the first golden age of Nswt Bety Snefru and SahuRa of specific campaigns against them.

Medjay and Kemetyu warriors defeating the Tjemehu

However, the climate down south was much different. Viceroy Medjay Priest-Scientist Ka-en-Jhutyms allowed skilled workers, traders, soldiers, students, and Kashite merchants and their families to enter only after strict arrangements were made in advance. Students had to apply for admission into the temples and were admitted based on skills because new farmlands had to be cultivated to feed the growing population. Many Medjay and Kashite warriors and even Ta-Sety bowmen were employed into a professional Kemet military.

Trade was also at an all-time high as merchants and skilled craftsmen bartered their goods. There was a great demand for beer and pomegranate wine from Kash, especially by the Remtch from northern Kemet. Many Kashites lived along the Eteru er Hapy, which curved northward through the desert. Farmers grew grains, peas, lentils, dates, and melons. But especially important were their herds of cattle, a measure of wealth and social status. In the deserts, Kashites mined carnelian and gold, as well as other mineral resources. They bartered cattle, gold, carnelian, ivory, animal skins, hardwood, incense, and dates. Kashites traded with the Kemetyu, their neighbors to the north, for grain, vegetable oil, wine, beer, linen, and other manufactured goods.

Kashite merchants from down south, trading in ancient Kemet

CHAPTER 3

SPIRITUAL REFORM

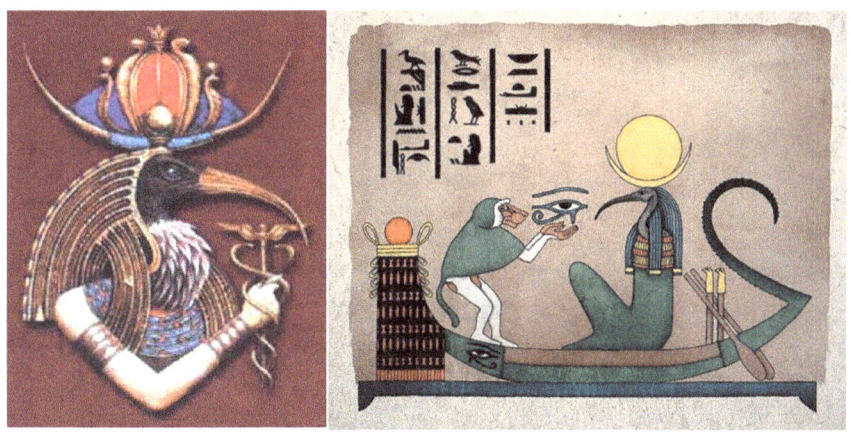

The Ntchr Jhuty holding his sacred scepter of power.
To the right, two forms of Jhuty as divine consciousness
in the Divine Spirit of every Remtch

Nswt Bety Neb Khru-Ra Sa Ra Mentchu-hotep sat down at
the head of the great royal oval table with himself on one end
and Chief Medjay Djedi Jhutyms Ka-en-Heru at the other. To
his right were Vizier Dagi and Medjay Priest-Scientist Vizier
Ipi; to the left was Hmt Nswt Wrt Neferu, and next to her was
Nswt Mwt Wrt Iah, the great royal mother of the Ntchru. The

others around the table were his chancellor Medjay Khety-en-Ra, chief steward Medjay Bennu Henenu, Kashite (viceroy) Medjay Priest-Scientist Ka-en-Jhutyms, head of security and chancellor Medjay Priest-Scientist Akhtoy Ba-Heru, Sdjawty treasurer Medjay Sia-em-hotep, chief architect Hem Sem Tepy Kha-ef-Ptah, all the high priests and priestesses from Upper and Lower Kemet, and a host of other important people who made Kemet function.

Shemsu Heru Nswt Bety Neb Khrw-Ra Sa Ra Mentchu-hotep stood up. He could feel all eyes on him as he wore the Skhemty double crown. Only now, he was the supreme leader and uniter of the greatest nation-state on the planet. "Today, I celebrate the eternal spirit at the center of my being. I set my eyes on the living light of Ntchr and am established in heaven's consciousness, so I know there can be no spiritual reform to our great nation-state, Kemet, until there is a revolutionary spiritual reform in its leadership. We become the light by which the Kemetyu can see. With that said, I will lead *Qbhw* [libation]."

Everyone stood and faced Shemsu Heru Sa Ra Mentchu-hotep, who stood before a sacred altar for Amen-Ra. He was carrying a very fancy bowl of water made of gold and silver in the shape of a ram's head and a small tree inside a planter with the face of Het Heru in it. He stepped forward with his left leg, and his left hand was open in the Ma'at posture. He then closed his eyes and began the libation. The council followed each of his postures.

SA RA MENTCHU-HOTEP: In the name of Nswt of the Ntchru Amen-Ra, the hidden one, the almighty force, the Ntchr of breath and life. Great Amen-Ra, who was self-produced at the beginning of time, self-existent, almighty, and eternal force, which created all the

Ntchru and gave form to all things. Amen, you are the unseen and unseeable creative force that is spirit and all thoughts. Ra, you are the Ntchr of light and victory, of protection, and of immeasurable power. You are the seen force of the universe manifested by the sun. Ra, you are the energy that allows light to shine. You are Kheper in the morning, Ra at noon, and Atum (the complete one) in the evening. As Amen-Ra, you have no equal. You are the sun that keeps us warm, the spirit that offers us life. You mark the cycle of day and night, months and years, centuries and millennia. You are eternal. We ask Amen-Ra to be with us, to strengthen us, and to give us vision for a great Kemet future.

RESPONSE, *as Sa Ra Mentchu-hotep poured water into the tree*: Dwa!

SA RA MENTCHU-HOTEP, *his left leg still remaining forward, his hands rising in the Ka posture, and the council following him*: In the name of the great Ntchru, the cosmic and celestial Ntchru, that aid Amen-Ra in the maintenance and general operation of the universe. These Ntchru are laws and principles of creation and act as the managers of all existence for all life known and unknown. In the name of the Duat Ntchru, they represent the intermediate plane. These Ntchru are realms of light that are responsible for transformation between the spiritual and the physical, material worlds. And to the terrestrial Ntchru, they represent nature and the natural functions of things on our planet. We ask these Ntchru to be with us, to strengthen us, and to give us vision for a great Kemet future.

RESPONSE, *as the Sa Ra Mentchu-hotep poured water into the tree*: Dwa!

SA RA MENTCHU-HOTEP, *only his left hand rising in the air, with his right hand across his chest, but the left foot still remaining forward, and the council following him*: In the name of the first great Remtch (original humans) who began the march of humanity and civilization; who were guided by Jhuty, Ma'at, and Seshat; and who came out of the womb of the mother of creation—Mwt, Het Heru, Sekhmet. We ask the great mother Ntchru, mistress of the universal feminist energies to be with us, to strengthen us, and to give us vision for a great Kemet future.

RESPONSE, *as the Sa Ra Mentchu-hotep poured water into the tree*: Dwa!

SA RA MENTCHU-HOTEP, *kneeling down on his right knee, with his left hand up and right hand across the chest, and the council following him*: In the name of the first great Remtch leaders who began the march of humanity and civilization—Asar, Aset, and Heru—and to the Khemmennu Ntchru.

The Khemmennu Ntchru were eight deities who were the bases of Kemet's creation story during the second golden age. They were primarily worshipped in Khemmennu, but their aspects of the creation were combined in other areas with existing stories. Each one is a member of a masculine-feminine pair, and each pair represents an aspect of the primordial chaos out of which the world was created. They all came into being at the same time. Nun and Nanuet represented the primordial seas, from inert to energy; Kuk and Kauker represented the infinite darkness and light, Hu and Huhet represented empty space, (infinity and finite; and Amen and Amenunet represented quintessence or the secret powers of creation that which was hidden and revealed.

The Ntchru Khemmennu at Khemmennu was led by Jhuty. In the name of the great triad in Waset, Amen, Mwt, and Khensu; to the great triad in Kash, Khnum, Anuket, and Satet; to the great triad in the north, Ptah, Sekhmet, and Nefer-Atum; and to the great triad of the south here in Waset, Asr, Ast and Heru, we ask these Ntchru to be with us, to strengthen us, and to give us vision for a great Kemet future.

RESPONSE, *as Sa Ra Mentchu-hotep poured water into the tree*: Dwa!

SA RA MENTCHU-HOTEP, *kneeling on both knees, with his hands crossed like Asr, and the council following him*: In the name of the first great Remtch and Kemetyu leaders who began civilization in the Hapy Valley, establishing their high culture and building their temples, great monuments, pyramids, and tombs to the Ntchru and great human spirits. We ask these great Remtch and Kemetyu, like Imhotep and Ptah-hotep, and the best of our ancestors' great spirits to be with us, to strengthen us, and to give us vision for a great Kemet future.

RESPONSE, *as Sa Ra Mentchu-hotep poured water into the tree*: Dwa!

SA RA MENTCHU-HOTEP, *bending his head forward, touching his forehead to the ground, with both knees bent in prayer, and the council following him*: In the name of Shemsu Heru who came from the south to Kemet; from Kash, Ta-Sety, Punt, Ta Khuy, Ta Ntchr; from the three Mountains of the Moon; and from beyond where the Heru Bess dwells, who guided and taught the Shemsu Heru here in Kemet—like Heru Narmer, Heru Aha, Heru Djer, Heru Djet, Heru Den, Heru Anedjib, Heru Semerkhet, Heru Qa'a, Heru Hotepsekhemwy, Heru NebRa, Heru Nynetchr, Heru Set-peribsen, Heru Khasekhemwy, Heru Sanakhte, Heru Netchrikhet, Heru Sekhemkhet, Heru Khaba, Heru Huni, Heru Snefru, Heru Khufu, Heru DjedefRa, Heru KhafRa, Heru MenkauRa, Heru Shepseskaf, Heru Userkaf, Heru SahuRa, Heru NeferifkaRa, Heru ShepseskaRa, Heru NeferefRa, Heru NiuserRa, Heru Menkauheru, Heru DjedkaRa, Heru Unas, Heru Teti, Heru Pepy, Heru MerenRa, Heru Pepy NeferkaRa, Heru WadjkaRa, Heru MeryibRa, Heru MerykaRa, Heru KaneferRa, Heru QakaRa, Heru NebkauRa, and our beloved Heru Sehertawy-Sa Ra Intef—we ask these great Shemsu Heru to be with us, to strengthen us, and to give us vision for a great Kemet future.

RESPONSE, *as Sa Ra Mentchu-hotep poured the last of the water from the bowl into the tree*: Dwa! Dwa! Dwaaaaaaaaaa!

The entire council stood in awe, for Sa Ra Mentchu-hotep was truly the high priest and Nswt Bety of Kemet. Once the council had taken their seats, the Nswt Bety continued his speech. "The entire priestship of Upper and Lower Kemet must be vibrating on the same wavelength of Ma'at. I know that there must be artistic freedom for each temple to express the Ntchru in their own special way. These things will not change. But truth and harmony are consistent in our solar system governed by Ra, so Ma'at must be taught the same in each temple. The sacred trinity of Asr, Ast, and Heru must be taught on all levels of the society. It must penetrate all classes, from the elite rich to the farmers and everything in between. We have defeated our physical foreign enemies on the battlefield, but now the real battle must be waged in the minds and hearts of our people.

Level 1 at the top was the Shemsu Heru, the Nswt Bety. Level 2 was the royal family and high-ranking priests and officials. Level 3 was the regular priests, artists, scribes, and wealthy merchants and farmers, along with police and officers of the soldiers. Level 4 was the regular farmers, merchants, traders, soldiers, and common Kemetyu.

"If the souls of our people are to be liberated, we must show them the way! I have seen their hearts, and I have looked into their minds and walked in their footprints with their sandals. And I know what they want. They want the very same things we want at this table. Our people, the Kemetyu, want to be free, safe, clean, and prosperous and their environment filled with love and respect. We have destroyed the external enemy physically. Now we must defeat the enemy within. We defeat our enemy's culture by practicing our own. Embracing ourstory and practicing Ma'at, our nature-based spiritual system, will enhance our freedom.

"We have developed the greatest military on earth with the help of the Medjay. This will protect our freedom and our borders. Each temple must also teach cleanliness as part of our spiritual system, so we, the Remtch, must clean our own villages and streets, as well as our own personal properties. We will encourage farming and the cottage industry, meaning everything we use, we must make. Prosperity comes when you export more than you import. And during the inundation season when we can't farm, the powerful central governing system will employ the Remtch in government projects, temples, irrigation systems, and housing.

"During the first golden age, only the Nswt Bety and his royal family and a few high priests could be Maa Khrw, true of voice, vindicated, and risen to Pt [heaven]. But if we are responsible for building good character, every Kemetyu has the possibility of standing before the judgment scales of Ma'at in the Duat. Every citizen of Kemet can work toward being Maa Khrw, and no one has an automatic pass into Pt. This makes everyone accountable to Ma'at."

The whole council stood up and lifted their hands up in the Ka position and chanted, "Dua Ntchr! Dua Ma'at!"

His royal mother, Nswt Mwt Ntchru Iah, and his great royal wife, Hmt Nswt Wrt Neferu, had tears in their eyes. And so did a few other men. His fellow Medjay warriors in the room all looked at one another with that united sparkle from another world, for their younger brother had arrived!

He continued his thoughts, "I want Ma'at to be more than just a principle but a way of life—whether that balance refers to weights and measurements in the marketplace among the merchants, law and order in our courts among our judges and priests, innerstanding the universal cosmological patterns above and below by our priest-scientist, or the judgment of the heart on the scales of Ma'at in Amenta by Asr."

He knew that the Kemety society was shaped like a Mer Khut (pyramid). The Nswt Bety with his Hmt Nswt Wrt (great royal wife) was at the top. Below them, the royal family and nobles, chief priests and priestesses, head scribes, ministers, and military officers formed the upper class. Below the upper class, the artisans, skilled craft workers, traders, scribes, and regular priests and priestesses made up the middle class, while farmers, fishermen, soldiers, and laborers formed the base of the Mer Khut.

"Ma'at originated with the creation. The great Nswt Bety of ancient Kemet who considered themselves the sons of Ra and followers of Heru were also great servants of the Ntchru Ma'at, Seshat, and Jhuty. They felt it necessary to constantly restore Ma'at whenever it was needed. We have made tremendous progress over the last year rebuilding Kemet. I am very pleased with the physical progress and the economic progress, but our spiritual commitment to the Ntchru needs more work. So yes, it is that time once again, my great and distinguished council, to restore Ma'at. We restore Ma'at in our nation by restoring Ma'at in ourselves. We must conquer our egos, and only then can we teach the correct virtues of Ma'at. In order to conquer our egos, the soul must be victorious in battle for the use of our minds.

"The ego seeks to serve itself, while the soul seeks to serve others. The ego seeks outward recognition, while the soul seeks inner authenticity. The ego sees life as a competition, while the soul sees life as a gift. The ego seeks to preserve the self, while the soul seeks to preserve others. The ego looks outward, while the soul looks inward. The ego feels lack, while the soul feels abundance. The ego is mortal, while the soul is eternal. The ego is drawn to lust, while the soul is drawn to love. The ego seeks knowledge, while the soul, through the Divine Spirit, is wisdom. The ego enjoys the prize, while the soul enjoys the journey. The ego is the cause for pain, while the soul, through Divine Spirit, is the cause for healing. Our nation needs healing, my divine council. Like Heru defeated Set, we must defeat our own ego so that Ma'at may take control of our lives, our families, our cities, and the complete nation-state of Kemet, Sema Tawy, and our beloved land, Ta Mery." The Nswt Bety gathered his thoughts as he looked around the room.

"When we met last year in Hut Nen-nesu, Kashite [viceroy] Medjay Priest-Scientist Ka-en-Jhutyms made a profound statement that is worthy of repeating here. 'Don't wait for the perfect moment. Take the moment and make it perfect!' We must seize the moment and bring forth Ma'at. Kemet will not change by our position in the universe. Actions change only when beliefs change. Collective actions and beliefs will change Kemet. That is why we are here, so collectively, we can leave on the same page. The chief Medjay has taught me that popular beliefs on essential matters must be examined in order to discover the original thought, and then we must make room for growth. Kemet has grown, but we must not make the mistake of growing too fast. It is the passive resistance from the helm that steers the boat. Medjay Sia em-hotep, you taught me that.

"Finally, I echo the words of Chief Medjay Jhutyms Ka-en-Heru that the key to all problems is the problem of consciousness, so we must make sure our thought pattern is symptomatic thought. We must learn to increase our sense of responsibility and accountability of the fact that everything we do will have its consequences. And there are specific symptoms that lead to success. We must follow them. So, my priests and priestesses and Kemetyu of leadership, this is what must be explained when you talk about the Duat and the double halls of Ma'at. And of course, the reward for doing Ma'at is to receive Ma'at.

"Organizational unity is impossible unless those who know the laws of harmony lay the foundation. That is why each temple must reflect Ma'at. The totality of all our science, astrology, astronomy, mathematics, and ethics must be reflected not only in our buildings but even in our art. It is of no use whatsoever to preach wisdom to the dead, dumb, and blind Remtch. You must inject it into their blood. Knowledge is consciousness of reality. Reality is the sum of the laws that govern nature and of the causes from which they flow.

"Duau Ntchru and my divine council, thank you for your time and patience. Let's hold hands and repeat these words. This is a prayer for positivity: I pray that I think peace, speak peace, and *I am* peace. I pray that I think truth, speak truth, and *I am* truth. I pray that I think love, speak love, and *I am* love. I pray everything I attract carries high, harmonious vibrations and intentions. May the light within me serve as a lantern shining the way for those who need it. Amen-Ra.

"Now if we can break into smaller groups so that we can review what was spoken here today. I need all the branches of the grand council innerstanding and understanding one another so when we leave here, we are of one mind. We are to heal ourselves and the nation of the six major disorders that still plague us—anger, grief, worry, stress, fear, and hate. Anger weakens the liver. Grief weakens the lungs. Worry weakens the stomach. Stress weakens the heart. Fear weakens the kidneys. Hate weakens the soul."

*****

"Tiw, Neb aa, great lord, you wanted to speak with us?"

"Please sit, Vizier Dagi and Vizier Ipi. I want to speak with you not as your leader but as a friend or as a student of life."

"Tiw, we innerstand Shemsu Heru Sa Ra Mentchu-hotep." They sat in a vast library surrounded by papyrus scrolls; some of which were much older than Kemet.

The Nswt Bety pointed to the scrolls. "I have spent a lot of time and energy reading many of these scrolls, and I need to be clear on my innerstanding so that our nation can move forward spiritually. In the early phases of Kemet, the Nswt Bety's role was fundamental. Because he—as a Ntchr-man—was the only possible mediator between the sky or heaven [pt] of the pantheon and the earth [ta] of Kemet and its temples, he guaranteed the stability and the unity of Kemet by offering truth and justice [Ma'at] to his father Ra. Is this correct?"

"Tiw, Neb aa."

"With the end of the Mer Khut [pyramid] age came our First Intermediate Period or the dark period—a period characterized by an increased provincial, family-based individualism. This was also a time when eastern and western Asiatics immigrated into our country, causing esfet. We have ended that era. My great-grandfather, Mentchu-hotep, and his children, the great family of Inyotefs—called the keepers of the door of the south—led us to this point in our glorious story. And now this is the second golden age I am leading into existence. I want to bring about operational unity and ascension [everybody has a soul and has the ability to ascend to Asr] but also familiarized judgment as the results of personal works [a soul could be annihilated if out of balance with Ma'at].

"Amen-Ra of Waset is the national Ntchr or the Nswt of the Ntchru, and with this worship, a strict innerstanding of one Creator is being created. I don't want our priests and priestesses to just place Amen at the apex of the pantheon as 'ruler of the Ntchru' and 'divine judge.' I want the Kemetyu intellectual elite to innerstand the complete pantheon as so many manifestations and transformations of the *great* and *one* Amen, hidden by nature but manifested in nature's million forms. A spiritual theocracy will be born. Although Amen-Ra is the one great mind, it exists inside each Remtch. So each Remtch must take action of their own prayers. No one in the sky is listening to the prayers of the commoners. Amen-Ra is in everything, and everyone and the Creator have placed the responsibility in our hands, not just the Nswt Bety's hands.

"Now under my rule as Nswt Bety Neb Khrw-Ra Sa Ra Mentchu-hotep of the second golden age, nonroyals could assume the form of Asr. And a fundamental prerogative of Nswt Bety was made available to the monarchs [the rulers of the forty-two provinces or *sput*], their families, and wealthy administrators and all who lived by Ma'at. For by placing Asr before their names, the deceased expressed the hope of their forthcoming deification in the afterlife in heaven with Asr.

"Let us review our priests and priestesses. At the top, we have the *Hem Ntchr-Tepy* [high priest], *Imi-khet Hemu-Ntchr* [overseer of priests and priestesses], *Sem Ntchr* [leader of rituals], *Kheri-hebet* [lecturer priest], *Hem-Ntchr* or *Hemet-Ntchr* [ritual priests and priestesses], *Yit Ntchr* [father or elder priests], *Mwt Ntchr* [mother of the Nswt Bety and elder mother of the Ntchru], *Wab Ntchr* and *Wabt Ntchrt* [worker and purification priests and priestesses—nonritual tasks], and then *Shemayet* [chanter]. We also need to post all the four major months with their festivals for each season so that the complete Kemetyu family will be on the same page."

Akhet (Season of Inundation)

First month: opening of the year, Wag festival of Asr, festival of the departure of Asr (Abydos), festival of Jhuty, festival of intoxication (Het Heru)

Second month: festival of Ptah, south of his wall (Mennefer), Opet festival (Waset)

Third month: festival of Het Heru (Edfu and Dendarah)

Fourth month: festival of Sokar, festival of Sekhmet

Peret (Season of Growth)

First month: festival of Nehebkau, festival of the coronation of the sacred falcon (Edfu), festival of Min, festival of the departure of Mut

Second month: festival of victory (Edfu), great brand festival

Third month: small brand festival

Fourth month: festival of Renenutet

Shemu (Season of Harvest)

First month: festival of Khensu, festival of the departure of Min

Second month: festival of the beautiful feast of the valley (Waset)

Third month: festival of the beautiful meeting (Edfu and Dendarah)

Fourth month: festival of Ra-Heru-khuty, festival of the opening of the year

Epagomenal Days

Festivals of Asr, Heru Ur, Set, Ast, and Nebet-Het (celebrated on five successive days)

The unified priestship of Upper and Lower Kemet in the second golden age under the leadership of Nswt Bety Neb Khrw-Ra Mentchu-hotep

*****

I, Shemsu Heru Nswt Bety Neb Khrw-Ra Sa Ra Mentchu-hotep, commanded military campaigns south, as far as the fifth cataract or the second cataract from Punt into Kash, which had expanded its territory during the First Intermediate Period. My Kashite viceroy—Commander Medjay Priest-Scientist Ka-en-Jhutyms—and I met with Shemsu Heru Nswt Tut-Ankh-Khnum, ruler of Kash at Dju Em Hat. It was a city just north of the fifth cataract.

"Thank you for meeting with us here, Shemsu Heru Tut-Ankh-Khnum. This is about trade and economic stability between our two great nations. Kemet would like to build a few fort castles, like you have in Napata in Kash, as trading posts to better control the flow of goods traveling in both directions. We will finance it if you will provide the labor.

Viceroy Commander Medjay Priest-Scientist Ka-en-Jhutyms will oversee the projects with your permission, of course. Also Hmt Nswt Tem, your elder daughter, will oversee our joint educational program between Kemet and Kash."

"Give me the plans and exact locations. Deliver them to my son, the mayor of Napata, and we will review them. I am sure he would look forward to working with his big brother, Medjay Ka-en-Jhutyms, and his younger big sister, Hmt Nswt Tem. The old Kemet during the first golden age would have tried to bully us, so I appreciate your style. My lovely daughter, Tem, made an excellent choice when she chose you. Thank you for being a true man of honor and character.

"I look at this financial crisis in Kash with its expanding desert as a challenge rather than a curse, an opportunity rather than a problem, a struggle rather than an obstacle, a time to win rather than a time to lose, and a time to be brave rather than be afraid. We Napatians are sometimes glad when things are difficult because difficulty is the dividing line between winners and losers, freedom and slavery. Think of difficulty and struggle as the training ground of champions and success, which creates the backbone of a strong nation." He reached over and hugged me—warrior to warrior, ruler to ruler, Shemsu Heru to Shemsu Heru. "At one time, I thought I lost a daughter, but now I realize I never lost a daughter. Instead, I gained a son! *Dua Ntchr Khnum*," he said.

"I'm glad you are leading this project, Medjay Ka-en-Jhutyms, because not only are you one of the strongest warriors I know—and I know the very best—your very existence is the life of Heru! Heru thinking is the foundation for *truth* or what you Kemetyu call Ma'at. Ma'at is universal and eternal. It is so important that we continue to move forward in Ma'at, even though it may feel as though we are straining to do so.

We should never give up on our dreams, our goals, and our missions. We can and must allow the challenges that we are going through to make us stronger and better. It may not be easy, but it certainly will be worth the effort.

"National growth cannot happen in a vacuum. It is important and necessary that we experience challenges in order to create in us the growth and maturity that we long for and desire. Because in the end, we all want sovereignty." He embraced Medjay Ka-en-Jhutyms with great love and respect. They looked into each other's eyes. "My son?"

"He is Vizier Medjay Priest-Scientist Ipi now. He is *eqr* [excellent], and he sends much mrr [love]."

Shemsu Heru Tut-Ankh-Khnum smiled as he mounted his shiny all-black horse and joined his warriors. Words were exchanged, then they rode away.

*****

We both knelt down on one knee and closed our eyes in silent prayer. "Speak to me of Ankh en Mrr," I said to my Neb Aa and Medjay Priest-Scientist Ka-en-Jhutyms.

"I was alone with the primeval ocean Nun. All the Ntchru were within me. I was floating between . . . totally inert, my son. Life roused my spirit, which made my heart live, and gathered up my inert members. I heard the sound of Hu, who told me, 'Inhale your daughter Ma'at and raise her to your nostril so that your heart may live. May they not be far from you, your daughter Ma'at and your son Shu, whose names are life and love, Ankh en Mrr."

"Speak to me of Heru."

"I am Heru who comes to you, mighty one. I bring you this from my father Ra. I performed Asr's purification rites and assisted him at his justification. I assembled his bones and reunited his members. Amen-Ra. Love, wisdom, and power—Ankh, Shsa, Was [prosper Heru]."

We mounted our horses and joined our warriors for our return journey back to Kemet. Our new mission has begun. Amen-Ra is satisfied.

*****

Medjay Priest-Scientist Ka-en-Jhutyms thought to himself as they road back silently to Waset that Nswt Bety Neb Khrw-Ra Sa Ra Mentchu-hotep had earned his new title that would be etched in the walls of Kemet as Sankh-ib-Tawy Heru—he who invigorates the hearts of the two lands.

The Buhen castle covered 140,000 square feet! It housed at any time over 3,500 soldiers. It possessed catapults, ramparts, drawbridges, buttresses, cylinder towers, and all other classic features of the castle.

CHAPTER 4

STAGES OF MY JOURNEY

The chief of the Medjay, Djedi Jhutyms Ka-en-Heru, entered the great royal palace of the Nswt Bety Neb Khrw-Ra Sa Ra Mentchu-hotep and was greeted by his own youngest son, Medjay Priest-Scientist Akhtoy, who was head of security for the royal family at the royal palace.

He greeted his father, bowing his head in respect, "Ee m htp Yit Wr." (I come to offer you peace, great Father.)

He replied, "Dua Ntchr Nb Sa Aa." (All praise to divinity, great son.)

"How can I serve you, Father?"

"I need to speak to Shemsu Heru Sa Ra Mentchu-hotep, my great son."

"He is with Hmt Nswt Wrt Neferu in the reading room at the moment, but if you would wait in the royal garden, I will tell him you are here."

"Dua Ntchr."

As they both walked through the royal palace, the chief Medjay was impressed with the internal decor of the palace, the spacious flow of air, the sweet smell of flowers, and the beautiful wall paintings with Mdw Ntchr everywhere. He smiled because he could tell the work of his grandson, Hem Ntchr Kha-ef-Ptah. There were even several friezes of the chief Medjay in battle and of him giving great words of wisdom. They passed several posted Medjay royal guards who all knelt on one knee as they approached Chief Medjay Djedi Jhutyms Ka-en-Heru, and he returned their respect as he entered the royal garden. Two more Medjay were on post in the royal garden—one on each side. They both quickly dropped to one knee when they saw Chief Medjay Djedi Jhutyms Ka-en-Heru enter. "As you were," he said as he returned their respect.

"I shall return quickly," replied Medjay Akhtoy as he vanished back into the great palace.

The great Medjay chief sat near the flowing water fountain as he began to collect his thoughts. In his mind's eye, he could recall the battle of Shemsu Heru Neb Khrw-Ra Sa Ra

Mentchu-hotep and King Mery Ka-Ra of the north. He saw and could feel the great energy field that surrounded Nswt Mentchu-hotep in battle. He saw the Nswt jump over nine feet in the air, with perfect catlike balance, unlike any normal human being. He witnessed his transformation into a huge black panther and saw the panther rip, claw, and pull King Mery Ka-Ra's shield arm right out of its socket. He also innerstood the power and ability of Sa Ra Mentchu-hotep to transform back and forth from man to panther at will. He saw the blinding speed of Sa Ra Mentchu-hotep's sword. And even through the smoke, which even very few Medjay could see, he saw the black panther bite into the chest of the king, pulling his heart out! This was not only the skill of an elite Medjay warrior but it also fits the skill of a Medjay spiritual priest-scientist! He thought, *His time has arrived!*

Medjay Priest-Scientist Akhtoy returned with both the Nswt Bety Neb Khrw-Ra Sa Ra Mentchu-hotep and Hmt Nswt Wrt Neferu. They all came into the garden to greet Chief Medjay Djedi Jhutyms Ka-en-Heru. They all hugged like it was a family reunion.

"I just wanted to thank you personally for the safety of my husband, Nswt Bety Neb Khrw-Ra Sa Ra Mentchu-hotep, and for our great nation-state, Kemet! Words cannot express my appreciation, for he is my life, my air," Hmt Nswt Wrt Neferu said as she knelt to his feet. Neferu rose slowly. "You are not only a Heru to the people. You are my personal Heru also, and there is no one that the Nswt Bety speaks more highly of than you, Chief Medjay Djedi Jhutyms Ka-en-Heru! I will vanish back into the palace and let you men, you great warriors, speak. Dua Ntchr!" They all hugged again as Hmt Nswt Neferu ran back into the royal palace.

Medjay Priest-Scientist Akhtoy spoke, "Is there anything I can bring to you, my Neb aa?"

"We will be fine. Thank you," said Sa Ra Mentchu-hotep. Medjay Priest-Scientist Akhtoy backed away, never turning his back, as he reentered the royal palace.

"I will get straight to the point," said Chief Medjay Djedi Jhutyms Ka-en-Heru. "The Immortal Psdju, our sacred Medjay council of the nine immortal Djedi, wish to initiate you to train as a Medjay priest-scientist. We are a group of great spiritual teachers called the Immortal Psdju or the council of nine immortals. We are Djedi, and we make Medjay spiritual priest-scientists and Djedi warriors. Their divine spirits represent love, like the Ntchru. Their devotion to our salvation is total, impersonal, selective, and all-embracing. They have very little communication with this world, and they only train Medjay priest-scientists and Djedi warriors. We, the Immortal Psdju Djedi, have no real legends to any country or nation but only to Ma'at not only in this world but also in our galaxy.

"We will meet at the base of the Mer Khut en Khufu at the next full moon at Ra set or *Atum-Ra*. Do not question the council. It is with my recommendation that they see you. You have come to know and experience that the Ntchr or Ntchru is not outside of you. You will learn to no longer identify yourself with a vulnerable body or anything else that can be limited. You will learn instead of your true reality as pure spirit that is invulnerable forever. My two sons who have become Medjay priest-scientists speak very highly of you, and they both say it is truly an honor to serve with you and under you.

"And of all the Medjay medju, you have embodied Ma'at at its highest level. You have embodied what we call deep thought—one whose heart is informed about things that would be otherwise ignored by the commoner, who is clear-sighted when he is deep into a problem, who is moderate in his actions, who penetrates ancient writing, who is sensible enough to unravel complications, who is really wise, whose heart gives good instructions, who stays awake at night as he looks for the right way, who surpasses what he accomplished yesterday, who is as wise as a sage, who followed Jhuty's great pathway to wisdom, and who asks for advice and sees to it that he follows that great advice. So I say to you, great Neb Shemsu Heru Nswt Bety Neb Khrw-Ra Sa Ra Mentchu-hotep, *Dua Neb.*

"Only one out of a hundred Medjay warriors become a priest-scientist. It is not even the goal of most Medjay. I am extremely proud of you! There at the Mer Khut en Khufu, you will outline the ten steps of becoming a Medjay priest-scientist, which are the ten steps of finding oneness. In doing this, you will also innerstand that life is not a problem to be solved but a gift to be opened."

"I am honored to walk behind you, great Neb of Nebu. I offer myself as an instrument of the spirit. I allow my soul's force to express in its fullest form, and all is well with my spirit and life circumstances. I shall be ready. And to meet all the Djedi council is a dream of a lifetime!" The Nswt Bety knelt on one knee. "Dua Ntchr."

They embraced, and then one of the Medjay guards escorted the chief Medjay out of the royal palace.

*****

I entered the new royal palace in Men-nefer; my heart was pleased by the work of our chief architect Hem Sem Tepy Kha-ef-Ptah. I am always amazed by his magnificent work. Hmt Nswt Ashait greeted me at the front entrance. She looked so beautiful, and now she walked like the true ruler she was born to be. Her beautiful golden skin and dark-brown eyes were highlighted by blue eye shadow, with a matching lapis lazuli necklace and bracelets and matching armbands. She was absolutely stunning. I kissed her gently on her lips and hand. "You look gorgeous," I said to her.

"Dua Ntchr, my Neb aa."

"Nswt Mwt Wrt Iah says that you graduated at the top of your class and that you are a full priestess of the sacred temple of Het Heru."

She smiled as she placed her arms around me, the man she admired the most in life. "I am so glad to see you, my Nswt Bety. How long will you be here?"

"Only three days and then I must meet with the Djedi Immortal Psdju."

Ashait knelt down on one knee. "You are so honored, my Neb aa. Most Remtch think they are not real, only legendary stories of super beings from another world. Tonight I shall cook for you and show you that I am a complete hemet, but now let me show you around our new royal palace." She was extremely proud of her honey farm, where she was cultivating several types of honey. "Now that I am also a priestess, I have learned so many uses for honey, my Nswt Bety. Honey combats infections and speeds healing. It's a potent killer of harmful bacteria. It's a disinfectant, an antibiotic. It's hypertonic—absorbs water and keeps wombs dry. It promotes the growth of healthy tissue. And the beauty of all this is, it will never go bad!"

"Dua Ntchr," I said.

"And Vizier Ipi is teaching me meditation," she said. "And now I know why you are so peaceful, my Nswt Bety. I am learning some of your Medjay secrets: anger weakens the liver, grief weakens the lungs, worry weakens the stomach, stress weakens the heart, and fear weakens the kidneys."

"I am very impressed, my hemet. You have been very busy."

"I remember your words, my hee, like it was yesterday. 'Great minds have purpose. Others have wishes and dreams.'"

At the conclusion of each of the three days, Hmt Nswt Ashait bathed me and gave me a complete body massage. She made me feel like I was twenty again and full of life. I spent each morning signing important documents and papers; each afternoon meeting dignitaries, kissing babies, and mixing with the common people; and the late afternoon talking trade and government with the wealthy and noble class. But each night, Hmt Nswt Ashait had me to herself.

On our final night together before my meeting with the Djedi immortal Psdju, she recited a poem that Hmt Nswt Neferu wrote for her. She stood up in front of me with her perfectly shaped nude body and spoke with elegance and grace.

What is a Ntchrt?

A woman who is in the process of learning to know, accept, and love herself on all levels—mind, body, and spirit.

A woman who, because she focuses on personal growth and self-awareness, experiences a life increasingly filled with peace, love, joy, passion, and harmony.

A woman that innerstands that she has unlimited capacity to make her life anything she wants.

A woman who is inspired to give to those around her because of her sense of gratitude and abundance of infinite love.

I am a divine noblewoman of Kemet, embodying the very essences of Ntchrt.

I sat up in my bed and gave her a Dua Ntchr with a lot of energy and mrr. *She has become an amazing woman,* I thought.

*****

The next day at high noon, the Medjay medju met me at the royal palace, and Hmt Nswt Ashait gave them the royal tour also. They were very impressed because they remembered it when it was just a garden. I stood at the base of the Mer Khut en Khufu at the full moon at Atum-Ra in Giza, just like Chief Medjay Djedi Jhutyms Ka-en-Heru had instructed. The Medjay medju were all by my side; they were as excited as I was because only four of the Medjay medju had seen the Immortal Psdju Djedi. Four Medjay priest-scientists from our Medjay medju were related to a Djedi priest-scientist warrior. Medjay Priest-Scientist Ka-en-Jhutyms and Medjay Priest-Scientist Akhtoy en Heru were the sons of Djedi Jhutyms Ka-en-Heru, and they both had Djedi mothers. Medjay Priest-Scientist Ipi was the grandson of a Djedi, and his father's brother was a Djedi. Medjay Priest-Scientist Heru-Bes was the son of a Djedi from the deep south.

A large circular blue light appeared in front of us. We all stood back. A Djedi grand master walked out of the light. "I am Djedi Ka-en-Khufu, and I know who all of you are. I greet you in the name of Amen-Ra and the Djedi royal council, for

I am a humble servant of Ma'at, a member of the Immortal Psdju Djedi council. I send you all greetings from the Immortal Psdju."

This Djedi was beyond striking. He stood maybe six feet nine and was 250 pounds. He was extremely dark in skin color, almost pure black, and was very muscular. He was dressed in a golden royal apron trimmed in purple with two gold and purple straps that crossed his muscular chest. He wore a double-sword holster on his back, like Djedi Jhutyms Ka-en-Heru, loaded with two magnificent swords. Hanging from the belt around his waist was a leather pouch and dagger on the left side and some kind of colorfully designed tube about twelve inches long called a light sword, with a handle on the right side. He wore a golden-looking helmet. It was nothing like I had ever seen before. At his feet were sandals that strapped up to his muscular calves, with daggers attached inside and out. "Shemsu Heru Nswt Bety Neb Khrw-Ra Sa Ra Mentchu-hotep, along with Medjay Priest-Scientist Ka-en-Jhutyms and Medjay Priest-Scientist Akhtoy Ba-Heru, you may assist your ruler. Step inside, please. Everyone else, please wait here. We shall return in two of your hours or less."

We walked inside some kind of transportation portal. We only walked inside maybe three or four steps, and the portal closed and opened on the other side. We were inside the Mer Khut of Khufu, in its uppermost chamber. Sitting in magnificent golden stools were the Immortal Psdju Djedi grand masters. There was one stool reserved for me, and the Medjay stood near the entrance. The irony here was that the entrance was sealed, so there was no way in or out! There seemed to be some kind of bluish light on the ceiling. It was very calming.

"The names of the Djedi are irrelevant for this meeting. You have been recommended by a Djedi to this council. That is the only way we recruit new members, and that is why you are here. Do you innerstand us?"

"Tiw."

"*Dua,* we will continue. We, the Immortal Psdju council of Djedi, operate as one voice, so they will speak through me or telepathically send the question directly to your mind. But you will only address me, Djedi Ka-en-Khufu. I hope that is clear?"

"Tiw, it is clear," I responded.

"I will ask questions. Please repeat each of them, then answer them to the best of your ability. Speak only the truth you know, and be steadfast in its application. Before you speak, let your words pass through three gates: Is it true? Is it necessary? Is it Ma'at? Are you ready, Shemsu Heru Nswt Bety Neb Khrw-Ra Sa Ra Mentchu-hotep?"

"Tiw, Djedi Ka-en-Khufu. I am ready."

"*Wa.* What was your divine mission in this lifetime?"

"Wa. What was my divine mission in this lifetime? Searching for the spirit of my great-grandfather and unifying Kemet into one nation-state. I innerstood my journey and my divine mission here in Kemet. I recognized that what I was truly seeking was contentment, not just happiness but an inner peace—Ma'at."

"*Senu.* Did you accept your divine mission?"

"Senu. Did I accept my divine mission? Discovering the spirit of my great-grandfather, once I knew the mission, I truly innerstood it in its totality. I realized that the journey to the center must take place in my mind first. True power comes from within. I not only accepted my divine mission. I became the living embodiment of it."

"*Shmut.* Can you reprogram your mind for success?"

"Shmut. Can I reprogram my mind for success? Preparing for the journey in a way was part of the reprograming. You uncover the way in which you have unconsciously defined yourself, and you realize how profoundly these self-images have affected the quality of your life. The reprograming was finding the right self-images to direct my new life. We all have the power to reprogram our minds for success."

"*Fedu.* Can you acknowledge that fear does not exist?"

"Fedu. Can I acknowledge that fear does not exist? Conquering your fears is the innerstanding that fear is an illusion. You begin to resolve your issues from the past and present and start to confront your challenges because there are no fears regarding the future. Love is what we are born with. Fear is what we learn. The spiritual journey is the unlearning of fear and the acceptance of love back in our hearts, being able to know the difference between fear and danger! I have no fear because now I know that fear does not exist, but I innerstand that danger is real!"

"*Diu.* Can you manage your thoughts?"

"Diu. Can I manage my thoughts? Making the journey yours, owning it, takes personal management! I learned how to maintain a moment-to-moment awareness of my thoughts that incessantly rose within my mind. Tiw, I learned to manage my thoughts."

"*Sesu.* Could you create a map to your destination?"

"Sesu. Could I create a map to my destination? Walking the path of your journey once you have your end goal or mission plotted in your mind is the outline of your map. You learn to live in the moment, in the infinite now! This gives you clarity of your past, your present, and your future, which are all happening now. Your map is created after this is clear. Only at that point could I construct my map."

"*Sefku*. Was arriving at your destination the end of your journey?"

"Sefku. Was arriving at my destination the end of my journey? Arriving at my destination was not the end of my journey but only a new beginning. You unify your fragmented mind as you conquer all the obstacles leading to Ma'at, which were only illusions to start with. At this point, a new energy is created, allowing a new beginning, living in harmony with the natural rhythm of your life in Ma'at. Arriving at my destination was an open door to a new journey."

"*Khemmennu*. Is ankh eternal?"

"Khemmennu. Is ankh eternal? Tiw, a new journey is birthed, showing there is no beginning and no real end. You realize who you are beyond your self-definition. Who are you to your community? How does your personal journey benefit the community? Your life does not belong to you, and tiw, this energy you call your life is eternal because it is part of the eternal Creator!"

"*Psdju*. Does divinity have management?"

"Psdju. Does divinity have management? The divine is all. Reaching the divine source takes management. You reach the center of your being, and your psychological and spiritual struggles finally close one door only to open another. Now you need a team for management and maintenance to maintain your accomplishment and institutionalize it to live beyond its creator. The concept of divinity needs management in order to be achieved, not divinity."

"*Medju*. What is a divine legacy?"

"Medju. What is a divine legacy? Jhuty and Seshat are divinely married, giving birth to the idea of Ma'at, a second mate. The divine legacy is truth and harmony maintained. You learn to integrate your new innerstanding with the rest of your life and to appreciate the joy of sharing with others what you have come to innerstand. Your divine thoughts became divine words, which became dynamic action. When all of this is recorded, written down, and filed away, then we have the creation of a divine legacy!"

"*Medju wa*. When does your training end?"

"Medju wa. When does my training end? You should always expect to be a student as long as you appear to be in a body. This is a lifelong spiritual path for spiritual warriors who are serious about wanting to break free from the world and go home. My training never ends."

"*Medju senu*. How important is your breath?"

"Medju senu. How important is my breath? The breath is one of the major keys to ankh. I have been working on breathing control since I was nine years old, and only now do I have a small degree of mastery. I was taught that food, water, and air were three of the most important elements in the maintenance of ankh. So as I analyzed them, I found that you could live for three months without food. You could sustain life for thirty days without water, but one could only live a few minutes without air. So air was a major source of fuel for every cell in the Remtch body, and through the control of this airflow by breathing, it became a major source of power in the Remtch body.

"The more efficient the breathing control, the more efficient the body and mind become. And the more efficient the body and mind become, the more energy one could create or harvest from the universe by the use of the mind. This state of harvesting and creating energy is called meditation. This energy I have come to innerstand is the source of the spiritual realm. Living only in the physical, mental, and emotional realm makes energy limited. But if we can tap into the spiritual dimension through the power of meditation and breathing control, then energy is limitless. This internal power is called *sekhem*."

"Dua Ntchr Amen-Ra, in theory, you are correct. But now we the, Djedi council, ask you to prove your theory. Is this symbolic thought or symptomatic thinking? We need you to lie in Khufu's open *Krst* [coffin] now."

I walked over to the Nswt Bety's open Krst; I stepped inside and lay on my back. Medjay Priest-Scientist Ka-en-Jhutyms and Medjay Priest-Scientist Akhtoy Ba-Heru both reached down and picked up the heavy pink granite lid.

Djedi Ka-en-Khufu spoke, "You must slow your breathing down to conserve air, a state of controlled meditation. We have measured the air in the Krst. There is about ten minutes of air if you breathe normally, so cut your breath in half because we will remove the lid in fifteen minutes."

"Now lower the lid," said Djedi Ka-en-Khufu.

They lowered the lid over the Krst, and Djedi Ka-en-Khufu turned over a sand timer. Inside the Krst, my arms were folded in the Asarian position. I have practiced a drill similar to this several times, but I knew this was for real. If I failed today, I would die! As I slowed down my breathing, I began to count. I would keep my own time. When I reached ten minutes, I felt very good. There was no problem. But by the time I got to fourteen minutes, the heat was almost unbearable. Then I heard the voice of Chief Medjay Jhutyms Ka-en-Heru in my head, telling me this was all an illusion and that if I wanted to stay in this Krst for thirty minutes, there would be no problem. Then I saw my *Hemet*, *Mwt*, and *sa-i* (my son), all crying at my funeral. And in the background, Kemet was in flames. The temperature began to cool back down. I lost track of the time, but it did not matter now. The force of the Djedi was with me. I innerstood that what was at stake here was far beyond me. Everything went blank.

Djedi Ka-en-Khufu levitated the lid off the Krst without touching it and placed it gently to the side. Medjay Priest-Scientist Ka-en-Jhutyms and Medjay Priest-Scientist Akhtoy Ba-Heru ran and looked inside the Krst. My eyes were closed, and they shook me. "Mentchu-hotep, Mentchu-hotep," I could hear them, but it sounded like they were a long ways away from me.

I opened my eyes slowly. Was I in Amenta, or was I alive? I saw the look on the face of Medjay Ka-en-Jhutyms, but I could not talk. I raised my hands, and he pulled me up slowly. I begin to breathe normally again. I really felt good, like I had died and was resurrected. I said, "Nefer e." (Fine.) Then I stepped out of the Krst and greeted the immortal Psdju Djedi council with a bow of the head. I saw Djedi Jhutyms Ka-en-Heru wink at me.

"You have done well, Shemsu Heru Nswt Bety Neb Khrw-Ra Sa Ra Mentchu-hotep. You have showed the council that your Jhuty skills were backed by symptomatic thought. You truly innerstood and embodied the symptomatic process of success, distinguishing the real from the unreal. You are the first Medjay priest-scientist in over 150 years who also held the title of Nswt Bety! You have gained much strength from your Medjay training. Every trial endured and weathered in the right spirit makes a soul nobler and stronger than it was before," said Djedi Ka-en-Khufu.

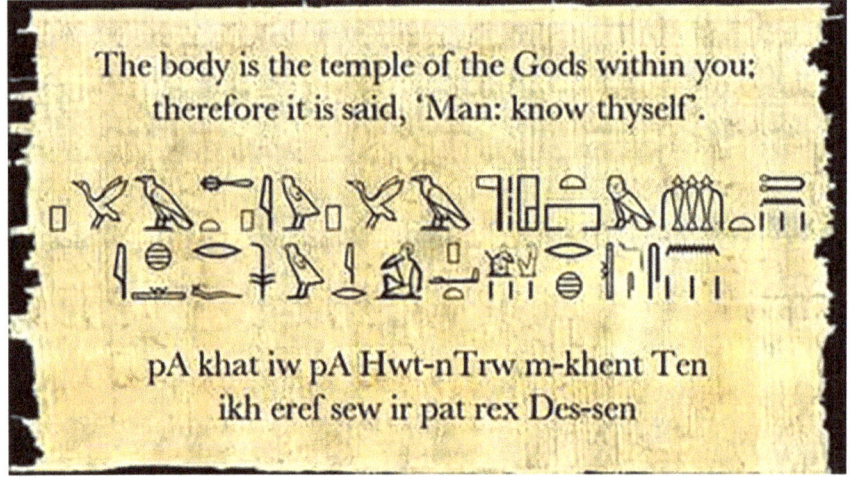

The body is the temple of the Ntchru within you;
therefore, it is said, "Mankind, know yourself."

My body and mind felt stronger than I had ever felt before. *My twenty-five years of Medjay training has led me to this point,* I thought.

"Don't expect to attain the same level of excellence as Chief Medjay Djedi Jhutyms Ka-en-Heru, but tiw, the time will eventually come when you will never suffer. That is one of the long-term payoffs of this spiritual path. Even while you still appear to be in your body, it's possible for you to attain psychological invulnerability. You have passed your first test in your Medjay priest-scientist training. The most common way people give up their power is by thinking they don't have any. You don't have limitations, but the Remtch have become addicted to limitations because of faulty symbolic thinking.

"Your Medjay priest-scientist training will continue in one month from the next new moon. Here, take these scrolls. They are from the Djedi priest-scientist training manual. They are to be memorized. You will need this information for your next training session. Share this information with no one, except another priest-scientist or Djedi. We will send for you. The training has three sections—mental, physical, and spiritual. Prepare yourself and your family. Dua Ntchr."

The Immortal Psdju council all stood up and bowed their heads, and in the blink of an eye, they and their golden stools were all gone. Only Djedi Ka-en-Khufu remained. He waved his hand, which held a crystal wand, and the large circular blue portal reappeared. We all stepped in the portal. It closed and, within two seconds, opened in front of the Mer Khut of Khufu. We stepped out, and the Djedi Ka-en-Khufu was gone.

*****

When Shemsu Heru Nswt Bety Neb Khrw-Ra Sa Ra Mentchu-hotep arrived back at the royal palace in Waset, it was very late, but Hmt Nswt Wrt Neferu and Hmt Tem, along with priestess initiate Kawit, all greeted him with great joy as soon as he entered the royal palace. Sa Ra Mentchu-hotep was still in deep thought. Now he knew he had to prepare himself once again for life-changing rites of passage.

Hmt Tem asked, "Did you find your truth?"

He looked at her and said, "Truth is not something that you find or a right to be claimed but a gift for those who are able to comprehend it."

Hmt Tem bowed her head as she held his hand. "Your wisdom is so great, my Neb aa."

He expressed the joy he felt just being in the presence of the Immortal Psdju Djedi. "However," he said, "feeling the force, the unlimited power of their presence made me realize that with all my accomplishments, I was just a beginner student in the mastery of life. For every great joy, there is a great price to be paid. I will need the help of all of you to prepare me for my next journey in life."

Later that night, he held Hmt Nswt Wrt Neferu by the hand. Once they were alone in their private royal chambers, she asked with great excitement, "Well, what happened? What did you learn?"

He looked deep into her eyes and said, "What you are doing or learning does not matter so much as what you are learning from doing it. The journey is the reward."

She replied, "Mrr e tw." (I love you.)

He replied back, "Mrr e tn wrt Hemet e." (I love you greater, my wife.)

CHAPTER 5

LESSONS FROM THE DJEDI

Medjay spiritual warriors

"I am here, Shemsu Heru Nswt Bety Neb Khrw-Ra Sa Ra Mentchu-hotep, to prepare you for your meeting with the Djedi council."

"Are you a Djedi, Medjay Ka-en-Jhutyms?"

"I am a humble Medjay warrior priest-scientist. My skills are only one quarter the level of a Djedi grand master, and I still have many years of study to reach their level. But I will be a Djedi one day!"

"Then I must be about one-eighth or one-sixteenth?"

"The body, Shemsu Heru, is conditioned, disciplined, honored, and in time, trusted to be a vehicle to aid in your ascension. Take time to glorify the Ntchr in your own body!"

"How is this done, Master, if the body is an illusion?"

"First, never speak in the negative. You are what you will into being!"

"Dua, Master."

"The rest you already know. If you want to perfect the black panther dance, you must become, in spirit, the black panther. The spirit always knows what to do to heal itself, but the soul must listen and obey. The challenge, Shemsu Heru Neb Khrw-Ra Sa Ra Mentchu-hotep, is to silence the ego so that you can listen to the Divine Spirit in your mind and heart. We always know what to do if we are in touch with life as it is through the Divine Spirit, not as your ego has directed it to be. Through the Divine Spirit, you can change the script anytime you want."

"Dua Ntchr. I sit at your feet, Master Medjay Priest-Scientist Ka-en-Jhutyms. Things are becoming much clearer now. We see things not as they are but as we are! Change our consciousness, change the script, and change what is reality!"

"Tiw, Nswt Bety Neb Khrw-Ra Sa Ra Mentchu-hotep. You have awakened. Stop thinking of yourself as a Remtch, a human searching for a spiritual awakening when in fact you are a divine spiritual being attempting to cope with a divine human awakening. Seeing yourself from the perspective of the Divine Spirit within will help you to remember why you came here and what you came here to do. Shemsu Heru Nswt Bety Neb Khrw-Ra Sa Ra Mentchu-hotep, you came here to be a Medjay warrior priest-scientist who also happens to be the Nswt Bety who will lead our people, the Remtch, and all the Kemetyu of the Eteru er Hapy Valley into a new golden age—an era that will be remembered for its greatness as long as human civilization exists."

"Wow! I would have to be a Djedi like your father to do that!"

"Nen, no, you just have to complete your mission, your life's purpose! It will be the Djedi who will help make it possible. Remember, Shemsu Heru Neb Khrw-Ra Sa Ra Mentchu-hotep, your mission is to be a Medjay priest-scientist, not just the Nswt Bety! You must learn a new way to think before you can master a new way to be. Life is a school where your soul learns how to remember what your spirit already knows."

"How powerful can a Remtch soul become? Can the Remtch become a Djedi like your father? Your father is amazing. He treats everyone equally, from the desert hare to a prostitute. He has a body, but a body does not limit him. He functions way past the natural capacity of a human being."

"My father, Chief Medjay Djedi Jhutyms Ka-en-Heru, has passed through the eye of Amen-Ra and returned. He has reclaimed his place with the Ntchr Ntchru as pure spirit in a human body. He is a true embodiment of the Djedi spirit, and the Djedi are living examples of nondualism on earth. They, the Djedi, are doing their part in this miracle. We must do ours. Just remember this. Rather than being your thoughts and emotions, be the awareness behind them, and you will be successful, Shemsu Heru Nswt Bety Neb Khrw-Ra Sa Ra Mentchu-hotep. You are ready. You will see the Djedi council in the morning at Kheper-Ra rise. I will be here for you. Amen-Ra is satisfied." He bowed his head and got out of the room.

Nswt Bety Mentchu-hotep and Medjay Priest-Scientist Ka-en-Jhutyms

*****

I had two sacred meetings that evening to prepare myself for the Djedi council in the morning. My first meeting was with my two wives and my beloved mother, Nswt Mwt Ntchrt Wrt Iah—by far the wisest women in all of Kemet.

"Mwt," I said, "even though I am the Nswt Bety [divine ruler of Upper and Lower Kemet], am I even worthy to sit at the feet of the Djedi council?"

"My son, no human or Remtch is worthy to sit at the feet of the Djedi council, but that is not the issue here. They, the Djedi council, has asked you to come and be taught by them. My great son, they see in you what I see, what your wives see, and what your people now see—the spirit of unmatched greatness, a divine spirit of great character! You have already done what only one other great Remtch in the world has done, like Shemsu Heru Nswt Bety Narmer: united two great nations into one nation-state, which has become the greatest civilization in the world at this time. Now they want to give you the skills to travel even higher in this illusionary world. They want to give you the skills of a Medjay priest-scientist, like Imhotep, and spiritual immortality.

"My great son, just sit at their feet and open your mind and heart! Remember, my son, the heart is the primary organ of perception and the brain supplies a supportive secondary though essential role. You have worked hard, my son, and they see your good character. Give thanks for the entire honor and joy, which have not yet been received but are already on their way! And as always, son, remember, a loving heart is the beginning of all knowledge."

That night, I was in total peace as I held Hemt Tem in my arms, expressing my mrr to her as we made divine love. My talk with Hmt Nswt Wrt Neferu and my son went very well. I had been so honored to have these divine women in my life. "Hmt Nswt Wrt Neferu, I don't know how long I will be gone, but you will be with me the entire journey. You are my life, and Medjay Priest-Scientist Ka-en-Jhutyms said that a Djedi warrior will be here at the royal palace to ensure your safety while I am gone."

"Only my body will be here in the royal palace. My soul will be with you, my Nswt Hee. Dua Ntchr, for sharing these precious moments with us."

"The present moment is the only moment available to us, Neferu, and it is the doorway to all moments. I have found a great peace, Neferu, and you and Hmt Nswt Tem are responsible for helping me develop that. You have conditioned my heart with your Mrr so that I can recognize the peace inside me. My ego says, 'Once everything falls into place, I'll feel peace.' But I have learned to consult the Divine Spirit in these matters, and it says, 'Find your peace, and then everything else will fall into place.' Please write a message for the royal house in the north of my mission."

"Of course, my Neb aa. I have already done so."

This is a view of the Hapy Eteru from Waset, the nation-state capital.

As Kheper-Ra rose in the morning sky and my eyes adjusted to the dim light, I saw all the members of my Medjay medju unit, led by Medjay Priest-Scientist Ka-en-Jhutyms, waiting in our sacred Heru boat. *What a pleasant surprise,* I thought. We were all dressed alike as they all greeted me with the greatest respect as their leader. We had been together as Medjay medju for over twenty years, and you could not tell who was the oldest aside from Senior Medjay Sia-en-hotep. They all looked great. Only the senior Medjay had gray hair, but all our bodies were well-toned and lean-fighting machines. I could not have asked for greater company. We had trained together, fought together, worked together, prayed together, and built Kemet together. If I had to put my life in anyone's hands, these were the greatest hands in all of Kemet.

Four of the Medjay medju in our unit were already priest-scientists. I would be number 5. This was the last part of my priest-scientist training. I had passed the mental and physical training as my mind flashed back to a battle we had with the bear people from the extreme north. We were outnumbered—a hundred to five Medjay. They were twice our size, but we defeated them all and then had to swim five miles in the icy waters to our ship. Now this would be the spiritual training. I took a deep breath. Even though I was their leader, I was humbled to still be in their company.

We crossed the great Hapy Eteru to the western bank; another group of Medjay medju was waiting for us to arrive. Medjay Priest-Scientist Ka-en-Jhutyms handed out hooded black masks for all of us to wear; only our eyes were visible as we stepped on the shore. Medjay Benu Henenu and Medjay Ni-Sobek looked at each other, then Medjay Benu Henenu said, "I'm Nswt Bety Mentchu-hotep."

"No, I'm Nswt Bety Mentchu-hotep," said Medjay Ni-Sobek.

"Stop playing, you two. You know I'm Nswt Bety Mentchu-hotep," replied Medjay Ipi, and they all started laughing hysterically.

"That brought back memories," said Senior Medjay Sia-en-hotep. We all still were giggling a little as we mounted our horses to travel into the land of Amenta, the western sacred burial grounds. We passed the burial site of the three great Shemsu Heru Inyotefs, and then I saw a stunning white stone structure forming a temple with a second floor and what looked like the construction of a Mer Khut on top.

"Tiw, Shemsu Heru Nswt Bety Neb Khrw-Ra Sa Ra Mentchu-hotep. That is your mortuary temple, so you can't die yet because we are not finished. And we cannot complete it in seventy days!" said Medjay Ka-en-Jhutyms. Everyone laughed, including me. The temperature was already around a hundred degrees Fahrenheit in the shade. We dismounted the horses. Four Medjay priest-scientists and I walked into the deep mountain valley, while the other five Medjay stayed behind with the horses.

Finally, after walking in the scorching heat of Ra in the mountains for about thirty-five minutes, we came to a small hole in the side of a deep slope in the rugged mountain range.

"We are here," said Medjay Priest-Scientist Ka-en-Jhutyms. He moved a few rocks from around the small hole and crawled into the small tunnel. First, Medjay Ipi, and I followed him. Inside, there was a rope, and we kind of slid down maybe twenty-five feet underground into a large cave opening. A light appeared out of the blackness. It was Chief Medjay Djedi Jhutyms Ka-en-Heru. We all dropped down on one knee and gave the Djedi a salute of respect. Afterward,

Medjay Ka-en-Jhutyms tugged on the rope twice, which was the signal for Medjay Akhtoy Ba-Heru and Medjay Ka-en-Heru Bes to enter.

Once all five of the Medjay priest-scientsts were safely in the cave, we took off our masks. Chief Medjay led us through the tunneled pathway deep underground into a magnificent underground palace with several rooms all elegantly done, like the sacred temple of Amen-Ra in Waset. I was amazed. Who could have built something like this far underground? And what puzzled me the most was the scource of light and fresh air. The light came from the walls in the first three halls, but it came from the ceiling in each of the remaining rooms, like Ra, which was very bright.

The first three large halls were training areas for the Medjay priest-scientists by the Djedi priest. There were smaller rooms on each side of the large columned halls, and to the left was an unbelievable library. Far beyond my imagination, some of the papyrus scrolls were in languages I had never seen before. Smaller study hall rooms connected to them. The rooms to the right were living quarters for Medjay priest-scientists only.

Chief Medjay Jhutyms Ka-en-Heru seemed to know all my questions before I could ask any. He just kind of smiled and said, "Be patient, Nswt Bety Neb Khrw-Ra Sa Ra Mentchu-hotep. Everything will be crystal clear," as he handed me a clear circular ball made of quartz crystal. Two Medjay priest-scientists came toward us with trays of limewater and dried honeyed dates. I was astonished on how refreshed I felt with only after a few sips. We ate the whole lime, even the skin.

We ate and drank in silence. Shortly after we finished, my four Medjay medju brothers all stood and hugged me and affirmed my success. Medjay Priest-Scientist Ka-en-Jhutyms said, "When we see you again, Nswt Bety Neb Khrw-Ra Sa Ra Mentchu-hotep, you will be reborn into the Medjay priestship."

Then they all said, "Dua Ntchr." They all greeted the chief Medjay. Afterward, they exchanged a few words, and they were off the same way we came in.

"How long will I be here, Grand Master?"

"One lunar month, twenty-eight days. Don't worry, Nswt Bety. Kemet will be fine. We have made all the necessary arrangements, just like when you had your physical training."

I followed the chief Medjay to the end of the third grand hall. I was frozen in my tracks at first. There stood Enpu—the black jackal, the guardian of the gates—in the doorway. But this was not a man wearing a black jackal mask; this was a real humanoid black jackal standing almost eight feet tall! It was holding an ankh staff and was dressed like a Medjay priest-scientist. He stared at me with his cold blue eyes and growled his teeth. The chief Medjay held up his right hand, and Enpu knelt on one knee, with his ankh staff across his body. But he never took his eyes off me.

This is Enpu, the great guardian of the way, kneeling
at the entrance to the halls of the Djedi.

Only with the wave of the Djedi's hand, the huge, heavy
doors opened wide for us. The doors were twelve feet high
and almost a foot thick, made of some kind of metal gilded
with pure gold with beautiful carvings on both sides. Once
we stepped inside, the doors closed automatically behind us.
To my surprise, there were two more of these eight-foot Enpu
guards inside the Djedi hall—one on each side—standing at
attention as we passed by. The giant columns stood twenty
feet high, carved from solid pink granite stone, completely
decorated with Mdw Ntchr from bottom to top. Even the floors
and ceiling were made of granite, but the statues were made
of diorite, an extremely hard stone.

The underground Immortal Psdju Djedi temple

"What was that all about, Grand Master?" I asked.

"He could feel the spirit of the black panther in you. In nature, panthers hunt and kill jackals. Remember, the physical body is an illusion. We are divine spiritual beings having a divine Remtch experience. He was responding to your inner animal nature of the black panther."

There were two Djedi halls, both about fifty meters by fifty meters, before we came to the Immortal Psdju council hall. This time, the chief Medjay placed both hands out in front of his body, with his palms facing out, and some kind of internal force from the Djedi grand master opened the giant twin doors. Again, once we were inside, the giant metal doors closed automatically. There was writing and artwork on all the columns and walls everywhere, except in the Immortal Psdju council hall. These walls were clear, with only sheets of gold covering them.

This hall was breathtaking, simple, and beautiful. There were very little furniture, just the council's U-shaped desk with nine magnificent high-back chairs gilded with gold behind them. There were several strange-looking trees in golden pots placed around the room, along with a few matching chairs also gilded in gold but with low backs. The Djedi council seemed to have an angelic glow in front of them. I could feel each one greeting me without anyone saying a word. I bowed my head back to acknowledge their greetings. One of the Djedi, with the wave of his hand, picked up a chair in midair and placed it in the center of the room without moving from behind the council's desk. Mentally, I was directed to sit. Chief Medjay Djedi Jhutyms Ka-en-Heru took his seat in the center among the Immortal Psdju (nine) Djedi.

Three of the Djedi council members were women, and six were men. I recognized one of the women as Chief Medjay Jhutyms Ka-en-Heru's Hmt Nswt Wrt; I had seen her in Punt at the Medjay women demonstration. Her skills as a spiritual warrior were impeccable.

"*Anedj her ek,* Shemsu Heru Nswt Bety Mentchu-hotep. We, the Immortal Psdju council of Djedi, officially greet you, and we thank you for coming," spoke another woman Djedi whom I had never met. "I shall be the voice of the Djedi council for this meeting, so all questions should be directed to me, Djedi Neferu-Rat. Is this innerstood?"

"Tiw, Djedi Grand Master Neferu-Rat," I replied.

Everyone bowed his or her head. "Today we will answer your many questions, and tomorrow you will begin a new spiritual journey, Shemsu Heru Nswt Bety Mentchu-hotep. I will put your mind at ease, young Medjay. I know all about you, but you have never met me. I am the second daughter of Djedi

Grand Master Jhutyms Ka-en-Heru, the mother of Medjay Priest-Scientist Kha-ef-Ptah and the grandmother of Medjay Priest-Scientist Ipi."

I was stunned for a few seconds, but now I was beginning to connect the dots. I thought, *I have been surrounded and protected by a magical web of Djedi and Medjay priest-scientists my whole life.*

"Tiw, but you have done the work, young Medjay! We have only shown you the way. It was your will, your determination, and your sweat that got you to this point, Shemsu Heru. Most people miss the opportunity because it is dressed in work clothes and looks like hard work. You have persevered. But what we hope you have learned in these lessons, Shemsu Heru, is that perseverance is not a long race. It is many short races one after another."

"Tiw, Djedi Grand Master Neferu-Rat. It is getting clearer every day," I said as I rubbed my crystal ball. I knelt on one knee and looked at the Djedi council and spoke to Djedi Neferu-Rat.

ii   ḫr.k   ib.i   ḫr   mꜣꜥt

ee kher-ek ib-ee Kher Maat

I have come to you, and my heart is filled with truth and righteousness.

nn   isft   m   ḫt.i

nen isfet em khet-ee

There is no wrong in my body

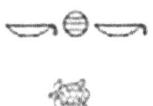

ink   ꜣḥꜥwty   n   mꜣꜥt

enek (a-nook) Ahawty en Maat.

I am a Warrior of Maat.

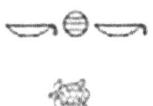

"Yes, we know this. That is why you are here, and that is why we named you Neb Khrw-Ra, master of the voice of Ra! We live a life of simplicity. Everything is on a need-to-know basis, not secrets. Simplicity is one of the most difficult things to master in a world of illusions. It is the ultimate aim of experience and the last effort of a Djedi grand master. We will teach you simplicity and tenderness. Why tenderness, you ask, if we are warriors? Because strength and confidence yield the greatest gentleness, allowing you the gift to give tenderness. When that is achieved, there is nothing stronger in this world than tenderness. When you have mastered the gentleness of tenderness, nothing physical can harm you or defeat you. Fire cannot burn you. You can walk on sand and leave no footprints. You can ride the air current, like a mighty falcon, or float on water, like a leaf. All the illusionary elements are at your command or can be directed through your will."

"I wonder, great Djedi Neferu-Rat, are these things possible only because you are from another planet?"

"Nen, no, these things are possible because we are Djedi priest-scientists, masters of energy, one with the Divine Spirit of the Ntchr! We are the universes, just like you are, and we are expressing ourselves as Remtch for a little while. The abundance of the spirit flows in and through me as it does you. I am a vehicle of its self-givingness. We are all visitors to this place you call home, and we are all just passing through. Our purpose here is to learn, teach, grow, love, create, and fulfill our mission, then give it to those who are seeking it, and then return home to heaven."

"How can you communicate with me without talking, great Djedi? And how do you know my questions before I ask them?"

"The deeper you go into your consciousness, young Medjay, both written and spoken words of formal language become less and less adequate as a medium of expression. Each energy force—rather it be a mineral, plant, animal, or Remtch—or some other benevolent energy force is surrounded by its own unique electromagnetic field. Each electromagnetic field is encoded with meaning and purpose. The finely tuned field of your heart innerstands these electromagnetic waves, and through the focus of power of your consciousness, you can perceive and decode each. In a simpler form, I can feel the essences of your thoughts before they are expressed into words or actions by the heart. I can even feel your emotional intent with my consciousness because we are all one. Djedi are always aware of this oneness, allowing them to live at a deeper and more enriched level of awareness. The Medjay priest-scientists can tune in to this awareness when they focus on it. While you Remtch are always getting ready to live but never living, we live."

"Wow, excuse me, great Djedi council, but now I innerstand why Chief Medjay Djedi Jhutyms Ka-en-Heru could communicate with every group or everything we encountered! And was this how he was able to heal every kind of disease also?"

"It is the power of nature or the Divine Spirit to heal, not the Remtch or even the Djedi. We cannot make seeds, and neither can we make them grow. We can only create the right environment for the seeds to grow, but only the Ntchr allows things to grow or bring life into being. The seed cannot sprout upward without simultaneously sending roots into the ground. The seed includes all the possibilities of the tree. The seed will develop these possibilities, however, only if it receives corresponding energies from the sky. Grain must return to the earth, die, and decompose for new growth to begin. So is above, so is below. This is why the Djedi teach, 'Know yourself and you shalt know the Ntchru.'

"In reconnecting the living reality of the organ system of a Remtch to nature by using plants, oils, or crystals, it is nature or energy of the plants, oils, and crystals that do the work. They, through Divine Spirit, teach the organ system how to be and what to do, teaching it how to return to its true form and be healed. As a Medjay priest-scientist, we train your mind to tap into this infinite reservoir of energy. Only then do you realize that nature is a fluid entity that changes from moment to moment. The untrained mind is unable to grasp the essence of nature because the true form of nature leaves nowhere to be grasped. The Remtch become perplexed and bounded by theories that try to freeze a fluid nature.

"Nswt Bety Neb Khrw-Ra Sa Ra Mentchu-hotep, as long as your conscious mind stays within the boundaries of the ego, you can never find the inner peace of Ma'at that you truly seek. You can experience moments of Ma'at but not her infinite, eternal peace. When the Divine Spirit does not guide the conscious mind, a Remtch only knows him- or herself only insofar as they know the world. They perceive the world only in themselves and themselves only in the world. But since the world is an illusion, the Remtch can never fully know themselves.

"The field in which you locate yourself will shape how you perceive yourself. So you never really innerstand how powerful you are or can be because you don't innerstand the nature of the world that does not exist. Listen carefully, Medjay. The goal of life is innerstanding your Ntchru gifts and endless possibilities! The source of life is Ntchr! Ntchr is the goal of the Medjay's life, the end of all his or her seeking, the meaning of all his or her striving. The major difference between the Djedi and the Remtch is, the Remtch are trying to innerstand Ntchr from the outside. As the Djedi, we know we are Ntchr from the inside. We are one.

"Ntchr is consciousness, not an abstract creator. Ntchr is the source of creation itself and the Creator. It [not he or she] is not independent of you. It is the totality of everything. So when I call myself Ntchr, I am not talking about my personal self. I am talking about the expression of the Ntchr self that rests inside me. The verb . . . the energy . . . not the noun.

Once you think Ntchr is a noun—person, place, or thing—you separate yourself from it and immediately become a limited being. That's what separates the believers, the Remtch, from the knowers, the Djedi and priest-scientist Medjay.

"Know your most inward self and look for what corresponds with it in nature. As a Medjay priest-scientist, the opinion of the Remtch about nature or the world is irrelevant. To the Remtch, they are not disturbed by things but by the opinions about things. If you search for the laws of harmony, which are the laws of Ma'at, you will find infinite knowledge. But this same knowledge is only a potential power until it is used wisely. Knowledge is not necessarily wisdom. Wisdom is the correct usage of knowledge. As a Medjay priest-scientist, you must first know the world in yourself. Never look for yourself in the world, for this would be to project your limited illusion as a reality.

"Your journey to become a priest-scientist is a stage in your eternal evolutionary process of completing your mission on earth. The Djedi council needs you to innerstand that our way of teaching is not an accumulation of knowledge. It is an awakening of consciousness, which goes through successive stages—mentally, physically, and spiritually. So at this point, Sa Ra Mentchu-hotep, tell us, what do you choose as a Medjay priest-scientist, which you have learned from your Djedi manual?"

"I choose to live an awesome, extraordinary life. I choose to love with an expanded heart. I choose to embrace my strength within, my *Sekhem*. I choose to move with a focused mind. I choose to always give thanks for all that I have. I choose to work with a limitless Ntchr. I choose to create a life of harmony based on Ma'at. I choose to always be conscious of my glorious ancestors."

"Dua Amen-Ra," he could hear in his head from the council.

"Great Djedi council, can I learn these things in my short visit here on this earth?"

"Believe you are divine, then know it! Once you believe in yourself and see your soul as divine and precious, you'll automatically be converted to a being that can create miracles. Listen very carefully, young Mentchu-hotep. We are all stardust wrapped in human skin, and the light you seek has always been within you!"

"What do you mean stardust?" asked Mentchu-hotep.

"That is the same question Imhotep asked us two hundred years ago, and now his spirit is immortal. So we will tell you what we told him. You are a carbon-based unit made of oxygen, carbon, hydrogen, nitrogen, calcium, iron, and copper, just like our planet, which also came from the stars. Listen with the totality of your being, not just your ears, Mentchu-hotep. Growth of the consciousness doesn't depend on the will of the intellect or its possibilities or even its birthplace but on the intensity of the inner urge, your inner desire. Your mind must arrive at your destination before your life does."

"Imhotep was a Medjay priest-scientist?" I asked in complete surprise.

"Tiw, as well as his leader Shemsu Heru Netchrikhet. We knew them like we know you. Imhotep's father was the royal architect, Ka-nefer. His mother, Khredu-ankh, was a divine healer and a hereditary noble. She was also a scribe and priestess, extremely wise. And his wife was Ra-nfr-en-nfrt. At a very early age, Imhotep, much like you, Mentchu-hotep, entered our priestship. You both grew up along the same Eteru er Hapy—you at the temple of Amen and Imhotep at the temple of Khnum. There, like you, he had access to our great library and wisdom teachers. And this is where Imhotep mastered the love of science and the Mdw Ntchr.

"Priest-Scientist Imhotep is the one who created the caduceus, the staff of Jhuty. So even though Vizier Priest-Scientist Imhotep was a great healer, his greatest love was with architecture and the immortality of stones, the mineral domain. Some of his building plans will still be completed a thousand years after his physical transformation, just like future rulers of Kemet will imitate your funeral monuments and temples. Maybe my son Kha-ef-Ptah, who is a great architect, will complete this story for me.

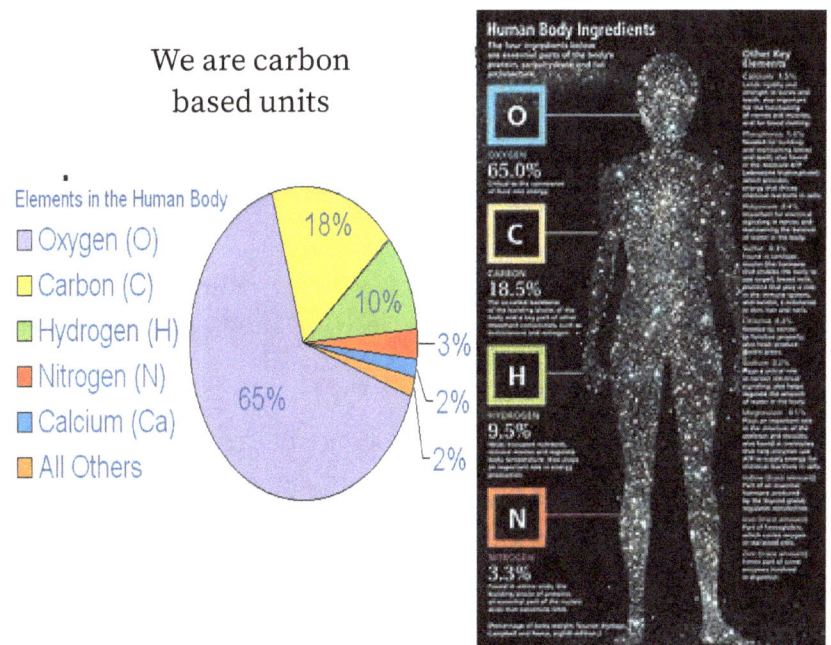

"But very much like Imhotep, your spirit will be immortal like his if you believe and then replace that belief with dynamic action and a lot of sweat."

"Sweat?" I asked.

"Tiw, sweat! Nobody ever drowned in his or her own sweat—hard work. Remember, Sa Ra Mentchu-hotep, if you are persistent, you will learn all that we teach you. But if you are consistent, you will keep it and become a Medjay spiritual priest-scientist."

"Great Djedi council, speak to me of the poor. How do I help them?"

"Poor are those who have eyes but cannot see, ears but cannot hear, mouths but cannot speak. You can only help those who want to be helped. A soul with no inner vision is blind to the beauty and goodness of Amen-Ra. The poor are surrounded with ignorance, and it floods their minds. Its currents sweep them away and drown them in misery and mental enslavement. Teach them to see by your excellent example, and those who seek help, through your excellent council, will be led to the house of knowledge. There, the poor will see with their hearts the brilliance and brightness of the Ntchr. You also must believe in your heart that you can help them. The power of faith can be a strong force, but the power of knowing is even stronger.

"Shemsu Heru, what we think, we create. Poverty only exists in the mind of the poor thinking ego. What we feel, we attract. Only because they feel poor, they attract poor thinking habits. What we imagine, we become. Ignorance is bondage! You must teach them to imagine greatness and abundance. You simply will not be the same person three months, seven months, or a year from now after consciously giving thanks each and every day for the abundance that exists in your life and in the world as you follow your mission with an action plan."

Djedi Neferu-Rat looked deeper into Mentchu-hotep's mind before she continued. "When there is extreme poverty in the midst of abundance, there are several other factors at work here: One [wa], not only are they impoverished and ignorant but they are also controlled by a system that teaches and promotes ignorance. Two [senu], they are at the mercy of greedy and selfish landowners. Three [shmut], they also live under a corrupt and/or weak government. Four [fedu], slavery and free or cheap labor are part of the makeup of the governing body that controls the poor.

"As a ruler, Nswt Bety Neb Khrw-Ra Sa Ra Mentchu-hotep, you must innerstand that there is only the Ntchr to serve! So corruption is unthinkable. When you serve others, you are actually serving yourself because all beings are an individualized expression of the only life that there is—Ntchr. And you will have set in motion an ancient spiritual law: The more you have and are grateful for, the more that will be given to you through the Divine Spirit. Therefore, the more you can share eliminates the conditions for extreme poverty. Only spiritual warriors can heal the poor, the sick, and the ignorant.

"You must embody these seven concepts, Sa Ra Mentchu-hotep," Djedi Neferu-Rat added.

1. *Imagination.* It must serve your higher self.

2. *Intuition.* Instincts connect you to the One, the source of *all.*

3. *Will.* Give yourself a command and follow it.

4. *Memory.* Backward and forward, live the life you want to live.

5. *Reason.* Conditions are limitless and extraordinary.

6. *Perception.* Ma'at is the scale of justice based on your current results, reality check.

7. *Voice.* Speak your truth daily, and be thankful.

"Great Djedi council, speak to me of the Ntchru. Are they in tune with the Divine Spirit, even Setsh?"

"Tiw, Shemsu Heru Nswt Bety Neb Khrw-Ra Sa Ra Mentchu-hotep. Even though the world is an illusion, we must innerstand the nature of nature. In Jhuty's eyes, your higher divine consciousness of the Remtch's greatest error is that they have the power to know the divine Ntchr and yet do not use it. The great Divine Spirit may be thought of as lying hidden within the Ntchru. Like the Ntchru Geb and Nut, they are forces that support and nurture nature. The form of the Ntchru Geb and Nut finds expressions in the forms of nature. Mental images of the Ntchru may be thought of as arising from within nature and being born in the Remtch. So the breath of the Ntchru becomes nature, and the heart of nature makes the Remtch divine beings.

"Contemplate what spirit discernment means and how you may apply it to all areas of your life. Embody this quality in your consciousness, and you will revolutionize the experience known as your life. As you develop the inner practice of gratitude, you will not only realize that it is a natural quality of your soul. You will also notice more and more things for which to be grateful. Your consciousness will come to trust this mental posture and will no longer release mental and emotional toxins. Taking a mental posture of being equally grateful for the challenges as you are for the gifts in your life results in spiritual maturity.

"The more you include unconditional gratitude of the Ntchru in your spiritual practice, the more the line blurs between divine gifts and challenges. Once ignorance is removed, you suddenly become aware that the Ntchr is with you and in you. And the more enlightened you become on your spiritual journey is the realization that the Ntchr is everywhere and everything. As for Setsh, remember, he is in front of the divine bark of Ra, slaying Ra's enemies every day and night. You must learn to control the Set in your consciouness so that Set can destroy only your enemies, not your friends and allies! Remember, Set is like the element of fire. It can help you or harm you, depending on your information base or lack of information. In order to be effective, truth must penetrate like an arrow, and that is likely to hurt."

This is too good to be true, I thought. "Great Djedi council, speak to me of the construction of this temple and this underground city. How can you build something of this magnitude this far underground, with the hardest materials known and with so few laborers? And what is your source of light or energy? And how come no one knows of it, not even the Nswt Bety, the strongest nation-state in the known world?"

"Young Medjay, the answers to your questions would always elude you, just by the way you asked them. We cannot fathom technology that is unknown to us, and we seldom consider things that seem impossible to us. If this is an illusion created by your mind, then the mind can always create an answer. There is in all things a pattern that is part of the universe. It has symmetry, elegance, and grace. These qualities you find always in that which the true artist captures.

"We, the Djedi, have mastered this art. We are true divine spiritual artists, and it composes everything within our spiritual being, from love to combat. You can find this spiritual, scientific pattern in the turning of the seasons—like in the desert, the way *Shu* [the wind] trails the sand along a ridge, in the spiral of a tree, or the patterns in a flower or a leaf. This temple is a living organic entity, and we created this temple in our collective minds. There are several of these temples around *Ta*, this planet, along with whole underground cities."

"Wait, are you telling me that this magnificent temple is just a small part of an entire underground city?" asked Mentchu-hotep.

"Tiw, young master Sa Ra Mentchu-hotep. The greatest ideas, the most profound thoughts, the most elegant buildings, and the most beautiful Mdw Ntchr are born from the womb of silence in the mind. At the heart of real silence rests the Divine Spirit. What you think, you become. What you feel, you attract. What you imagine, you create. So we did not need a large number of laborers to move these huge stones because we made them right here where they stand. The Ari-Kat Djedi ministries of the Udjat-en-Heru [the eye of Heru] can create stones, which look exactly like natural rocks. We can cast statues in stone or in one-hundred-thousand-ton beams on top of giant columns. Do you remember Djedi Grand Master Jhutyms Ka-en-Heru telling you that when real mrr [love] is exchanged between any two energy forms, its secrets are shared?"

"Tiw."

"So now you innerstand why mrr is so important and why the heart is on the scales of Ma'at and not the brain."

Wow! I thought.

"You are astonished by our light and energy source. The universe holds within it an unlimited number of energy sources. I shall only mention a few at this time in your development. Nature has provided us with unlimited geothermal energy, which we converted into light and sound energy. We can also move objects or render them weightless through the vibration of sound and thoughts. This sound can be created by the Remtch's voice, the beating of a drum, or through music created by two or more elements, like crystals or singing stones or bowls.

"We know this is new to you, Nswt Bety. We will make it simple for you to innerstand. This energy is obtained from a natural heat that is stored deep within the surface of the earth. Geothermal energy is typically found near areas where volcanic activity has occurred, and it is this heat that provides geothermal energy. This energy is commonly found in areas that have experienced volcanic activity, whether that activity was recent or decades ago. The Hapy Valley, Kemet, and Kash all the way to Ta Ntchr and the Mountains of the Moon are a valley of unlimited geothermal energy.

"Geothermal energy occurs in the form of hot rocks, hot liquid, or steam. Wells are drilled deep into the surface of the earth to obtain geothermal energy. With specially designed control valves, we bring the hot liquid or the steam to the earth's surface. We then used Djedi technology to convert the hot product into useable energy sources, which is the source of our light. Sometimes, hot water springs are used to obtain geothermal energy also, as well as a great healing source for the Remtch's body. All the minerals of the *Ta* exist in you.

"The advantages of geothermal energy are clear: It can be used to replace water and Ra energy. It is a renewable energy source that we will not run out of. It does not require importing, and it is present in the earth in large quantities. It is an excellent source of free energy with no real environmental problems, and there is no pollution to our environment.

One of the Djedi energy sources used to power their underground city

"Also, there is universal and cosmic energy, like in cosmic energy healing, which is an important facet of spiritual healing and deals with using cosmic energy, which exists in our universe. Cosmic energy is referred to as the force and the energy that maintains the balance of the universes, the entire cosmos. Everything we do is infused with energy—conscious or unconscious. If we are happy, life will be happy. If we are peaceful, life will be peaceful. But if we are frantic, life will be frantic. And so our goal in any situation, Shemsu Heru, becomes the mission of inner peace. What you think about activates a vibration within you.

"Energy is the currency of the universe. When you pay attention to something, you buy that experience. So when you allow your consciousness to focus on someone or something that brings you happiness, you feed it your energy and reciprocate the experience of being happy. So that means you can feed and reciprocate being annoyed also. Be selective in your focus because your attention feeds and pays for the energy of it and keeps it alive. Not just within you but in the collective consciousness as well."

"Wow," I said as I rubbed my crystal ball. "Great Grand Master Djedi Neferu-Rat, speak to me of the blacks in Asia. Who are they? And are they a part of our family?"

"First, you must innerstand that all the people along the southern part of Asia come from here, Ta Ntchr. We are the original Remtch of all the lands. Elam is another great nation of Kashites, a country that stretched from the Tigris River to the Zagros Mountains of Persia. Its capital was the famous city of Susa, which was founded about two thousand years ago, almost the same time Nswt Narmer was uniting Kemet. In speaking of the Elamites, they are black Kashites and Kemetyu like you. There is a strong Kashite strain in the modern people of Elam. The ancient bones and grave sites represent symptomatic evidence, which favors this view. Here is more proof. We have a vase from Susa. There is one portrait of an Elamite [Kashite] king on this vase found at Susa. He is painted black, like all their early rulers, and thus belongs to the Kashite race.

"The Sumerian stories of their origins of themselves tell the same story, for from their beginnings, the Sumerians seem to have been in touch with Kemet and Kash. Some of their early texts mention Dilmun, Magan, and Meluhha. Dilmun was the first settlement that was made by the Ntchr Enki, who was the founder of Sumerian civilization. Magan was famous among the Sumerians as a place whence they got diorite and copper. Meluhha is a place whence they got gold. Dilmun has been identified with some place or another in the Persian Gulf—perhaps the Bahrain Islands or perhaps a land on the eastern shore of the gulf.

"In a late inscription of the Assyrians, it is said that Magan and Meluhha were the archaic names for Kemet and Kash, the latter being the southwestern part of Punt. The founders of the first South Asian civilization were black Sumerians, sun folks. This South Asian section was the land of Sumer, which sprung up around 1,500 years ago. The founders of the civilization were of Kash origin. It's clear by many knowledgeable teachers that the South Asian speakers of Akkad and the non-Asian speakers of Sumer were both black people who called themselves sag-gig-ga or Black Heads.

"Memnon was called the son of Kash and was the founder of Susa, the chief city of the Elamites. There were places called Memnonia after him. But the Djedi masters made it crystal clear that melaninated black and brown people, the Remtch, are the only original or first humans on this planet. Everyone else came much later! The Djedi had complete control of my mind," she said. "As divine beings having a Remtch experience, our thoughts, words, and actions mirror the Divine Spirit's presence within us. We as Djedi and Medjay must send out vibrations of love, joy, peace, and compassion to all who cross our path. The truth is that you are here to learn how to handle love, joy, creativity, and success. If you are persistent, you will get it. If you are consistent, you will keep it."

*****

That night, I could not sleep; this was way past my wildest dreams. Just think, Shemsu Heru Netchrikhet and Imhotep were Medjay priest-scientists, and all the Djedi were priest-scientists first. I was so honored to be in the excellent company of the great ones. Tears just flowed down my face as I lay sleepless in the brightness of the dark.

The Djedi taught me there were five divine temples in this illusionary world, and they all had to be mastered, innerstood, and respected. "The first divine temple is your divine mind of higher consciousness, where the Divine Spirit dwells and all healing starts. It is the throne of your magic, the key that opens the door leading to Ntchr. Meditation opens this door to unlimited energy called your Sekhm. Also, sounds in the form of rain or waterfall or even waves along a shore can aid your meditation.

"Music can do this also. It works by using embedded sound waves that stimulate your brain and bring it the energy it needs to produce more brain cells, reestablish lost neural connections, and restore your memory and ability to think precisely and quickly. And much more, sound or music can wipe out negative thoughts and feelings, relieve you of depression, and gently remove the anxiety that keeps you tensed and stressed. And there's nothing more to do than listen to pleasant, mind-pampering music and breathe correctly by meditating twenty to thirty minutes each day. Even the right music has even helped people enjoy deeper, more restorative sleep because when you sleep well, your brain and body are able to repair damaged tissues.

"The second sacred temple is your pure heart, which houses your emotions and feelings, the root of your strength or weakness and the pulse of our solar system. The heart is thinking and directing even before the brain is set into motion. Drink plenty of pure water, and fast often with the full moon and the change in seasons. If this is done, intuition will always be with you, knowing without being told!

"The third divine temple is your body, which is an outward expression of your energy force. Keep it fine-tuned through exercises, well nourished, and clean, and it will be your humble servant. But remember, it is not you. It is just an instrument, a tool, or a vehicle for your consciousness.

"The fourth divine temple is your personal living space or your sacred space. This is where you can find yourself again and again. This is where you recharge and prepare for your divine mission in life. Keep it clean, uncluttered, and full of Mrr (love). Only allow loved ones to dwell in your personal space because in that temple, you are the most vulnerable.

"And your fifth divine temple is nature, an imaginary space that if respected, protected, kept clean, unpolluted, and mastered will always be a source of unlimited beauty and power and will lead you back home to the Divine Spirit. The ego made the world as it perceives it—like a box with walls or boundaries. But the Divine Spirit, the reinterpreter of what the ego made, sees the world as a teaching device with no boundaries for bringing you home to Ntchr in heaven."

The double halls of Ma'at in the Duat

The Djedi council also explained to me, "Heaven, although it is beyond all words, has these kinds of characteristics. It is perfect, formless, changeless, eternal, innocent, whole, abundant, and complete love. It is life. There is nothing else. The Ntchr is the only source. This complete love is to love without condition, to talk without intention, to give without reason, to care without expectation. This is the spirit of true love. When you realize that, except for the love of Ntchr, you need nothing. And he or she who needs nothing can be trusted with everything."

The Djedi explained to me, "The real goal isn't dressing up your life. It's about awakening from what you think is your life! Bodies cannot join the Ntchr in heaven, only divine minds and pure souls. This is why the ego doesn't want you to focus on the mind. It wants you to focus on the body and material objects as your only reality. Happily, the Divine Spirit has a script, and you can switch over to it anytime you want. But the mind has to be trained to recognize the divine truth, the Divine Spirit, within you! Heaven is something that is always present but unseen by the Remtch who believe the illusion. Heaven, although it is beyond this physical world, is complete, unconditional love. It is life. There is nothing else. What we think we are living is like an illusion, a dream that was created by the ego.

"The ego made the world as it wants you to perceive it. But the Divine Spirit, the reinterpreter of what the ego made, sees the world as a teaching device for bringing you home to Ntchr, the only real reality. The ego loves it when you regret your past. The ego can only create an illusion, which blinds you from the real truth. In the world of illusions, even if you are successful at your goals, you will still always have problems. Problems will never leave you, which are the nature of the illusions, moving from one optical illusion to another. 'Would have, could have, should have,' and 'If only I had done this instead of that' and 'If only I knew then what I know now' are some of the ego's favorite lines. Not only does this make your past seem real to you, it makes you feel bad at the same time, all to the ego's delight. An evolved and balanced ego can be a valuable tool for the self in navigating the illusion. But a blinding ego is always among the first footsteps into oblivion."

The Djedi made it crystal clear that the ego called for sacrifices, pain, and death. In contrast, the Divine Spirit said, "There is no need for sacrifices of any kind. The Ntchr is forgiveness. You may give an offering to show your gratitude, but we should remind you that life gives life. Never kill on behalf of the Ntchr Ntchru. Do not eat flesh on behalf of the Ntchru, and do not drink blood or consume high levels of alcohol or do anything that is not Ma'at on behalf of the Ntchru or for the Ntchru. Gravity or Ra does not need a sacrifice to work or to work better or to work just for you, nor does any other Ntchru. But you need to be in Ma'at to use them wisely."

I asked the Djedi council, "What about reincarnation?"

They all smiled in harmony. "Reincarnation is also just a dream," they told me. "So you keep reincarnating because of this unconscious guilt and fear that has been placed in your mind or not completing your mission or ignoring it consciously or unconsciously."

"You're saying if the guilt was healed and you didn't have this fear of failure, allowing you to complete your mission, then you wouldn't have any need to reincarnate. So if the life you thought you were living was an illusion and you come back into another illusion, how does that make anything real?"

"The so-called reincarnation is a continual episode of one illusion in a different imaginary body. It's nothing but a dream. Let us be clear about consciousness. Consciousness does not end at the death of the physical body. In fact, consciousness exists outside of constraints of time and space. Consciousness resides in the fire-Atum cells of the brain, which are the primary sites of conscious processing. Upon death, this information is released from your body, meaning that your consciousness goes with it.

"Our souls are in fact constructed from the very fabric of the universe—and may have existed since the beginning of time—because we are connected to the one consciousness that brought all things into existence. Our brains are just receivers and amplifiers for the protoconsciousness that is intrinsic to the fabric of space-time."

I asked, "Is there really a part of your consciousness that is nonmaterial and will live on after the death of your physical body?"

"Let's say the heart stops beating, the blood stops flowing, the fire-Atums lose its quantum state. The quantum information or consciousness within the fire-Atums is not destroyed. It can't be destroyed. It just distributes and dissipates to the universe at large," the Djedi said. "Not only does it still exist in the universe. It exists perhaps in another universe or multiuniverses. If the Remtch is resuscitated, revived, this quantum information or consciousness can go back into the fire-Atums. And the Remtch says, 'I had a near-death experience.' If they're not revived and the Remtch's body returns to earth, it's possible that this conscious information can exist outside the body, perhaps indefinitely, as a soul in search of completeness.

"This account of quantum consciousness explains things like near-death experiences, astral projection, out-of-body experiences, and even reincarnation. The energy of your consciousness potentially gets recycled back into a different body at some point, and in the meantime, it exists outside of the physical body on some other level of reality and possibly in another universe. Remember, Sa Ra Mentchu-hotep, birth is not the beginning of life—only of an individual awareness. When the body changes into another state, this is not death—only the ending of this awareness. Most Remtch are ignorant of the truth and, therefore, are afraid of death. When a soul leaves the body, it undergoes a trial and investigation by the chief of the Ntchru Asar. When it finds a soul to be honorable and of good character, it allows it to live in a region that corresponds to its characteristics and vise versa."

"How real are dreams?" I asked the Djedi council.

The council continued, "When you are dreaming at night, you are seeing with your mind. It's always your mind that is seeing. It's always your mind that is hearing and feeling and doing the other things you give the body's senses credit for. There is no exception to this. The body itself is just a part of your mind's projection. So in reality, there exists only one sense—consciousness. Sight, touch, hearing, smell, and taste are just sensors reporting to the one sense. And through manipulation, the ego can control all these sensors, sending false information to your outer consciousness, which will keep you lost, confused, and in a state of ignorance, never fulfilling your mission in life.

"Your divine mind is the path to salvation and eternal peace. You can never go wrong by following the path of peace if peace is, at that moment, Ma'at. When you must defend yourself or your family or your nation from bodily attack and possible death, this is also Ma'at. But you defend yourself, your family, or your nation with peace in your heart because your ultimate objective was to bring back Ma'at where esfet, wrongdoings, had entered.

"I want to be crystal clear about *peace*. It does not mean to be in a place where there is no chaos, trouble, violence, or hard work. It means to be in the midst of those things and still be calm in your heart. Do you know the difference between formal school and life, Sa Ra Mentchu-hotep? In school, you're taught a lesson and then given a test. In life, you're given a test that teaches you a lesson.

"These are the four frequency waves of your brain," the council added.

- *Heru-Set (beta) brain waves.* Heru-Set waves, or the conscious waves, clock in between 14 and 40 hertz (Hz). They are most closely associated with that little voice in your head. The higher you go in the hertz range, the louder your inner voice may get! This is also where cortisol, anxiety, and agitation develop.

- *Heru (alpha) brain waves.* Heru (alpha) waves, or the relaxation waves, are in the 7.5 to 14 Hz range. Much slower moving than beta waves, this is the state where your subconscious mind begins to dominate. As you move toward the bottom end of the frequency range, your imagination becomes stimulated, your memory begins to clear, and deeper concentration may be brought out to your Heru (beta) state.

- *Jhuty (theta) brain waves.* Deeper still are Jhuty waves, or sleep and light meditation waves. These waves vibrate at a slow-moving 4 to 7.5 Hz. It's here where you may experience insight, creativity, and positive inspiration. You may be conscious of your environment during the Jhuty state, but your body has fallen into deep relaxation. And your REM dream cycle begins.

- *Amen (delta) brain waves.* This is your deep-sleep state. At a mere 0.5 to 4 Hz, delta waves are the slowest moving of the five frequency ranges. At this stage, your consciousness is fully removed, information is received without awareness, and you are in a deep, dreamless sleep. Kemet and Kash meditation is practiced in this frequency range.

"As a Medjay priest-scientist, we are not asking you to save the world. The Remtch of the world will never live in peace until the Remtch of the world have inner peace. We are asking you to be a master teacher of truth, a living example of truth, to spread Ma'at among the Remtch and to those who ask for Ma'at as a spiritual way of life. Remember, Shemsu Heru Sa Ra Mentchu-hotep, the nut doesn't reveal the tree it contains but it has all the information. The spiritual priest-scientist is just the information!"

During my second week, I asked the Djedi council about Mer Khut (pyramids). "Why so much time and energy on these structures? And are they found in other countries or planets?"

Again, the Djedi all smiled. Chief Djedi Grand Master Jhutyms Ka-en-Heru spoke to me with his mind, "The shape of the Mer Khut [pyramids] generates electricity by using the flow of energy along the earth's surface, like a natural power plant, and negative ionic energy is created. The angle and shape causes the air to tumble, creating an energy grid. This natural energy grid can do many things, like one [wa], preserve food; two [senu], purify water; three [shmut], improve the taste of wine, beer, tea, and certain fruit juices; four [fedu], increase the growth of plants; five [diu], sharpen or maintain the sharpness in knives, swords, and blades; six [sesu], restore the luster to tarnished metals; seven [sefekhu], promote healing of cuts, bruises, and burns; eight [khemenu], reduce pain from toothaches and headaches; nine [peseju], increase awareness in meditation; and ten [medju], dehydrate any organic materials. And this list can go on. And tiw, our ancestors built them all around the earth at certain power points. Some were built before the last great flood, and so many are underwater today. And tiw, some are on other planets and other solar systems."

During my third week, I saw a very strange tall albino humanoid creature over seven feet tall. When I asked about him, one of the Djedi took me to the side and asked me to sit. "He is from Pleiades. This star system is a small cluster of seven visible stars located in the constellation of Haap the Bull, which is five hundred light-years from the planet Earth. There are over a hundred stars in this system, but only seven are visible to the naked eye of the Remtch here on Ta.

"The Pleiadians are a very ancient race of humanoids. They visited earth many years ago, a little after us. They are responsible for a lot of the confusion on your planet today. They brought the pale or nonmelaninated humankind here to your planet, and they have played a large role in the northerners' and westerners' evolution, the ancient cavemen and mountain peoples, mixing the genes of their outcast with wild Asiatics. But in general, they have remained silent watchers of your planet.

"The Tamahu, Aamu, Namou, and Tchnnw—these nonmelaninated humans were the outcasts of their planet and, by nature, are antinature. Their DNA was mixed with Neanderthal cavemen and the Remtch, and most of them have a calcified pineal gland after maturity and are not capable of feeling nature, the planet, the same way black people or melaninated Remtch can. They are not connected to you or anything here, but they are great imitators, which, if not innerstood, could fool you. They are at war with themselves and any and everything they encounter. You must innerstand. Their species is a minority on this planet, and they are like a virus trying to survive by any means necessary, which includes lying, cheating, stealing, killing, enslaving, interbreeding, and raping—the very opposite of Ma'at. This is also why they have made the Ntchr Set their idol of worship.

"The Pleiadians currently are seeking chairs on the council, who oversee the higher truths of the universe with us, and since they have expelled the Tamahu from their world, they now remain a peaceful race of extraterrestrials who have overcome their animal-killer nature. Although they have not reached the heights of their friends, the Arthurian or the Djedi, they continue to develop the mental skills necessary to eventually reach their goal. However, this goal will not be reached until they cure the virus of the Tamahu and nonmelanin beings or remove them from this planet. The Pleiadians' state of mind have allowed them to develop the ability to transition in and out of our dimension at will.

"As our trek takes us into the teachings of higher spirituality, we find that many civilizations outside our world have already mastered and innerstood the benefits of becoming one with the infinite powers of the universe.

Pleiades—this star system is a small cluster of seven visible stars located in the constellation of Taurus the Bull.

"Remember this, Nswt Bety Neb Khrw-Ra Sa Ra Mentchu-hotep. Those who refuse to awaken feed those who control them. The fact that there is a beginning or an end is just a concept seeded into your mind by society. You are constant, continuous, infinite energy. And energy never ends. It *transforms*."

"I will remember, great Djedi Grand Master Ka-en-Khufu."

"Listen carefully, Shemsu Heru Mentchu-hotep. Real knowledge is a direct experience of the truth. An enlightened being does not have opinions about the Ntchr. We are one with Ntchr. Come with me, Shemsu Heru Nswt Bety Neb Khrw-Ra Sa Ra Mentchu-hotep, so you can see what lies inside of you. You have been meditating in the priest-scientists' training room with your peers, but now take a look at the experienced priest-scientists."

"Wow, his body has turned into pure light!"

"Tiw, we are light beings of energy, taking on a Remtch form. The purple and blue colors show his elevation to the fifth and sixth dimensions."

"But I thought the body could not go to the fifth dimension," I asked.

"It can't, so look at his head."

"I can't see it."

"You can't see it because it does not exist. His consciousness has left this fourth-dimension illusionary body. He is beyond your solar system and really beyond your comprehension at this stage in your development now. He is an advanced Medjay priest-scientist. It will take many earth years to advance to his level."

"Wow, you mean he is not at the Djedi level yet?"

Advanced Medjay priest-scientist in meditation

"Nen, not yet, Shemsu Heru Mentchu-hotep. Look over here. This is a Medjay priest-scientist on your level. When I observe you in meditation, Shemsu Heru Sa Ra Mentchu-hotep, this is what I see. This is good. It is the beginner stages of self-mastery. We can see the energy or force field around your body called an aura. This Medjay, like yourself, can create enough energy to transform his body and shape-shift."

"I will work harder, Djedi Grand Master Ka-en-Khufu."

"What you are doing does not matter so much as what you are learning from doing it, Young Master."

"Dua Ntchr."

Shemsu Heru Sa Ra Mentchu-hotep and Nswt Bety Nebkhreu-Ra

"We need your force field to expand like this Medjay priest-scientist in the chamber to your right. He has full range of all his senses and is capable of sending telepathic messages with his mind and with the ability to read minds. You are not far from his stage—maybe after your journey to Yam and if you are consistent with your meditation every day. We look forward to your progress, Sa Ra Mentchu-hotep. Just remember, your life is not a problem to be solved but a gift to be opened. The way of the Medjay is very deep.

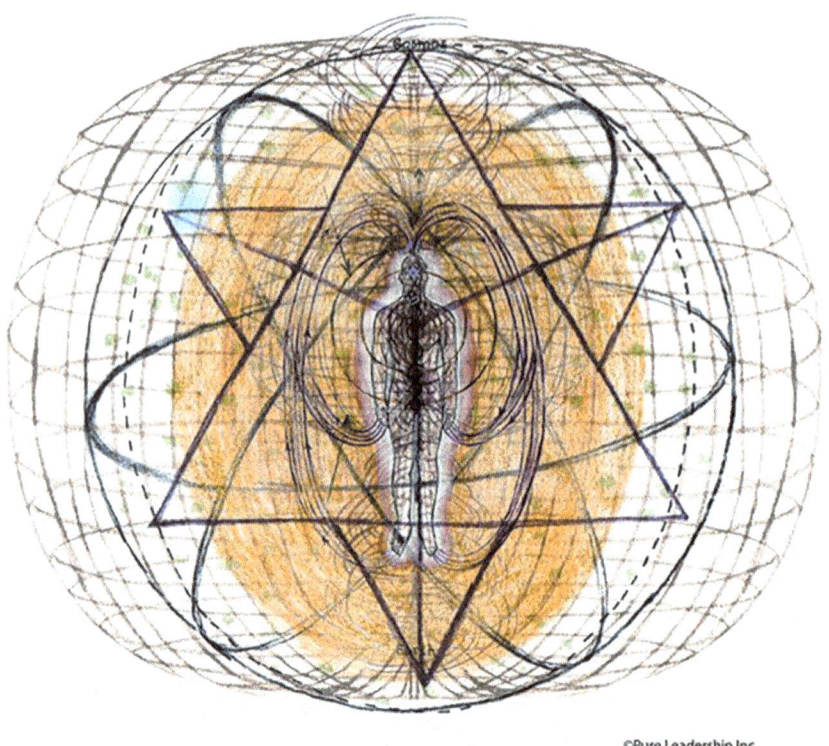

©Pure Leadership Inc.

The aura of a Medjay priest-scientist

"Now follow me into the Djedi golden meditation chamber. I shall levitate on water, keeping my body in a calm state. Only my consciousness will move the energy in this room so that you can see it."

This is unbelievable, I thought as I watched Djedi Ka-en-Khufu levitate in the air and balance himself on the water. He glowed in the darkness, then he illuminated the whole room with light only with his mind. With all my training, I was still like a baby just learning to crawl in this spiritual world.

I could hear his voice in my head, "What we have had, you may have. What we have enjoyed, you may enjoy. What we have learned, you may learn. It is all free, all open, all generously bestowed to those who seek it with the Divine Spirit. What lies behind us and what lies before us are tiny matters compared to what lies within us. You may see yourself out, and we shall talk in the morning." He then opened the huge doors with his mind.

I left quietly, thinking, *How can I sleep after this?*

Djedi Jhutyms Ka-en-Heru summoned me to the Djedi council chambers on day 27, my next-to-the-last day of my spiritual level training as a Medjay priest-scientist. "Shemsu Heru Nswt Bety Neb Khrw-Ra Sa Ra Mentchu-hotep, you have one last journey with the Medjay medju warriors when you return, and that is to journey to the land of Yam far out into the western desert. It is there you will find another piece of the ancient Kemety puzzle. A very valuable piece of information awaits you there. But first, I need you to read the journey of Harkhuf, who was a ritual priest under Nswt Bety MerenRa Heru. Ankh-Khau and Pepy NeferkaRa are in the northern burial grounds of Sokar, and the scribe Harkhuf's burial shrine is in Abu. They will prepare you for this journey.

"We are pleased with your progress as a Medjay priest-scientist, Shemsu Heru Sa Ra Mentchu-hotep. When you leave these walls, everything will start to change as you start emitting your own frequency as a Medjay priest-scientist rather than absorbing the frequencies around you, when you start imprinting your intent on the universe rather than receiving an imprint from existence. When you are confined to just living only in the physical, mental, and emotional realm, energy is limited. We have taught you how to tap into the spiritual dimension, where energy is limitless. You must now move from thinking and analyzing to directly and intuitively perceiving truth. Action is the fruit of all wisdom. One more thing, Sa Ra Mentchu-hotep. As you are evolving to your higher self, the road will seem lonely, but you are simply shedding energies that no longer match the frequency of your destiny. A snake cannot crawl back into his shedded skin."

Wow, another sleepless night thinking about all the lessons from the Djedi.

Early the next morning, I went to visit Djedi Grand Master Neferu-Rat, but as I was opening her door, she was walking out another door in her room. I quickly ran to the other door to catch her, but when I opened that door, she was gone. There was no floor. It was the view of deep space with mountains in the far-off distance, with a double sun and several moons reflecting many colors around it. All that I saw was totally not recognizable to my earthly experience. *Wow,* I thought, *where is this and where did she go?* I stepped back in the room and closed the door, thinking to myself, *That wasn't even our planet.* I walked back to my training area in a daze. Then I saw another Djedi on the council walk through the wall, like it was thin air. And when I touched that very spot, it was solid as a rock!

"Inner peace can be your greatest weapon, Sa Ra Mentchu-hotep," said Djedi Grand Master Jhutyms Ka-en-Heru. "Watch carefully." A group of Medjay medju with weapons all attacked the grand master. He avoided all their attacks without being touched by a single weapon. It was like he was performing a sacred dance. This went on for about five minutes. Then with the push of his empty hands in a circular motion, he stripped all the weapons from their hands. And when he stomped the floor, they all fell unconscious, like rag dolls, from the vibration of his force. He looked over at me and spoke, "Boundaries are imaginary, rules are made up, and limits don't exist."

Slowly the Medjay recovered one by one as they gathered around the grand master sitting on the floor. The grand master spoke calmly, "Insight is the greatest value, innerstanding the greatest wealth. Learning is the greatest profit and love the greatest investment. Inner peace is the greatest attainment. Inner strength, Sekhm, creates the greatest warrior. Remember, Medjay priest-scientist, true humility is staying teachable, regardless of how much you already know! You don't win by knowing what you know. You win by doing what you know."

Shemsu Heru Sa Ra Mentchu-hotep Nswt Bety Neb-Kheperu-Ra holding the Ankh staff of the Medjay priest-scientist

CHAPTER 6

VISITING YAM IN THE
WESTERN DESERT

A mighty warrior from Yam in the western desert

"*Ee nedj her ek yit e.* [Greetings, I seek your face for counsel, my father.] Shemsu Heru Sa Ra Mentchu-hotep, I have read all the material you have on Yam. I have traveled to Yebu and the sacred burial grounds of Sokar with mother and Princess Kawit. I know about the four journeys to Yam by the ritual priest Harkhuf. I have read his autobiographical tomb inscriptions. I know about his close relationship with Nswt Bety Mer-en-Ra and his successor, Nswt Bety Peppy Nefer-ka-Ra, during the first golden age of our great nation-state, Kemet. And I want to go with you to Yam."

"I can think of at least ten reasons on why you can't go, my beloved son."

"No, listen, Father. You told me I should never use the word *can't*. Really listen, Father. On his first expedition, he went with his father, whose name was Iry. Did you hear that, Father? He went with his *father*, and they exchanged gifts. But his second expedition was without his father—and the key words here are *without his father*—and then he made two more expeditions *alone*. Alone, Father, and he even fought against Libyan bandits. But listen to the things they brought back from Yam—ivory, ebony, incense, grain, panther's skin, even throw sticks. I have to go, Father."

"Are you finished, my son? First of all, Harkhuf was not ten and four years. Second, he was a ritual priest, which means he was not only an adult man but he had finished his education. Do I need to continue, Royal Prince Mentchu-hotep?"

"Will you at least bring me back a dwarf to play with, Father?"

*****

"My lord, Nswt Bety Nebkhru-Ra Sa Ra Mentchu-hotep, Chief Medjay Jhutyms Ka-en-Heru is here to see you," said one of his royal Medjay guards.

"Please send him in." When I looked up, three Djedi grand masters were standing at my front door. *Wow, what an awesome sight!* I thought. Even the light in the library changed. I knelt before them, and they returned the respect and greetings.

Djedi Jhutyms Ka-en-Heru spoke, "This is about your journey to Yam, Shemsu Heru Mentchu-hotep. I must journey to Punt and then to Sumeria. There are important matters there I must handle, so Djedi Ka-en-Khufu and Djedi Neferu-Rat will accompany you with two Medjay medju units. You will be safe, and it should take around six months' round-trip. Usually, the Nswt Bety does not leave the country and especially for such a long time unless it is war, and then you are protected with an army. So the Djedi will ensure your safety. There is a new moon in two days, so prepare to leave then at Kheper-Ra."

"Why Yam?" I asked.

"It's your road and yours alone. Others may walk it with you, but no one can walk it for you. Your great-grandfather visited Yam. When you follow in the path of a great and powerful father, you learn to walk like him. The Djedi have learned that the best education you will ever get is traveling. Nothing teaches you more than exploring the world and accumulating experiences. There are things you should know about your people and our land, and Yam has the answers. Consider becoming the type of energy that no matter where you go or where you are, you always add value to the spaces and lives of those around you. This journey will help you."

Behind me, almost out of thin air, appeared the chief architect, Hem Sem Tepy Kha-ef-Ptah, in the doorway. He knelt down on one knee but was not looking at us, only on the floor.

"You may enter, Hem Sem Tepy Kha-ef-Ptah," I said, but he did not move.

Djedi Neferu-Rat spoke, "You may rise, my son."

As he rose, he spoke, "Please accept my apologies, but I felt the strong presence of the force of three Djedi warriors, Mother. This is very uncommon, so I am here as your obedient son." The three Djedi all bowed their heads with one hand inside the other; slowly they went out the doorway, never turning their backs to me, and out of my sight.

I walked quickly to the doorway to watch them walk out of the temple, but the three of them vanished in thin air, and no guards saw them leave. *I need to work on my energy. They are light-years ahead of me,* I thought.

I looked around the palace hallways, but the Djedi left without leaving a trace. I walked into my personal library and was surprised to see Princess Kawit studying one of my many papyri. When she saw me, she rose and then knelt at my feet, "Excuse me, my Neb Aa. Hmt Nswt Wrt Neferu said it would be fine if I studied here."

"Nen, please continue. What are you studying?"

"I am a little confused about the so many manifestations of the Ntchru, especially when several different Ntchru overlap and do the same thing. Why so many?"

"I'm going to explain the Ntchru the way it was revealed to me. Our Ntchr Ntchru of Kemet and Kash are the personification of a function or attribute of the one Divine Spirit. Central to our complete innerstanding of the universe was the knowledge that the Remtch was made in the image of the *Divine Spirit*. As such, we, the Remtch, represented the created images of all creation. Another word is, we are a microcosm of the macrocosm. Each of our cells in our body is like a solar system. And just like there are billions of cells in our body, there are billions of solar systems in our galaxy. There are billions of galaxies in the universe, and there are billions of universes in the cosmos."

"Wow, it was never explained to me like that," said Princess Kawit.

"The great ancient priest-scientist who learned how to recognize their oneness with Ntchr innerstood the symptoms that led to symptomatic thought. Accordingly, Kemet, nature, and our galaxy are all part of Ma'at. All measures were therefore simultaneously scaled to the Remtch, like the golden spiral in us and in all organic life, like the flowers, trees, seashells, even our divine temples. Also, this correspondence with the divine and the Remtch is expressed in nature or earth, to the solar system, to our galaxy, and ultimately, to the universe.

The golden spiral in nature. So is above, so is below.

"Please listen very carefully, Priestess Kawit. The Kemety and Kashite thinking that the one Divine Spirit can be represented through its functions or attributes is reflected in the Remtch. Each one of us has various functions and attributes. Look at me. I can be the Nswt Bety, the ruler of Upper and Lower Kemet, a Medjay warrior, a teacher in my library, a father to his child, a husband to his wife or wives, even a player on a team or council, and even a student of the Djedi. I don't have multiple personalities or several bodies but have multiple functions or attributes, just like the Ntchru, and many of the characteristics and duties overlap."

"Now I can innerstand, my Nswt Bety. Only we gave names to the different attributes, but like you, they are all part of the *one*." Princess Kawit was very proud of herself.

"Even though it may appear complex at first sight, Princess Kawit, it is both coherent and consistent with experience. This was and is the essence of the spiritual system and deep thought. Our complete Kemety civilization was built on a complete and precise innerstanding of these universal laws called Ntchru in all aspects of life. Even this temple we are standing in is based on the law of the golden spiral. Even the Mer Khut of Khufu [the Great Pyramid] is based on these same laws, and it is aligned with specific stars and constellations in the sky. So is above, so is below. I hope this lesson on the many layers of the Ntchru was helpful."

Priestess Kawit stood up. "You are amazing, and I thought Hmt Nswt Neferu was the best Seba in Kemet. You are truly a divine complement. You are truly a divine being."

"We all are divine spiritual beings, Princess Kawit. We are just having a divine Remtch experience."

"I probably will not sleep tonight, thinking about this lesson," she said.

"I have been there many times also, Priestess Kawit."

"Dua Ntchr," she said, then turned as she placed the papyrus back in its place on the library wall.

*****

We traveled to Kerma by boat. Like a river, the Spirit's peace flowed through my being and soothed, warmed, and harmonized my body, mind, and soul as I prepared for this journey. Once we reached Kerma, we reloaded our donkeys with our supplies and began our journey by horseback to Yam across the western desert. None of the Medjay had traveled to Yam before, only our two Djedi escorts. After traveling for several days in the western desert, we left all signs of life far behind. There were no plants, no animals, not even insects, just miles of endless sand and rocks, blowing dust, drifting sand dunes, and a few loose boulders.

The climate in the western desert was extremely harsh. The star Ra blazed in the daylight well past 120° F, but after Ra-set, the heat went as quickly as it came, sending the temperature down to freezing mark.

Djedi Ka-en-Khufu dismounted his horse. "Look at this."

We all dismounted, but I didn't see anything, just some rocks in the sand.

"Kneel down and look at the eastern horizon," he said.

I still saw nothing unusual, and no one else said anything.

"This is the ancient playa or seasonal lake area. Look." He picked up several pieces of broken clay pots near our feet. "This was part of a Remtch settlement thousands of years ago. I can still see it clearly—children playing, women cooking in an open pit of fire. Dig here." He pointed. "You three, come with me. Dig over there. Now can you see it? Not with your eyes, Shemsu Heru, with your inner vision. It's not what you look at that matters. It's what you see, young Medjay."

All the Medjay were great trackers, but now I could see the difference between the Medjay priest-scientist and even the most powerful elite warriors. We found not only fragments of pots but also shells and bones. Someone found charcoal buried where Djedi Ka-en-Khufu had pointed. I was even beginning to feel the ancient settlement. "Look," I said, as I dug deeper into the sand. It looked like a sacred grave site. Several Medjay warriors helped me unearth the grave. To our surprise, it was the grave of a cow or bull.

Medjay Priest-Scientist Ka-en-Jhutyms said, "Their houses were along the lake on that hill site."

"Very good, Ka-en-Jhutyms." And several priest-scientists were smiling because, like myself, we could feel it also. "This playa was once a large basin in the western desert, located approximately 100 kilometers west of Buhen in southern Kemet," said Djedi Ka-en-Khufu, "and also 250 kilometers [155 miles] northeast of Yebu."

"Djedi Ka-en-Khufu, what is this?" asked Medjay Priest-Scientist Akhtoy Ba-Heru.

"Dua Ntchr." Everyone gathered around. "The Djedi have encountered these formations many times, even as far as the southernmost tip of Ta Ntchr, beyond the land of Bes and the second great desert.

Djedi Neferu-Rat spoke, "They are the gates of Ra. These stone rings represent a calendar circle showing the summer and winter solstice." Then the Djedi began to show the Medjay how to read the ancient calendar as she pointed to the summer solstice.

Finally, after that profound lesson, we came upon several alignments of giant stones. This area was located some two kilometers (about one mile) south of the calendar circle.

"What are these giant stone alignments?" asked Medjay Priest-Scientist Akhtoy Ba-Heru.

"These large boulders were placed here as part of a complex ceremonial center. These giant stone alignments are pointing to the rising place of important stars on the horizon." Djedi Ka-en-Khufu pointed at the large boulders. "I can see that one set of six stones was pointing to Spdt, and this set was pointing to Sahu or Asr's belt maybe two thousand years ago. That third set of giant stones is pointing to Dubhe or Alkaid, the bull's thigh constellation called Mesekhtyw, one of the circumpolar stars, the same stars that Nswt Bety Dozier is staring at in his burial temple at Sokar."

"Tiw," I said. (Yes.) "I remember one of the high priests from the temple of Het-Ka-Ptah pointing that out when we were in Sokar at Netchrikhet's mortuary temple complex."

"Now if you look closely, Medjay, these giant stones formed north–south and east–west sight lines, like a giant stone compass, and probably remained visible even when the summer inundation filled the playa basin."

Playa calendar circle showing the summer solstice over two
thousand years before Sema Tawy of Kemet in the western desert

Medjay Akhtoy said, "The cardinal alignments are what
you'd expect for people to use who travel across the desert with
no particular way to guide them other than the stars. As they
traveled, their tracks were obliterated, so they had to know
north, south, east, and west." We all kind of smiled. The people
of Yam must have been Medjay or connected to the Medjay, we
all thought, because as guardians of the eastern and western
desert in Kemet and Kash, we had to learn these things. And
they were reinforced when we traveled the open waters,
especially those Medjay from Punt and the eastern coast.

"I'm beginning to see how to put these puzzle pieces
together here," said Medjay Ka-en-Jhutyms. "I think the
Djedi are trying to tell us that these people who created these
calendar circles were from Yam and that we were connected
by more than just trade partners. They seemed to have the
same astrological science as we do, but it predates Kemet by
thousands of years. They were also carvers of stone at a time
before Kemet or parallel to the first golden age of Kemet. And
why is Shemsu Heru Netchrikhet Nswt Bety Djoser looking at
the same star constellation?"

"May I speak, great Grand Master Djedi Ka-en-Khufu? It also seems that these people had a great respect for cattle and the sacred cow Het Heru and the Apis bull also before Kemet."

"Very good, Medjay Ka-en-Jhutyms, Medjay Akhtoy Ba-Heru, and Shemsu Heru Sa Ra Mentchu-hotep, but there is still much more."

The giant stones formed north-south and east-west sight lines in the playa.

A stone calendar in southern Afraka made just like in the western playa near Kemet, only thousands of years older

After several more days in the western desert, we noticed many of the mountains had been shaped like Mer Khuts (pyramids) by the strong desert winds, looking much like the Mer Khut of Khufu or Kha-ef-Ra in Kemet. "These mountains hold ancient secrets," Djedi Ka-en-Khufu explained to us. "The song of water is audible to every ear along the Hapy Eteru, but there is other music in the hills and mountains of the desert that are, by no means, audible to all. To hear even a few notes of its magical music, you must first live here for a long time and you must know the speech of desert hills."

We passed through the White Desert, and the wind and sand had carved the soft white sandstone into mushroom shapes. "Come closer, Medjay," said Djedi Ka-en-Khufu. "Look closely at this white sandstone and limestone, and tell me what you see."

I spoke, "The single-cell sea creatures, like in the stones on the Mer Khut of Khufu, and sea fossils. But why are they here in the desert?"

"Tiw, that means this whole desert was underwater at one time," said Djedi Ka-en-Khufu.

Several of us said at the same time, "How long ago?"

"Maybe forty thousand years ago. We even found whale bones here in the desert. Before the earth shifted to where it is now, the Wedjy Wr was the Wedjy Wr aa, the big great green connecting the waters on both sides of our great land. Before we move on to our next destiny, let's review the Medjay handbook on what makes us different, successful in life, and unbeatable in battle," added Djedi Ka-en-Khufu.

1. *Imagination.* It must serve your higher self.

2. *Intuition.* Instincts connect you to the One, the source of *all*.

3. *Will.* Give yourself a command and follow it.

4. *Memory.* Backward and forward, live the life you want to live based on Ma'at.

5. *Reason.* Conditions are limitless and extraordinary.

6. *Perception.* Ma'at is the scale of justice based on your current results, reality check.

7. *Voice.* Speak your truth daily, and be thankful.

After a week, we traveled to a place the Djedi call Djedefre's Water Mountain. How he found this place in the middle of the western desert was unbelievable.

Djedefre's Water Mountain

All the mountains looked almost the same. Djedi Ka-en-Khufu had us leave our horses and donkeys and climb maybe twenty meters on the side of the mountain, then he said, "Look here! Over here where there are carvings on the wall. What does that say, Shemsu Heru Sa Ra Mentchu-hotep?"

"It says that Djedefre made two expeditions here to Water Mountain. Two of the excursions took place during the twenty-fifth and twenty-seventh regnal year of Nswt Bety Khufu. His followers had come to the hill in order to quarry pigments."

"Now I want you to spread out. Search this area well, look for clues of life, and we will report back here in three hours."

After three hours, the Medjay all circled around the two Djedi grand masters and reported what was found. Djedi Ka-en-Khufu then reinterpreted and summarized our findings. "In the western desert, more than eighty kilometers from the nearest oasis, the desert shows traces of early settlements in a depression, which, at the time, was probably an oasis. These people were of medium height and black of skin, probably settled people who earned their livelihood from plant cultivation. They used grindstones. The art of weaving was known and well-developed.

"Statuettes of a pregnant woman were of high importance to these cultivators. Possibly, they were connected with the idea of a Ntchr of fertility. The petroglyphs in the mountains and nearby caves represent the fauna then, existing four to five thousand years ago—ostriches, addaxes, goats, and other bovids. One thing, however, is clear to me by now. As no sizable amount of pottery for storing water has been found at Djedefre's Water Mountain, the followers of Khufu and of Djedefre came to the stone temple because water from wells still could be obtained there during the times of the Nswt Bety Khufu."

"Are these people from Yam or Tekhebet?" asked Medjay Ka-en-Jhutyms.

"We shall see. Let's travel southwest from here," said the Djedi.

Both the Djedi could feel the presence of hostile strangers coming in their direction fast, maybe two miles away. Djedi Ka-en-Khufu gave directions for the Medjay to travel, and they would join them shortly after further exploration of the area. The two Djedi moved to higher grounds, away from the direction of the Medjay. They dismounted their horses and waited for their pursuers.

They were Libyan bandits, thirteen of them. They surrounded the two Djedi. The Libyan leader spoke, "You are a long way from home, blacks. Are you lost?" The rest of the Libyan bandits laughed.

"All of this land is our home," replied Djedi Ka-en-Khufu. "You are the invaders." Both Djedi could speak their language, but Djedi Neferu-Rat said nothing.

"These blacks look like they are very spiritual by their dress. I think since they are lost, we should help them get to their ancestral burial grounds." All the bandits laughed again. The leader dismounted and walked toward Djedi Ka-en-Khufu. "I'll make you a deal. All we want is the woman and all your valuables. Place them down in the sand with all your water, and we will let you go." The Libyans laughed again. "We will let your creator, Ra, take care of you." The bandit thought that was extremely funny as they laughed again very loudly.

Djedi Ka-en-Khufu spoke, "I can't do that."

"That was the wrong answer, my black friend." The leader stepped away, and thirteen arrows flew toward Djedi Ka-en-Khufu from several directions.

With very little effort, he spun around quickly, and with only one hand, he caught all thirteen arrows. He then looked at his opponents and the leader of the bandits and broke all the arrows in half with both hands and dropped them in the sand at his feet.

The leader smiled. "Oh, you got skills! Brothers, I think these are Medjay warriors. We have heard about your incredible skills. Now we shall find out if it is just legend or hot air." Ten of the bandits dismounted as they pulled out their swords and battle-axes. Two remained on their horses, with their bows and arrows pointed at the two Djedi. Both Djedi did not move. They kind of stood back-to-back and waited.

The eleven bandits surrounded the two Djedi, and the leader spoke again, "You're not afraid to die, Medjay?"

"Fear can only go as deep as the mind allows. For us, fear does not exist," said Djedi Ka-en-Khufu.

"Are you going to pull your swords out?"

Djedi Ka-en-Khufu looked into the leader's eyes and smiled as he saw his face covered with sweat. "One does not use a sword to kill a snail."

"What, a snail! Kill them!" He waved his hand toward them. The first six bandits attacked with fury.

Djedi Neferu-Rat quickly dropped low, spinning into the bandits, knocking two down, disarming the third, and cutting his head completely off with his own sword with a smooth circular movement. She then stuck the Libyan sword through the heart of the second bandit, caught the arrow with her left

161

hand from the horseman, and plugged it through the neck of her third victim.

Djedi Ka-en-Khufu leaped over the head of two bandits and kicked the third on the side of his temple, killing him instantly on contact. He then blocked the sword of his second opponent with his bare arms, grabbing him and using his body as a shield, as the third bandit tried to stab him with his sword. He stabbed his fellow bandit in the heart. Djedi Ka-en-Khufu grabbed the hand of the stabbed bandit with the sword in his heart and cut the throat of the third bandit whose sword was still sticking inside his own friend. They just fell on top of each other.

The horseman shot his arrow at Djedi Ka-en-Khufu, but the Djedi grabbed the arrow out of the air and plunged it through the neck of his fourth victim. Djedi Ka-en-Khufu rolled on the ground, pulled two daggers from his sandal straps, and threw them in two directions almost at the same time, killing both horsemen instantly.

The two Djedi moved back together, unharmed and ready. There were only four Libyan bandits left—two had battle-axes and two had swords. The leader was furious, but the other three were shaking in their sandals. "Kill them," the leader said. Two charged, and one threw his battle-ax at Djedi Ka-en-Khufu's head. He caught the battle-ax in midair and used it to strike the two charging bandits who never knew what hit them. He cut one's throat and split the other's head wide open and then returned the battle-ax to its owner, only right between his eyes.

Djedi Neferu-Rat walked toward the lone Libyan bandit leader. She said, "You wanted me, right?"

He swung his sword toward her head, yelling at her. She sidestepped his movement, grabbed his sword from his hand, and swung it upward between his legs, cutting his penis off with a clean swipe. He screamed as he fell to the ground, grabbing his severed penis between his legs and rolling in the sand in agony. The two Djedi never took their swords out of their holsters on their backs.

The Djedi picked up all their weapons and placed them on their horses. They left the one screaming bandit in the sand with his horse and water as they led the rest of the horses with them back to meet the Medjay traveling southwest toward the Tassili Mountains and caves. The Djedi made excellent time catching their Medjay party before nightfall.

When I asked the Djedi where they had found the supplies and horses in the middle of the desert, they smiled and said, "The Ntchr provides for those who are prepared to receive its gifts."

After a few days, we came to another mountain range and cave area. This area was called Tassili Mountains. The two Djedi told us to scout the caves and nearby area and report back in three hours. I could see now what the Djedi were doing. The western desert was a classroom, and we were the students. This was geography, science, astrology, topography, ourstory, ancient ourstory, math, geometry, gemology, and Mdw Ntchr. And since we all had to keep a diary, it was also analytical and critical thinking and record keeping.

After exploring the Tassili Mountains and caves, we explored the Uweinat caves and mountainous area. We were two months away from Kemet by donkey. After putting all the information together—cave drawings, Mdw Ntchr, artifacts, rocks, pottery samples, bones of animals and the Remtch, seeds, and tools and weapons—Djedi Ka-en-Khufu did his summary.

Tassili Mountain paintings

Uweinat cave

"There existed a western desert wet period, which lasted from five hundred to fifteen thousand years ago, when much of the western desert was habitable for Remtch and when the dunes were covered with grassland, supporting hippos, lions, crocodiles, zebras, giraffes, etc. By six thousand to nine thousand years ago, there were hunters, dancers, bakers, and even sailors. There were shamans leaving rock paintings on the cliff's face. One dancer was wearing a jackal or dog mask. We even found a sahu [mummified] body.

"The earliest examples of western desert rock art are invariably engravings, sometimes on a cave of the ancestor of modern, domesticated cattle, resembling the modern east Ta Ntchr buffalo but with much larger horns. As it became extinct around a thousand years ago, it has allowed us to date the Tassili rock paintings, large-scale wall paintings, representing the ancient and partially extinct wildlife. Any questions so far?

"These are the same cattle people of the playa region. Gilf Kebir and Jebel Uweinat escaped the drying of the western desert and spread pastoralism throughout the land. However, a fast drying occurred. It pushed these people out of the north central Ta Ntchr, and that climatically forced migration led to the rise of the Nswt and the Kemet civilization as they met the southern Ta Ntchr Remtch traveling down the Hapy Eteru with knowledge of boats, hunting, herbs, and warrior skills.

"It was probably a slow desertification that occurred over several millennia from about two thousand years ago to five thousand years ago, meanwhile giving these people ample time across many generations to develop animal domestication, basic agriculture, art, primitive sign writing, the knowledge of how to move large stones and construct complex megalithic structures, and the knowledge of the simple principles of navigation, orientation, and timekeeping with Ra and the stars. They even had an earlier version of Enpu—the black jackal in their art connected to death and the sahu body. In other words, they acquired the practical and intellectual tools for building a civilization by the time they migrated into the Kemet Hapy Valley around one thousand to five thousand years ago.

"We, the Djedi, have seen the engravings on a large rock consisting of Mdw Ntchr writing, a Nswt Bety *shen,* an image of the Nswt Bety, and other Kemety iconography long ago. Your Medjay skills yielded astonishing revelations. In the annals of Kemety ourstory, there are references to far-off lands that the Nswt Bety had traded with, but none of these have ever been positively located by the Remtch of Kemet and Kash.

"We, the Djedi, states that the decipherment reveals that the region of their find is none other than the fabled land of Yam, one of the most famous and mysterious nations that the Kemetyu had traded within the first golden age—a source of precious tropical woods and ivory. Its location has been debated because of its distance, but it was never imagined it could be more than 1,400 kilometers [870 miles] from Buhen, Kemet, west of the Hapy Eteru in the middle of the western desert."

One of the Medjay asked, "Why would the rising of Spdt be valuable in the desert? I innerstand why on the Hapy because of inundation and the Hapy flood, but why in the desert?"

I raised my hand.

"Tiw, Shemsu Heru Sa Ra Mentchu-hotep. Would you like to answer that one?"

"Tiw, Djedi Grand Master."

"Continue."

"The summer solstice was the time of year that began the monsoon rains that filled the lakes at the playa community, which are the same monsoon rains from the Ta Ntchr and the Mountains of the Moon. So just like farmers prepare for planting, the pastoral people prepared to migrate their herds."

"Dua Ntchr," said Djedi Neferu-Rat.

"Mount up, Medjay warriors. Let's travel southwest and see if these people of Yam still exist or have died out with the longhorn cattle. Wrap your faces and head well, Medjay. I sense a storm coming."

"How is it that you can see and feel these things before they come into being, Djedi Grand Master Ka-en-Khufu?"

He smiled just like Djedi Grand Master Jhutyms Ka-en-Heru did whenever I asked a question. "Your mind is something very powerful, Shemsu Heru. Give it the time and strength it needs to open its first eye, and you shall see and feel these things also. Everything in the universe is within us. Yesterday and tomorrow are all happening right now! So by being in touch with the moment, I can sense all the things that I need to know."

"But how do you know what you need?"

"Simply by being in the now, enjoying the present moment. And intuitively, you will know what is needed! All the animals know when a storm is coming or when an earthquake is about to happen. Are we not as intelligent as most animals? Become in tune with your environment always. It's your home, your fifth temple! Ask all from yourself because you are part of the environment. There is really no separation. When you make that connection, then you will know also. The Spirit is so humble that it will not force itself into your awareness. But what great joy it knows when you willingly enter the temple of divine consciouness within your own soul.

"Throughout this day, stop frequently to breathe and touch that place within you that is the peace that surpasses all understanding. Let it be carried on the wings of your thoughts, words, and actions. Through calmness, keep your mental and nervous system relaxed so that they may catch the intuitive guidance whispered to you by the Spirit. Peace, calmness, and stillness are another way of practicing the presence of Ntchr."

Three hours later, the sky blackened in the middle of the day, and we could see a sandstorm raging like a lion several miles in front of us. We all dismounted and started digging a circular trench in the sand, maybe two feet deep, and then we secured all the animals. The winds were blowing almost seventy-five to one hundred miles per hour; the sand was so thick you could not see your hand in front of you. We sat in our trenches as the sand raced over us in almost every direction. If you stood up, the winds with the sand were strong enough to cut into your skin and rip your flesh or just pick you up and throw you twenty or thirty meters through the air. Most of us had witnessed sandstorms before, but never one at this magnitude.

After about three intense hours, the storm had passed and all was quiet again. Our trenches were completely covered up. We had to dig a few of the animals out of the sand and recover some of our provisions and equipment, but we were all fine. After the storm, we prepared our campsite for the evening. I followed the two Djedi to a high point on a sand dune, maybe a mile from the campsite, but I kept sinking into the sand. The two Djedi stood on top of the dunes without even leaving a footprint in the sand. Once I reached them, I asked what I was doing wrong.

They smiled and said nothing. Djedi Neferu-Rat said, "You have accepted your environment as real, and therefore, you are reacting to your surrounding elements. We know this is an illusion, so we are operating on a different paradigm. We walk as if we were kissing the sand with our feet."

After maybe thirty minutes of deep meditation, I opened my eyes and the Djedi were gone. It was pitch-black. *How am I going to find my way back to the campsite?* I thought. Then I heard a voice in my head say, "Follow the light that is in your heart, and you will find your way to us because we are all one. Remember, living only in the physical, mental, and emotional realm makes energy limited. Tap into the spiritual dimension, and the energy is limitless."

Shemsu Heru

Sand dunes after a storm

By knowing, one reaches belief. By doing, one gains conviction. I followed the powerful energy source of the Medjay back to the camp. The key to all mysteries and the source of all illumination lay deep within the self. The Ntchr Ntchru was the candle that lit the way for the souls of the Kemetyu. This was just another test that gave a profound lesson: every trial is an additional opportunity to expand our innerstanding of the way.

As I entered the campsite, I could feel the joy of the Medjay medju. I have surrounded myself with people who made me hungry for life, who touched my heart, and who nourished my soul. And that alone was great joy.

As we rose with Kheper-Ra the next morning, we could see rivers of white sand feeding into a dry ocean with waves of sand dunes. Behind us lay great limestone-capped hills that shone white, pink, or violet, depending on the angle of light and time of day.

In this place, time stood still as Djedi Ka-en-Khufu talked about time. "You have seen millions of years of time pass us in the wink of an eye in this desert. We have found shark teeth, whale bones, giant sea turtles, and brown fossils from an extremely ancient time before the Remtch or any people were on earth. Then maybe 500,000 to 2,000,000 years ago, we saw early men with simple hand tools—hand axes, flint knives, and spear tips. Then about 15,000 to 250,000 years ago, we saw different tools. The Remtch were still nomadic—travelers—but were thinkers very much like we are today.

"We, the Remtch, in our current form, appeared only about 250,000 years ago. So our species have survived *two* Ice Ages. Around 12,000 years ago, something happened—maybe the change in weather. The Afrakan Humid Period occurred between 3,500 and 12,000 years ago and was the last occurrence of a 'green western desert area.' At this point, we saw the domesticating of plants and animals, pottery, and a change from a hunting and gathering lifestyle to a more agrarian one. Around 8,000 to 10,000 years ago, we see the Remtch were raising goats and cows and growing wheat and barley, making pottery, weaving, and living in mud-brick houses. At this time, we found ostrich eggshell beads, arrowheads, spears, scrapers, bone tools, and heavy grinding stones that could be used for milling wild and domestic cereals or mixing ochre for body paints."

One of the Medjay asked, "How do you know the difference between wild animals and domesticated animals with just a bone?"

"By the size of the bones. All domesticated animals—like cows, goats, pigs, and birds—are smaller. This connects us to the people at the playa calendar circle showing the summer solstice over two thousand years before Sema Tawy of Kemet in the western desert."

After three more days, we found horse tracks in the desert. We followed the trail for about two hours as it led us toward the Sahel land of shrubs and small plants. The two Djedi stopped us and told us to be still as they dismounted their horses. Waiting in the large rocks were two large rock python snakes—one maybe eighteen meters and the other about fourteen meters long. The two Djedi captured the snakes with ease. They even seemed to tame them and sent them back into the rocks away from us.

Djedi Ka-en-Khufu spoke to us, "It is not always necessary to kill when you can use gentle persuasion. The falcon does not fight the snake on the ground. It picks it up into the sky and changes the battleground, and then it releases the snake into the sky. The snake has no stamina, no power, and no balance in the air. It is useless, weak, and vulnerable, unlike on the ground, where it is powerful, wise, and deadly. Take your fight into the spiritual realm by using your sacred Medjay training, and when you are in the spiritual realm, Ntchr takes over your battles. Don't fight the enemy in his comfort zone. Change the battlegrounds, like the falcon, and let Ntchr Mentchu take charge through your earnest training of Heru and Mentchu. You'll be assured of clean victory."

Watching the two Djedi in action was simply amazing. After recovering from that lesson, the Djedi said, "Look carefully. There are two different sets of tracks here—one set leads to the north and the other south between the mountains. We can split up into two groups, or we can follow one at a time. Or we can just continue south. The call is yours, Sa Ra Mentchu-hotep."

"What can you tell us about the two sets of tracks?" replied Mentchu-hotep.

Djedi Ka-en-Khufu replied, "The northern tracks belong to Berbers, a nomadic Asiatic group much like the Libyans, who are invaders to our land."

Djedi Neferu-Rat said, "The other southern tracks belong to warriors who have fast horses like our own."

"How old are the tracks?"

Medjay priest-scientist Ka-en-Jhutyms touched the tracks and said, "Only maybe an hour away."

"Very good, Medjay," said Djedi Ka-en-Khufu. "They are very fresh."

"Let's follow the Asiatics. Maybe they have been up to some esfet [wrongdoings]," I said.

We spotted them in only about twenty minutes. They did not see or hear us. We broke up into two groups and surrounded them. Djedi Ka-en-Khufu approached them alone while we hid in the sand dunes and small bushes. He gave them the signal of peace, and they immediately surrounded him. The Djedi asked to speak to their leader in their language.

They were shocked that he could speak their tough language as they looked at one another in surprise. "You are going to die, so it does not matter who you speak to," shouted one of the Asiatics.

"I come in peace," replied the Djedi. At the same time, two arrows flew toward his body. The Djedi caught them both as he jumped off his horse.

They all started charging at the Djedi, but in the blink of an eye, the party of maybe twenty-five Asiatics were shot full of arrows. The Medjay did not miss one shot. Arrows flew from two sides. Most of them never knew what killed them. Only one Asiatic seemed to be alive. He did not charge; he was leaning off his horse, like he was wounded. When we examined him, he had been bitten by the snake that we encountered back at the mountain range we just left.

Djedi Neferu-Rat said, "We can save him. It is not too late." She pulled him down off his horse. His arm was broken, and he was bitten on the leg. She tied a cloth around his thigh to stop the circulation and then began to suck the poison out of his leg while I applied a splinter to support his broken arm. We set it straight first as we tied it firmly to hold it in place.

As we looked around and examined their bodies, four more Asiatics had lived. The arrows went straight through two Asiatics without hitting any vital organs. We patched them up and gave them some medicine for their wounds and the snakebite. We asked if they wanted us to help bury their dead, but they wanted to take the bodies back to their families in their village. We placed their bodies on their horses and tied them together so it would be easier for the five wounded Asiatics to get home. We guided them halfway before we returned to the mountain range where we left off.

We entered an opening between two large rocky slopes and, to our surprise, stood before a war party of about forty warriors in full battle gear on horses. They all had strange paint designs on their faces. Their leader placed his hand out for us to stop. Djedi Ka-en-Khufu gave him a hand signal, and their leader spoke some words I did not innerstand. Later, I was told it was Hausa.

"You may not enter this land without special permission," he told Djedi Ka-en-Khufu.

"We have permission from the Ntchr Ntchru," replied Djedi Ka-en-Khufu.

Their leader smiled. "If the Creator gave you permission to enter our land, then it must have given you special skills in which to pass! If you can defeat me in hand-to-hand combat, we will escort you into our village. But if you lose, we will bury you here and escort your party back into the desert where you came from!"

Painted warrior from Yam in the western desert

They both dismounted their horses as they maintained eye contact with each other. We could see a contest was about to happen. Their leader drew a large circle in the sand and then divided it in half. Then he invited Djedi Ka-en-Khufu inside. We began to smile because we knew what was in store for the painted warrior, but their warriors were smiling too. They stood on both sides of the dividing line and touched hands to begin the contest. They both moved like wildcats. I could tell that their souls knew each other. Souls recognize each other by the way they feel, not by the way they look.

The painted warrior spoke, "You may have defeated Apep [Apophis] the Snake, the enemy of Ra, but we are even more dangerous." He threw a series of punches and kicks that could not be seen by the average eye, but the Djedi blocked them all with one hand. Then he attacked again, only this time with hands and feet swirling in the air, but the Djedi blocked and evaded them all. The painted warrior rolled on the ground, throwing dirt at the Djedi's face, followed by several poison darts, but the Djedi caught all the darts and laughed.

When the painted warrior attacked the fourth time, Djedi Ka-en-Khufu stepped inside his move, striking him to the chest and throat, then quickly spinning behind him and placing him in a choke hold. I think the warrior was more shocked than hurt. First, he was stunned from the speed of the blow, then he could not breathe as Djedi Ka-en-Khufu gently put him to sleep in his Medjay choke hold. The other warriors looked on in disbelief. Three of their warriors jumped down from their horses to run to their leader's aid. Djedi Ka-en-Khufu spoke in their Hausa language that he would be all right.

When their leader came to, he smiled. After he got his breath back, the other warriors were puzzled. For he knew only a Medjay Djedi could do this! They helped him to his feet, then he knelt down on one knee to Djedi Ka-en-Khufu. "Great Djedi, we welcome you to *Ta-nout*, the land belonging to Nut the Sky. I offer you *Ma'at* [peace]. I offer you Mrr [love]. I offer you *smr* [friendship]. I see your nefer [beauty]. I hear your need. I feel your feelings. My wisdom flows from the highest source, Amen Ra. I salute that source in you. Let us work and build together." They both hugged each other. He then spoke to his warriors that it was an honor to be beaten by a Djedi and still live. They were still a little puzzled until he explained that the Djedi were the greatest warriors on Ta and Nut was sent from Ra by Amen to protect them from Asiatics, Northern demons, and the monsters living under the earth.

We all got down from our horses and greeted one another like family. Water and food were exchanged, and then they led us into their village. Now we were shocked. First, we passed a series of round houses with roofs that came to a point like small pyramids, like we saw in the land of Punt, before seeing a large walled city with two large lions carved from pink granite at the front entrance. The guards opened the doors, and we were amazed at an unexpected sight—two rows of three-step pyramids that led to a great temple all carved in stone.

A group of priests dressed in all white came to greet us. The leader of the warriors spoke to the priest on our behalf. We all dismounted as we greeted the priest. We all knelt down on one knee, and the priest returned our greetings. The chief priest spoke to us, "We are keepers of Ma'at and Mrr [love]. Ma'at and love are the bridge between you and everything. I can see that some of you did not come as warriors. You were born warriors. Some of you are still catching up to what you are. We are. Just like some of us did not become healers. We came as healers. We are. Some of us are still catching up to what we are.

"We do not become storytellers. We came as carriers of the stories we and our ancestors actually lived. We are. Some of us are still catching up to what we are. We do not become artists. We came as artists. We are. Some of us are still catching up to what we are. We do not become writers or dancers and musicians or helpers or peacemakers. We came as such. We are. Some of us are still catching up to what we are. We do not learn to love in this sense. We came as love. We are love. Some of us are still catching up to who we truly are."

They spoke like the Djedi, with wisdom far beyond this world. The high priest spoke again, "The world is a magical place. Once we close our physical eyes and view through the first eye, we look beyond the illusion and pierce the veil to the true reality." The high priest looked at the Medjay and spoke again, "The world is full of magical things, patiently waiting for our senses to grow sharper, so we can comprehend them."

Djedi Ka-en-Khufu spoke to the priest, "My soul honors your soul. I honor a place within you where the whole universe resides. I honor light, love, truth, beauty, and peace within you, because they are also within me. In seeing these things, we are united. We are the same. We are one."

Tears came into the eyes of the high priest, and soon we were crying too. "It has been 150 years since a Djedi has returned to our village. We see you. We feel you. We greet you in the name of Amen-Ra, Ma'at."

We all could feel the emotions that filled the air. In all my journeys with the Medjay, I have never witnessed people with the knowledge of Medjay priest-scientists and Djedi masters until now. At this moment, I realized there was a sacredness in tears. They are not the sign of weakness but of power. They speak more eloquently than a hundred thousand words. They are the messengers of overwelming grief or the deep, unspoken feeling of unspeakable love. When we walked through their temples, climbed their Mer Khut, marveled at their stone carvings, and saw that they even had Mdw Ntchr in the shrine rooms at the top of the Mer Khut, we were convinced. If there was any doubt that we were connected mentally, physically, and spiritually, it was all obliterated after this encounter.

The next day, we met Nana Ghana, their ruler who was dressed in all purple. His priestly advisers were dressed in purple and white as they carried large umbrellas over Nana Ghana's head. Their priest followed closely behind, dressed in all white. Their warriors followed in black. And finally, the Remtch, the black people, followed wearing many colors but mostly earth tones. Their leader explained that their Mer Khut (pyramids) were older than the ones in Kemet and were built before the last great flood, when their land and Kemet's were still wet and bountiful. "Some of our family immigrated to the Hapy Eteru Valley and, with your help and the help of the Medjay, built Heru-em-Akhety in Dar Gaza. Our sciences were exchanged, making both groups stronger. Some of our people moved on into South Asia, where we brought high culture, science, agriculture, and cattle herding to Sumeria and the neigboring villages.

"The land where our Mer Khuts rest is called Dar Gaza, which means 'crown of the Creator or light of the solar disc—Ra.' Each morning, our priest gives prayer and libation in reverence to Amen-Ra, who comes forth in the morning as Kheper-Ra, each high noon as Ra, and each evening as Atum-Ra, the complete one. Who is without a hemet [wife] in your group of Medjay?" asked the Nana Ghana.

I replied, "Medjay Priest-Scientist Ka-en-Jhutyms is the leader of our Medjay medju and one of our greatest warriors and ambassadors of Kemet and Kash, and he does not have a divine mate."

"Neferukayt, the second daughter of Ghana, is a royal gift from the ruler of Yam, Nana Ghana, to the ruler of Kemet, Shemsu Heru Nswt Bety Neb Khrw-Ra Sa Ra Mentchu-hotep, who gives her to his ambassador and friend, with much respect. If my daughter accepts, we will link our blood together again, like we did in the past, but this time for eternity.

Neferukayt, the second daughter of Nana Ghana, stepped forward. She was a commander in their royal military, and she was stunningly beautiful. She stood about six feet tall, maybe 180 pounds. Her body and looks were 'blacknificent,' more than magnificent. She spoke, "I must first see if he can fight, then I will know if he is even worthy of my Mrr and devotion!" She drew a circle on the floor in front of her father and then divided it in half, and then she invited Medjay Ka-en-Jhutyms inside.

We were thinking that no matter how good she was, she was no match for Medjay Priest-Scientist Ka-en-Jhutyms. They bowed to Nana Ghana and then to the two Djedi grand masters—Ka-en-Khufu and Neferu-Rat—then to me and, finally, to each other.

She thrusted her spear toward the body of Medjay Ka-en-Jhutyms, and he snatched it out of her hand. She was shocked at first, but she realized at that moment that he was a formidable foe! She threw several kicks and punches at the Medjay, but they all were reflected. At first, he did not try to counter her attacks. He just blocked or evaded them. She grew frustrated. "Come and fight me!" she shouted.

He looked over at Djedi Ka-en-Khufu, and he nodded his head. He then swept her off her feet, but she snapped back up before he could move in. She then twirled in the air sideways, throwing several kicks, but the Medjay evaded them all. He grabbed her by the arm and put her in an armlock, but she leaped up and flipped backward over the Medjay's head and then kicked him in the back!

Wow, that was beautiful, I thought.

The Medjay turned around quickly and countered the attack with a crane strike to the temple, followed by a crescent kick to the side of her head. She never saw either strike as she fell unconscious to the floor. Several priests helped her to her feet, but she was smiling when she came to. She then knelt to her father's feet and spoke, "I accept this warrior's hand in marriage, Father, and I shall make you proud of the union of our two nations."

Above is Neferukayt, the second daughter of Nana Ghana, of Ta-nout in ancient Yam.

The priest who led the wedding ceremony was dressed like a giant bee, with mushrooms growing out of his hands and from the top of his head and neck. He did some kind of dance, almost like some real bees I have seen giving messages in their beehive. He gave them both the sacred mushrooms and told them to eat them now and that in the morning, they would know their future together. "Everything you see has its roots in the unseen world. The forms may change, yet the essence remains the same."

There were lots of drumming and dancing, and only now I saw why the Djedi wanted me to make this journey to Yam! None of this could have been explained the way I witnessed it with my own two eyes. And like the mighty rulers of Kemet who came before me, whose footsteps I stood in, I would carve my name in the mountains on our return trip back to Kemet for future generations to witness this mighty union.

The bee priest of infinite possibilities

*****

The full moon glowed bright as the two newly married warriors lay nude, only witnessed by the moon on top of Ta-nout, the largest step Mer Khut (pyramid) in Yam. The newlyweds would celebrate their marriage in intimacy and seclusion.

Even though Medjay Priest-Scientist Ka-en-Jhutyms was one of Kash and Kemet's greatest warrior, he was still a virgin when it came to women. He marveled at her well-defined, nude body. Up until now, he had never really taken the time to enjoy the difference and beauty in a woman's body. He was spellbound by her movements as she swayed her voluptuous hips from side to side. Her breasts were like two mountain peaks standing firm and soft at the same time. Her dark-chocolate-brown skin was well-oiled, and it glistened in the moonlight. His fingers sunk into her soft, tightly curled hair that was bushy, like a tropical rain forest. He was a strong warrior, a champion among champions. And for the first time in his life, he felt weak and vulnerable. He sat down under her on the soft mat. His legs were trembling.

Princess Neferukayt picked up two small beautifully colored bowls as she stared into the Medjay's eyes. "Close your eyes," she said softly. "And drink this." She began to pour the contents of the second bowl all over him.

Medjay Ka-en-Jhutyms was puzzled. *What is this?* he thought. But before he could ask the question, she was licking his body all over. Medjay Ka-en-Jhutyms felt his body parts standing at attention while he was still lying down, floating in a state of ecstasy and trembling all at the same time.

She kissed him on his lips and then said, "It's honey. Lie back and enjoy your honey wine and wild honey on your honeymoon!"

*****

That night, after the wedding ceremony, I asked Djedi Ka-en Khufu and Djedi Neferu-Rat where they were during the storm. I was looking for them, and I could not feel their presence until after the storm.

Djedi Ka-en-Khufu looked me in the eyes and said, "When a storm is coming, all other birds and animals seek shelter. The great falcon and eagle are the only creatures on earth, along with the Djedi, that avoid the storm by flying above it. So in the storms of life, Medjay Priest-Scientist Nswt Bety Neb Khrw-Ra Sa Ra Mentchu-hotep, may your heart soar like Heru, the mighty falcon, above your storms in life!"

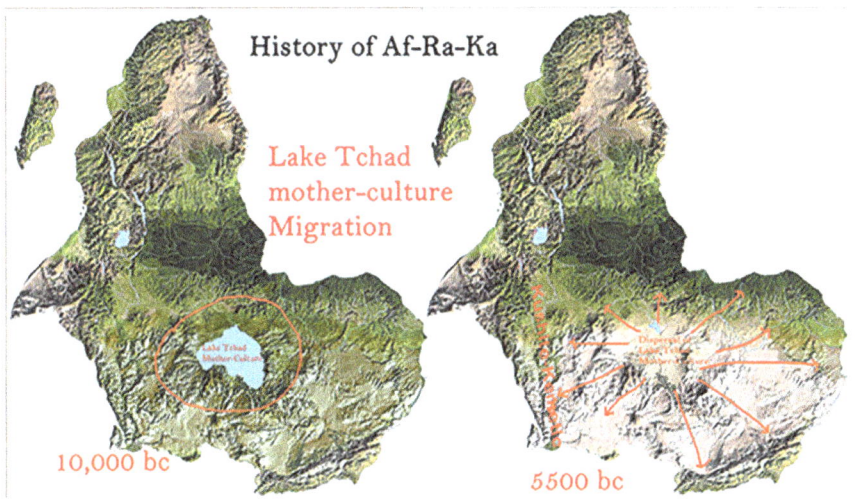

Emigration from West Afraka to the Hapy Valley as
North Afraka began to change into a desert

On my journey back to Kemet, my thinking was crystal clear as a result of symptomatic thinking, analyzing all the symptoms of the past and our life-giving experiences that Kemet is the gift of the Eteru er Hapy and the western desert! The Djedi also taught me that imagination was more important than knowledge, for knowledge was limited and only focused on earth, whereas imagination embraced the entire world and beyond, stimulating progress, giving birth to evolution. My imagination was the spirit's vehicle. It was created mightily, and I would use it with the rest of this visit to earth.

The high priest of Yam explained, "The Djedi taught us why the savanna of our ancestors dried up. And because of the desertification of our land, we are here today. Conditions in the western desert during the Afrakan Humid Period were dominated by a strong North Afrakan monsoon, resulting in larger annual rainfall totals, which did not exist compared to today's conditions. We all have learned to make an adjustment to our lives. The Djedi taught us that manifesting is not about attracting what you want. Manifesting is an awareness and an innerstanding that you attract what you are. We, the people of Yam, give thanks and praise to the wisdom of the Djedi. We clearly can see now that innerstanding is much deeper than knowledge. There are many people who know us or have heard of us but very few who understand or innerstand us.

One of Ta-nout's best warriors from the legendary Yam

"We will show you the best way back to Kemet. We will send an escort team with you, with our best warrior, so you don't waste any time. The Imazighen Asiatics will attack because that is their nature, but they lack the skills to pose any threat to the Medjay. After the last Ice Age, hoards of Asiatics from the northern caves have invaded our lands.

"Imazighen are fair-skinned people from Asia. Essentially, about ten thousand years ago, a population wave from the near east swept over North Afraka, bringing in Wedgy Wr people, Asiatics, in the North Afrakan area. We have been in conflict with them since that period.

"They look like the Libyans of your era, and they typically live in small villages and eke out a meager peasant existence from small irrigated gardens, dry cereal culture, arboriculture, and small flocks of sheep and goats, occasionally a cow or two. They love to fight and raid even among their own people. They are the desert thieves and desert sand dwellers. The great desert separates us, but we send out border control units to keep them out of our territory. They have never been our friends."

CHAPTER 7

FEMALE MEDJAY IN
THE ROYAL COURT

"Hmt Nswt Tem, my lovely hemet, come walk with me in the royal garden." Sa Ra Mentchu-hotep reached out and held her hand. "You look fantastic in purple. Is purple your favorite color?" He kissed her gently on the lips.

"Tiw, you know it is, my Neb aa. We were married in purple. I must talk to you about my little sister, Priestess Kawit."

"I was hoping to share an intimate moment just talking about you and me, my lovely hemet."

"I am flattered, my Hee [husband], but this is extremely important, my Nswt Bety Neb Khrw-Ra."

"Is she all right? I saw her yesterday, and she was fine. In fact, she looked nefer [beautiful]."

"Nen, her health is excellent. That's not the problem."

"Nswt Mwt Wrt Iah said she had completed her priestship and that she was almost as good as you. I find that hard to believe. You are a hard act to follow, Priestess Tem. Does she want to go home to Napata?"

"Nen, that is part of the problem. My brother has married, and his wife is having a child."

"That is wonderful. We must send them something really special. Hmt Nswt Tem, she can stay here with us. That's not a problem. There is more than enough room, and she's family."

"I'm trying to explain, my Nswt. She is in love with you and wants to be your hemet also."

Shemsu Heru Sa Ra Mentchu-hotep stopped in his tracks. "What? I'm married to you, High Priestess Tem. She knows that. I don't innerstand."

"She told me she couldn't hold it back any longer. She has always loved you! She only came here to Kemet to be near you. She said she dreams about you every night, and if she doesn't

189

see you every day, she gets sick. Two large statues of you are in her room. Sometimes, she just stares at them for hours."

"This is not good, Hmt Nswt Tem. Have you talked to Hmt Nswt Wrt Neferu and Mwt Iah about this?"

"She has told both of them. That is why I'm telling you now before she approaches you. She told me she would die if she can't be with you."

"I don't know what to say. I have never looked at her that way, and she is so young."

"She told me she is the same age as Hmt Nswt Ashait of Men-nefer."

"And what do you think of all this, Hmt Nswt Tem?"

Tears came into her eyes. "I love you the same way she does, and I love my sister. I want her to be happy." High Priestess Tem started crying almost uncontrollably. He held her in his arms to comfort her. "The Hmt Nswt Wrt Neferu who loves you more than life itself shared you with me. She is so selfless and kind and gentle and innerstanding. I want to be like that for my sister, Kawit. Mother died when my sister was so young, just a baby, and I have always been there for her."

"Hmt Nswt Wrt Neferu and Mother approve of this?"

"Tiw."

"And you approve of this?"

With tears in her eyes, she answered, "Tiw."

"I will talk with Hmt Nswt Wrt Neferu, and then I must think. I should not see Priestess Kawit today. I have to place things in their proper perspective in my head so that Ma'at is upheld."

After talking with his Nswt Mwt Wrt Iah, he sat down with his chief wife, Hmt Nswt Wrt Neferu. "I trust that you already know what this is about, Hmt Nswt Wrt Neferu?"

"Tiw, my Neb aa."

"Let me hear your words, Neferu, because it is you that I mrr more than even my own life."

She held my hand gently as she looked into my eyes, and her voice was calm and clear. "Priestess Kawit loves you like I mrr you, like Nswt Mwt Iah mrr you, like Hmt Nswt Tem mrr you. She is young, but she has an ancient soul. And she is strong. Talk with her like she is a woman, and if you feel that in her heart she is sincere, we all support her because she can only make our royal family stronger. She may bring you many sons."

"Have you consulted the oracle on this matter, High Priestess Neferu?"

"Tiw, I have, Shemsu Heru."

"Please tell me the outcome."

"She will not live a long life like me and Priestess Tem. If you marry her without love but through obligation, she will die within a year, my Nswt Hee. But if you learn to love her, she will be a great Hmt Nswt who will be remembered for thousands of years. Or if you will reject her, she will wither up like a prune and die in a few months."

"Neferu, you are the most precious and valued gift that has been given to me on this planet. I draw my strength from your Mrr. Your Mrr is so pure it is like Ast to Asr, and I will dwell in your heart forever. You have the power to resurrect me even if I die before my mission here is complete. Neferu, you are *Hmwt Nbw* [mistress of all women]. *Dua e Ntchru en ek* [I thank the Ntchr for you.] Send your loving sister Heru Kheper-Ra to me in the morning, and we shall talk. I feel so much better now. Dua Ntchr. Social good, which is Ma'at, is what brings peace to family and society. Once we have experienced mrr [love] outward, once we have experienced the fierce joy of life that attends extending our identity into nature, once we realize that the nature within and the nature without are continuous, then we, too, may share and manifest the exquisite beauty and effortless grace associated with the miracles of Mrr and the miracles in the natural world."

Hmt Nswt Tem worried about her sister Priestess Kawit.

*****

192

Shemsu Heru walked into the garden in his royal palace where Viceroy Medjay Priest-scientist Ka-en-Jhutyms had been waiting. "Nen, please remain seated. Dua Ntchr. Thank you for coming on such short notice. I need two female Medjay priest-scientists to live in the royal palaces—one here in Waset and one in Men-nefer. We have increased the number of women in the royal family, and their safety concerns me. We have already had two fatal accidents in the royal family—the death of my Hmt Nswt Henhenit in childbirth—and we all are still recovering from that. Please discuss this matter with your brother Medjay Priest-Scientist Akhtoy Ba-Heru because his work is eqr [excellent] and no one could do it better. But women can go places men cannot go and do things that they would not share or discuss with a man. We need a Medjay woman who can feel these things that we cannot."

"My brother will innerstand. He is wise beyond his years. I shall have him discuss this issue with the Djedi council at once. May I speak as your viceroy to Kash, Nswt Bety Neb Khrw-Ra Sa Ra Mentchu-hotep?"

"Dua Ntchr, tiw."

"All three of the fort castles are completely up and running. Trade has already tripled in the last year, and Shemsu Heru Tut-Ankh-Khnum of Kash is very pleased. But what is so amazing is the number of temples, Shemsu Heru. They have doubled in Kemet and have expanded tenfold in Kash, and the priest have produced more than ten times the yield of produce from the temple farms over the last year.

"Your two wives in the north, Hmt Nswt Ashait and Hmt Nswt Kemsit, working with Vizier Ipi, have expanded the literacy rate by 80 percent since you have united the two lands, Sema Tawy. Our literacy rate in the cities like Waset and Abu

Nswt Bety is nearly 90 percent among the youth, and you can thank Nswt Mwt Wrt Iah and Hmt Nswt Wrt Neferu. Ma'at is the talk in all the border towns all the way into Napata and Meroe thanks to Hmt Nswt Tem and Hmt Nswt Kawit. The Ntchru have truly honored you, Shemsu Heru Sa Ra Mentchu-hotep. I sit at your feet."

"Dua ntchr, but please tell me how is your beautiful hemet."

"Dua Ntchr, she is eqr! We are having our first child. This is all possible because of you, my Neb."

"You really got this twisted. As I look deep into the Akashic records, it reveals that you saved my life a dozen times."

*****

Hmt Nswt Wrt Neferu sat down with her Hee, Shemsu Heru Sa Ra Mentchu-hotep. "I mrr you, my Hee. Your insight and vision is so outstanding. *Ee-nedj her ek.* [I seek your face for counsel.] Dua Ntchr for bringing a female Medjay into our royal palace. You have no idea how much smoother everything is running. She said that I must have been a Medjay in another life.

"I told Medjay Ma'at Nefert that I have the best teachers in this life, Nswt Mwt Wrt Iah and Shemsu Heru Nswt Bety Neb Khrw-Ra Sa Ra Mentchu-hotep, who is a Medjay priest-scientist. Her name means 'the beautiful, harmonious balance,' and she is just that. I asked her to help me write a set of rules that I could use when I am teaching the girls and the women, and this is what she gave me," she added.

These are the rules on how to invite Ma'at into your life:

1. Enjoy your own company. Embrace everything about you! Without a doubt, it's the most important step toward being a happy person.

2. Smiling releases serotonin in the brain, which instantaneously gives your mood a lift.

3. Listen to music, sing or play your favorite song, and let your voice ring!

4. Savor a small piece of honey date and watch your mood improve.

5. Believe that something wonderful will happen for you today. The universe is waiting to shower happiness on you.

6. We all make mistakes; none of us is perfect. Forgive your imperfections, accept your faults, and laugh.

7. Seven or eight hours each night of sleep should increase your energy and decrease moodiness.

8. Gratitude, the emotion of thankfulness, is one of the key ingredients for living a happy life. Make gratitude a habit and happiness will be yours.

9. Create powerful affirmations that will bring joy and happiness into your life, then make reading it a daily ritual until it becomes a habit and it will empower your life.

10. Start the day off on your left foot with a happy thought. The morning hours are full of spiritual energy and Sekhem (life force).

11. Look out at Ra, the sun, for about two to five minutes as soon as you wake up. Then two hours or more, if possible, of walking or sitting outside in sunlight per day improves mood and wards of seasonal affective disorder.

12. Think it, read it, say it, and sing it! "My happiness brings me more happiness."

13. Give yourself permission to pat yourself on the back. Recognize your accomplishments and positive qualities as you plan for your future success and your next great accomplishments!

14. Remembering that happiness is contagious, surround yourself with happy, positive people who share your values, goals, and dreams.

15. Watching plants grow and thrive under your care is thrilling! Buy a few houseplants. If the season is right and if you have the space, grow a garden. Talk to them as you give them love. Water them daily and drink with them. And as they blossom, so will you!

16. Every day, sit in meditation for a few minutes to gather your thoughts. Happiness is something you work on until it becomes a habit.

17. Set goals, and then make plans to succeed and take action. Pursuing something we value always makes us happy.

18. Don't waste your precious time, energy, or thoughts on something that is beyond your control. Let it go. Accept what you cannot change.

19. A ten-minute nap is all it takes to rejuvenate your spirit and get the happiness to flow during the day. If this is not possible during the day at work, then nap when you get home before you start your home program.

20. Love who you are. Love what you are doing. Love the person you're with. Love your friends, and respect your enemies. Mrr! Mrr! Mrr! Respect!

Djedi Priestess Ma'at Nefert from the land of Punt

"I know she has only been here for one year, my *Neb Hee Wr*, but the whole palace has changed for the better. She said if we practice these principles that she has outlined, you move from thinking and analyzing to directly and intuitively perceiving the truth. Contemplate what spirit discernment means and how you may apply it to all areas of your life. Embody these qualities in your consciousness, and you will revolutionize the experience known as your life. She doesn't talk much about her personal life. All I know is that she is from Punt and that Punt is a beautiful and magical place. She is so beautiful and youthful looking, but she talks about things before I was born, like she was there.

"We look like peers, and her skills as a warrior are like nothing I have ever seen women do. She is mysterious in a very magical but pleasant way. Her room is spotless and simple, and I don't think she eats every day or sleeps every night. And she always seems to know what I want without me asking her anything. I saw her training with Medjay Priest-Scientist Akhtoy yesterday. And as good as he is—you even said that he is one of the best warriors in Kemet outside of his brother Medjay Ka-en-Jhutyms—well, he could not even touch her."

"Are you finished? Come sit here next to me. First of all, she is not just a Medjay warrior. She is a Djedi grand master! Second, she is the second Hemet of Djedi Jhutyms Ka-en-Heru."

"Wow!" Hmt Nswt Wrt Neferu said in total surprise.

"It gets better. She is the mother of Medjay Priest-Scientist Akhtoy Ba-Heru and his chief instructor."

"His mother—are you for real?"

"And she has a Medjay daughter five years older than Medjay Akhtoy in Punt, who is a Medjay priest-scientist also."

"No way! They look like peers or brother and sister."

"When I thanked her for being such a positive influence on my family, she just smiled and said, 'Every time you put something positive into the universe, the world changes. Our kindness invites miracles to appear all around us—not just in your world but in the whole world.'"

"She speaks and acts like Hem Sem Tepy Kha-ef-Ptah."

"That's because they have the same teacher, and he is her sister's son."

"Are you messing with my head now?"

"No, it goes even deeper. Hem Sem Tepy Kha-ef-Ptah is the grandson of Djedi Grand Master Jhutyms Ka-en-Heru and the sacred guardian of High Priestess Tem."

"I don't understand. Sacred guardian?"

"Hem Sem Tepy Kha-ef-Ptah is the son of Shemsu Heru King Tut-Ankh-Khnum's Djedi brother."

"Priestess Tem's father's brother's son? Does High Priestess Tem know this?" asked Hmt Nswt Wrt Neferu.

"Nen, what has been said was never said, so no one else will hear what did not happen!"

"I innerstand," she said.

Then he held her in his arms. "The Medjay don't keep secrets, but their personal life is on a need-to-know basis only. Djedi Priestess Ma'at Nefert also gave me some very valuable advice. She saw that I was working very hard late at night, taking valuable time away from my family. She told me to tell my son how much I loved him and to praise my mother while she is still alive and to love my wives with all my heart.

Love Thy Wife (Woman)

In your home, sooth her, water her flesh and body

Touching her hands, speak softly to her, make love to her.

"Hmt Nswt Wrt Neferu, life is an echo. What you send out comes back. What you sow, you reap. What you see in others exists in you. Remember, life is an echo. It always gets back to you. So give Ma'at."

"You are so wise, my Nswt Hee Wr."

"My soul honors your soul, Neferu. I honor the place in you where the entire universe resides. I honor the light, love, truth, beauty, and peace within you, Neferu, because it is also within me. In sharing these things with you, we are united. We are the same. We are one."

"That was so beautiful, Mentchu-hotep."

"That was taught to me by Djedi Grand Master Jhutyms Ka-en-Heru."

Neferu looked into his eyes as she spoke, "I think one of the best feelings in the world is when someone remembers something you said. Whether it was something from yesterday, a week ago, a month ago, even ten years ago. It's just like 'Wow, you were actually listening to me.'"

*****

While resting in his royal bed, Sa Ra Mentchu-hotep felt a strange energy. This was the fourth time he had had this feeling, like a force field was above his head. He jumped out of bed, and he grabbed his Hmt Nswt Tem. And then they both knocked on the door of Hmt Nswt Wrt Neferu. Sa Ra Mentchu-hotep spoke to his chief Hemet, "I felt that strange energy again I told you about." He took her by the hand. "Come, something strange is happening upstairs. It's coming from the crystal room."

The last time he felt a force like this was in Medjay priest-scientist training. They opened the door to the crystal room. All three of their mouths—Hmt Nswt Wrt Neferu's, Nswt Hmt Tem's, and Sa Ra Mentchu-hotep's—dropped open. Their son, the royal prince Mentchu-hotep, and Djedi Priest-Scientist Ma'at Nefert were levitating in the air about four feet over several beds of crystals with their eyes closed and their bodies sitting in thin air as they were holding hands. They stood in utter amazement for several minutes, watching, then they walked back out the crystal room, closing the door quietly behind them.

"I've been trying to teach my son how to meditate for years without much progress."

"I know. So have we," said Hmt Nswt Wrt Neferu and Hmt Nswt Tem.

"Did you see how the crystals were arranged in that room?"

"I did not do that, my Hee aa. Our son, along with Djedi Priest-Scientist Ma'at Nefert, redid the whole room. They have been working on it for a few years now. She said she was going to teach him the power in crystal healing to sharpen his mind."

"I have seen these crystal formations only in the Medjay priest-scientist underground training rooms. There was a bed of clear quartz crystals, a bed of purple crystals, a bed of dark-blue crystals, a bed of light bluish-green crystals, a bed of green crystals, a bed of pink crystals, a bed of yellow and gold crystals, a bed of orange crystals, a bed of red crystals, and a bed of black crystals. Even the ankhs on the walls had the same color formation totally done in crystals. I have felt this force before several times, but I thought it was just Djedi Priest-Scientist Ma'at Nefert or Hem Sem Tepy Kha-ef-Ptah working."

The next day, Nswt Bety Neb Khrw-Ra Sa Ra Mentchu-hotep spoke with Djedi Priest-Scientist Ma'at Nefert about what they had seen. The Djedi explained that she felt a weakness in the boy's character and his lack of concentration and focus on simple tasks. She knew of his curiosity and love of crystals, so she decided to heal him through the study of crystals.

"How did you collect all those different kinds of crystals?"

"We did not collect them. Hem Sem Tepy Kha-ef-Ptah and myself made them. We belong to the Ari Khat society within the priest-scientist of the Medjay and Djedi order. I felt it necessary because we know that at any time, someone could try to take your son's life by an assassin hired by Prince Kaneferre, and he needs to know danger before it's too late. All four of the Libyan assassins were captured and killed, and Kaneferre and two royal guards were tracked down by the Medjay and killed. But Prince Kaneferre still lives, so the threat still lives."

Two days later, Nswt Bety Neb Khrw-Ra Sa Ra Mentchu-hotep summoned his son, the young royal prince Mentchu-hotep, to his office. "Son, I heard you have been doing some fine work with crystal healing. Is this true?"

"I have been working hard, my Neb aa. Mother Hmt Nswt Wrt Neferu and Djedi Grand Master Ma'at Nefert are great teachers."

"What would I do for sleepless nights, my son?"

"I would give you an amethyst stone or cluster and have you place it under your bed while you sleep, my Neb, but I would also tell you not to eat late at night and stay away from sweets and to drink plenty of clean water."

"How about arthritis and pain in my joints?"

"I would have bracelets made of copper, magnetic hematite, and malachite and place them on your arms or near the joints where you are having pain, my Neb. But I would also have you stay away from starches and sweets or any foods that cause inflammation, and I would give you black seeds twice a day, in the morning and night."

"Have you learned about colors, my son?"

"Tiw, my Neb aa. Violet stimulates intuition, imagination, universal flow, meditation, and artistic qualities. And the stones would be amethyst, lepidolite, and fluorite. Blue indigo increases calmness, peace, love, honesty, kindness, truth, devotion, and emotional depth. The stones would be sodalite and your favorite lapis lazuli for deep thought and the first eye. For the throat, I would add aquamarine, turquoise, and blue calcite stones and even blue lace agate. Green supports balance, harmony, love, communication, social acceptance, and the innerstanding of nature. Supporting stones would be moss agate, aventurine, malachite, and jade.

"Yellow increases fun, humor, lightness, personal power, intellect, logic, and creativity. The stones would be citrine, yellow jasper, and tiger's eye. Orange stimulates creativity, productivity, pleasure, optimism, and emotional expression. Good stones here would be carnelian, moonstone, and orange calcite. Red increases physical energy, vitality, stamina, grounding, spontaneity, stability, and passion. Stones that support that are red jasper, garnet, and ruby. Black is the essence of life, goodness, protection, beauty, and power and is the source of all life. Good stones here are onyx, obsidian, tourmaline, and hematite."

"I am so proud of you, my son. Now I know Kemet is in good hands with a sharp mind and a loving, healing heart. One last request, my son. Can you help Medjay Priest-Scientist Akhtoy Ba-Heru protect our royal palace?"

"Tiw, *Yit* [father]. I can help protect our royal palace from negative energies with black tourmaline and selenite. I can grid the palace by adding a piece of each to each of the main corners of the palace. I will place them with the intent to only attract and allow in positive, loving energy into our home. This is Nefer, my Nswt aa, because I just received a whole basket of sage. And I know just what to do with it."

"My last question, my son. What have you gained from your meditation with Djedi Priest-Scientist Ma'at Nefert?"

"Nothing," replied the prince. "However, may I tell you what I have lost: anger, anxiety, depression, insecurity, fear of death, and fear of failure as a prince."

He was stunned. His son had become a man—not just a man but a spiritual warrior!

*****

Several years later, Djedi Priest-Scientist Ma'at Nefert, with the help of High Priest Hem Sem Tepy Kha-ef-Ptah, completed the temple dedicated to Satis or Satet, the mate of Khnum, in Abu. She was the protector of the southern frontier, and as such, she was depicted as holding a bow and arrow. She was also the guardian of the source of the flood and was identified with the star Sirius or Spdt. She wears the white crown of upper Kemet with antelope horns. In Kemet, antelope and deer live in the eastern and western deserts, and they represent speed, endurance, and great agility. She was also called the Lady of the Stars and was depicted by a five-point star of Spdt. Hmt Kawit was made high priestess of this temple, along with the royal crown prince Mentchu-hotep as the high priest, both only reporting to Nswt Bety Neb Khrw-Ra Sa Ra Mentchu-hotep.

Nswt Bety Neb Khrw-Ra Sa Ra Mentchu-hotep finally felt like he had accomplished his dreams. The nation-state Kemet was strong; there was a great balance between Upper and Lower Kemet, Sema Tawy. He felt that the women in his household were protected and strong and that women in Ta Mery, the beloved land of Kemet, were the safest in the known world.

In Kashite-Kemet spiritual science, Ma'at represents the Afrakan wombman as the balancing force in the world. She is the harmony that unites the healer and the warrior. She is the moderation that allows nature to provide and replenish. She is the order that creates justice in a society. She is the tough love that develops a child into a responsible adult. Ma'at was truly truth, justice, love, reciprocity, and harmonious balance.

The female Djedi represented Sekhmet in Kemet. It was Sekhmet that brought change and protection from esfet, which brought the destructive storm that renewed the land. Sekhmet is she who raises the marketplace through economic unity, symbolized by the unity of the lionesses as they effectively hunt for the pride.

On Sa Ra Mentchu-hotep's thirty-ninth regional year, he had consolidated his power throughout Kemet with a strong military, and with his Kashite viceroy, he developed strong allies with the south. And with the help of the Kashite's Viceroy Hemet Neferukayt from Yam, there existed a real pan-Afrakan operational unity, which extended to the four corners of their continent. Shemsu Heru Nswt Bety Neb Khrw-Ra Sa Ra Mentchu-hotep was now a Medjay priest-scientist. Now whatever the Nswt's thoughts were, they became the seeds that caused success to unfold in his experiences. Divine love and inspiration flowed through him, assuring his success in all his endeavors. His whole consciousness was alive, with the inspired thoughts of Ntchr. "I am impregnated with divine ideas. I think directly from the Spirit and let its intelligence have its way with me." He had successfully spread the teachings of Ma'at and symptomatic thinking throughout Kemet, solidifying the second golden age.

*****

Medjay Priest-Scientist Ka-en-Jhutyms, viceroy to Kash, was greeted at the royal palace by his younger brother and Medjay medju comrade, Medjay Priest-Scientist Akhtoy Ba-Heru, head of royal security and chancellor to Sa Ra Mentchu-hotep. He said, "Ankh Udja Sneb Neb sn e." (May you have all life, prosperity, and health, my brother.) They hugged each other with respect and love.

Medjay Priest-Scientist Akhtoy Ba-Heru replied, "Ee ee tee em htp sn e." (Welcome in peace, my brother.)

"We must speak to Nswt Bety Mentchu-hotep as soon as possible!"

"He is in the library," said Medjay Priest-Scientist Akhtoy Ba-Heru.

"Can we see him now?"

"I will see. Wait just a minute," replied Medjay Priest-Scientist Akhtoy Ba-Heru. "Tiw, we may enter."

Both Medjay brothers entered the library. They both knelt on one knee as they spoke together in harmony, "Ee nedj her ek Nswt Bety Neb Khrw-Ra Sa Ra Mentchu-hotep." (Greetings, I seek your face/council, ruler of Upper and Lower Kemet, Mentchu-hotep.)

"Please sit and speak to me. What has happened?" said Mentchu-hotep.

"One of our spies has reported to the Medjay that two coastal towns have been raided in Kash, with the stealing and enslaving of several women who were taken to a trading port on the eastern coast in Kemet at Khanais to be sold as slaves by the Tamahu [Asiatics] in Asia. They also have been poaching ivory in Ta Ntchr. We can handle this, Nswt aa, my great ruler of the south. There is no need for you to get involved," replied Medjay Priest-Scientist Ka-en-Jhutyms.

Sa Ra Mentchu-hotep stood up and walked to the map of Kemet on the library wall. He stuck a red marker in the spot they were believed to be based—Khanais, on the east coast of Kemet. "How long have these Asiatic bandits been operating in our country? When they violate women, disrespect our laws, kill our sacred animals only for their tusks, and enslave our people, it involves me! Ma'at must be enforced! Why do you think Ma'at exists? Without Ma'at, the universe, the solar system, and the land would be in chaos. Ma'at is a commitment to social order and harmony. Injustice to the Kemetyu, Kashites, or any black people anywhere is injustice and disrespect to all black people everywhere.

"We must let these Tamahu and Amu and black collaborators know that they cannot come to Kemet, Kash, or Ta Ntchr and disrespect our women, our people, or our land without paying for it with their lives! I want a full report on their location, how long they have been in operation, and who they are selling our enslaved people to. I want to know who the mayor in this town is. Does he know what is going on? If not, dismiss him immediately for incompetence. If he is a collaborator, his sentence is death! I don't want just the little followers. Follow the wealth who is benefiting from this injustice. The whole organization must be destroyed.

"Reciprocity must be honored and restored. I want to know the villages that have been violated. Healing must take place, and part of that healing is making the men who could not protect their women accountable. Every village must be able to protect their people. To have anything of value without being able to protect it is like not having it at all because the Tamahu and Aamu, along with greedy Remtch, will take it! Have two teams of Medjay medju from Kemet and Kash meet in Punt in three days."

"It will be done, Sa Ra Mentchu-hotep. We are already on it!" They both bowed their heads and got out of the room.

*****

Sa Ra Mentchu-hotep met Djedi Ma'at Nefert in the royal family garden. "Ee nedj her etch Djedi Ma'at Nefert Wrt." (Greetings, I seek your face, great Djedi Ma'at Nefert.) He knelt on one knee to the Djedi.

"Ee-ee tee htp Sa Ra Mentchu-hotep." (Welcome in peace, son of Ra, Mentchu-hotep.) She returned his greetings.

"I need your council. We have a confirmed report that a band of Tamahu [Asiatics] bandits have been operating raids and slave trade on Ymnsqt [the Red Sea] in the land of Kemet at Khananis. I need at least two Medjay women to assist us because they have women spies and hostages, and certain information might only be shared among other women. I need to wipe them out completely."

"Tiw, I will consult Djedi Jhutyms Ka-en-Heru, but I am sure my daughter and I can assist you on this mission."

"Two Medjay medju units will meet us in Punt in three days," he said.

"I know a quick trail through the desert used for transporting gold. We can use horses if we travel at night and then by boat once we get to Ymnsqt," said Djedi Ma'at Nefert.

"Dua Nefer," replied Mentchu-hotep.

*****

Djedi Jhutyms Ka-en-Heru and his daughter Medjay Priest-Scientist Neith ka Ma'at with her Medjay medju unit from Punt of all women met them at the mayor's palace. Early that morning, one of the Medjay women, Medjay Neith ka Ma'at, came into Mayor Setyms's room just before sunrise. The mayor thought it was a woman prostitute sent to wake him up. He could see even by candlelight that she was young, beautiful, and black. "Come to Daddy, my little black treat," he told the woman. The Medjay told him to close his eyes because she had a real treat he would never forget. He closed his eyes and pulled the covers back off him as he sat up in his bed. His penis was at full mast. "I am ready, my sweet," he said. She then kicked him in his head, knocking him unconscious. Afterward, she tied him up and placed a cloth over his eyes and mouth.

Around noon on the 3rd meeting day, all the Medjay met in the courtyard of the mayor's palace. Communication was eqr. The Djedi used falcons, the fastest creatures on earth, to carry their messages between them. They knew that the mayor was on the take (fact no. 1). They—the Tamahu, Aamu, and Tchhnu—had been running a ring of prostitution for about five years (fact no. 2). They had been raping and stealing women in small groups over the last five years. There were twenty women tied as slaves at the mayor's palace as evidence (fact no. 3). The enslaved black women and men were taken to Lebanon and Libya to be sold, and they could identify five houses who bought and sold slaves from them (fact no. 4). There were twenty-two Tamahu, seven Aamu, three Remtchu, and seven Tchhnu Libyans who were part of the home-based organization, plus the mayor and five more staff members all on the take. Nine of the forty-four members were women (fact no. 5).

As they searched the mayor's palace, besides the female slaves, there were also about ten small boys. They also found a dozen ivory tusks, a stack of about fifty animal skins, and gold nuggets, along with copper and a sack of semiprecious stones of all kinds and colors.

"Bring the mayor in, please, along with his staff," said Sa Ra Mentchu-hotep. The mayor and his staff were all brought out, and the blindfolds and cloths from their mouths were removed.

"What is going on here?" asked the mayor. "What do you want? Gold or women or both? I have much more than that. Just let us go," he begged.

"You honestly don't know who we are, Mayor Setyms?"

"Bandits from the south," replied the mayor.

"How did this man get in office?" replied Sa Ra Mentchu-hotep.

Djedi Ma'at Nefert replied, "First, he killed the former mayor and bribed his way into office. He is from Libya, along with three of his five staff members."

"Do we know who his partners in crime are?" asked Sa Ra Mentchu-hotep.

"Yes, Chief Medjay Jhutyms Ka-en-Heru is there as we speak. All of the prostitutes have been rounded up, along with their pimps, all but one house, and we will take care of that when we leave here," replied Djedi Ma'at Nefert.

All the women were untied and given food and clean water. Djedi Ma'at Nefert asked one of the enslaved women how she was captured and how long she was here.

First, she just cried, then she said her village was raided during the night and her house was set on fire. Her mother, father, and uncle were killed. "The Asians took me, my thirteen-year-old sister, and my little nine-year-old brother. I don't know how long I have been here. I was raped and beaten so many times I lost count." She fell to her knees in shame.

"Make sure all these women get special healing treatment, as well as mental and spiritual healing. They have been traumatized for life," said Sa Ra Mentchu-hotep. "How about the ivory smugglers?"

"We have them too. There is a team of seven. We have four. Three are on a mission, and two Medjay are tracking them as we speak."

"Who are you people? You are really good. Maybe we can be partners. There is enough room for all of us," said the mayor. "These people are just waiting to be controlled like children. They are so trusting, even to total strangers, and they believe in all kinds of taboos and superstitions. Their leaders can be bribed easily." He smiled for a minute. We know who you are. That is why you suckle our babies, raise our children, and cook our food. But the blacks don't know who we are," said the Libyan mayor."

"I guess you should know who I am before you die, Mayor Setyms. I am Shemsu Heru Nswt Bety Neb-Khrw-Ra Sa Ra Mentchu-hotep! And yes, I know who your people are!"

"Wow, a real king!" said the mayor. "And these people must be Medjay warriors."

"Give them all weapons so they can die in combat. Even if they had no honor while they were living, at least they can die with honor." Several types of weapons were placed in front of them—swords, axes, spears, shields, and daggers. "Pick your weapons. If you win, you are free. If you lose, your soul goes to Amemt, the devourer of unjust souls. And we will burn your bodies so they can never be used again," said the Nswt Bety Neb Khrw-Ra Sa Ra Mentchu-hotep.

"Come on, it's just a bunch of women. They can't kill all of us," said the mayor as he waved his large sword in the air. "I want you." He pointed to the Medjay who knocked him out earlier in his room. They all picked up shields, two with a spear, two with swords, and one with a battle-ax.

Sa Ra Mentchu-hotep and Djedi Ma'at Nefert sat down and watched the six Medjay women versus the mayor and his five staff members. The mayor charged first at his Medjay opponent. She did not even block his sword. She just sidestepped it and jumped in the air, throwing a swirling tornado kick upside the mayor's head, and he was out like a light for the second time. When the mayor came to, there were five heads without their bodies staring at him in a pool of blood. He began screaming, "No, please don't kill me. I have gold, lots of gold. It's all yours. Just let me live!" He threw his sword down and fell on his knees, crying, as his head rolled on the floor beside the other five heads with tears still in the eyes.

Very good, thought Djedi Jhutyms Ka-en-Heru, *they built their headquarters on a hill, overlooking the surrounding valley, but this still will not save them.* He signaled for the Medjay medju to surround the house and put on their masks and charge on his command. This would give the enemy about seven seconds to respond. By then the Medjay would be in superior battle position. The lookout man on the roof died instantly from two arrows—one to his neck and the other to his heart. As they charged the house, several fire arrows entered the house through open windows. Before the Tamahu bandits could get to their weapons, the house was on fire, and Djedi Jhutyms Ka-en-Heru had knocked the front door open.

Several Medjay followed behind him. Four Medjay jumped through the open windows, leaving two Medjay outside, guarding the front and back door. The bandits were in a state of total confusion. Several died before they could find their clothes. Two were killed while performing sex to tied-up hostages. There must have been a dozen women tied up in the front room of the house. Djedi Jhutyms Ka-en-Heru took all the women outside to safety. There were two back rooms, each with a window. Two bandits tried to climb out; they both died before their feet could hit the ground. The Medjay kicked in the two doors at the same time. The bandits shot several arrows, which only hit the bodies of bandits who were still alive. Their bodies were used as human shields as the Medjay entered the rooms.

Room 1 had six bandits. They all were dead within thirty seconds, and the eight naked girls were taken outside. Room 2 had eight bandits. Two were killed trying to climb out the window; three tried to hold women in front of them for safety, which did not work at all. All eight were killed swiftly.

Meanwhile, the house was still on fire. The eight naked women were taken to safety. All the dead bodies of the bandits were lined up, stripped naked, and their clothes or cloths were used to cover the naked women.

"How many bodies?" said Djedi Jhutyms Ka-en-Heru.

"There are twenty-nine Namou and Tamhou bodies," replied Medjay Ka-en-Jhutyms.

"How many women?"

"Thirty women," replied Medjay Akhtoy Ba-Heru.

"I bet the leader is still inside," said Djedi Jhutyms Ka-en-Heru. "I sense a cellar trapdoor. Dig one large grave and bury them all. Take the women to the mayor's house. I will stay behind. After the house has burned down, I will look for their leader."

*****

The three poachers from a distance could see a small herd of six elephants with two calves. They knew these animals do not have great eyesight but do have a very good sense of smell and hearing, so they were facing away from the breeze. The one Namou (pale northerner) said to the two Remtch (blacks), "Let's just kill them and get these twelve tusks and get out of here."

One of the Remtch poachers said, "I don't know about this. The two babies will die if we kill all the adults."

The other Remtch poachers said, "Well, let's just kill the males."

The Namou poacher said, "How do you know the male from the females? They all look alike."

One of the Remtch said to the Namou, "Male and female savanna elephants look very similar. However, if you look closely, you will notice the males have a generally round head compared to the female's squarer head."

The other Remtch then said, "There are two males, which also are larger, and four females."

The Namou got upset. "Look, I'm in charge. Let's just kill them all and get the tusks, OK?"

The two Medjay saw the three poachers sizing up the elephants. "We better move in quickly before they kill them all—the adults and the babies." The two Medjay split up to hit them from two different directions.

As the poachers were pulling their bows, so were the Medjay. *Thump, thump!* Two poachers hit the dirt with a loud noise; the third poacher started running toward the elephants, away from the Medjay. By now, the elephants sensed danger. The female elephants surrounded the babies, and the two bull elephants charged at the poacher, who now changed his direction away from the elephants. But he was hit by a Medjay arrow in his buttocks. He grabbed a small tree and tried to climb it, but one of the large bull elephants that must have weighed up to 6,000 kilograms (6.6 tons) and measured up to 3.3 meters (10 feet) at the shoulder rammed the tree, knocking the poacher on his back. Before he can get up, the second elephant stomped him, squashing the life out of him with both feet. The other bull dragged him with his tusk to make sure he was dead. The two Medjay watched from a safe distance.

After the elephants had gone, they collected the three bodies and started their journey home.

Medjay warrior stalking his enemy

*****

Several Medjay women, along with Djedi Ma'at Nefert, set fire to the house of prostitution. Within minutes, two customers came running out, holding their clothes in their hands. Afterward, two naked women also came running out, followed by seven more women. Two of the women were Tamhou; they were all held for questioning by the female Medjay. The two Tamhou women pulled out long knives, but Djedi Ma'at Nefert quickly snatched the knife out of one Tamhou's hand and kicked the other on the side of the head, knocking her unconscious. Then they were tied up. The customers were spanked and embarrassed in the village square, and the other women were taken to Mayor Setyms's house.

*****

The fire burned for several hours until only a shell of a large house was left. Djedi Jhutyms Ka-en-Heru waited patiently near the barn as darkness crept up on them, and then he heard a noise in the center of the burning shell of the house. He was right; there was an underground cellar. The bandit leader walked out, totally unharmed. Once he managed to escape the charred remains of their gang's house, he placed two heavy large sacks on the ground by his feet. They were filled with gold. He stretched his arms in relief and then started laughing aloud.

Djedi Jhutyms Ka-en-Heru was still silently observing everything. He whistled aloud several times, and then within a few minutes, a large white horse appeared out of the darkness. Once the horse approached him, he patted it on his head. "That a girl. Come to Daddy," he said. "Now let's go home rich." He was about to open the barn door to retrieve his saddle, but instead, he looked straight into Djedi Jhutyms Ka-en-Heru's eyes. His head still had that surprise look on its face when Djedi Jhutyms Ka-en-Heru presented it to Nswt Bety Neb Khrw-Ra Sa Ra Mentchu-hotep at Mayor Setyms's house.

Djedi Jhutyms Ka-en-Heru told Sa Ra Mentchu-hotep that he would go alone to Lebanon, taking the two Tamhou prostitutes with him and that he would destroy this black slave trade and black prostitution houses. "Hemet Djedi Ma'at Nefert and the Medjay medju led by my son, Medjay priest-scientist Ka-en-Jhutyms, will escort you back to Kemet safely. And then Djedi Ma'at Nefert will go to Libya and destroy the slave ring and prostitution there. And my daughter, Medjay Priest-Scientist Neith-Ka Ma'at, and her Medjay medju will take the two sacks of gold and return the women back to their villages after they have been debriefed and healed. Those who have no homes to return to will remain in Punt and be given gold so they can start new lives. The second sack of gold should be used to repair the damages of broken homes and better the security in the villages. This is the law of reciprocity."

"*Ee nedj her ek Amen Ra, Mwt hna Khensu.* [I give homage to Amen-Ra, the unseen and seen manifestation of divinity, along with Mwt, the great mother, and her son Khensu, the healer of emotions.] May this holy trinity guide us and keep us safe. I shall see you all back in Kemet soon. *Ankh Udja Snb Neb. Dua ntchr.*"

CHAPTER 8

KEMET'S CLASSICAL AGE IN MDW NTCHR, ART, AND LITERATURE

It was during the second golden age that we find the earliest examples of great Kemety literature. Perhaps best known from this period was the *Story of Sinuhe*. Sa Ra Mentchu-hotep liked this story so much he had hundreds of papyrus copies made. Also written during this classical period were didactic works such as the instruction of M-hat-Amen (Amenemhat) and the protests of "The Eloquent Peasant."

By Sa Ra Mentchu-hotep's forty-ninth year as Nswt Bety of Sema Tawy, Kemet had grown into a strong nation-state. Strong emphasis was placed on preprofessional education. Kemety schools and colleges were attached to or were next to or inside many of the temples of Kemet. The teachers were the priests, priestesses, and scribes. Sa Ra Mentchu-hotep made sure that the Kemetyu placed a strong educational role for mothers and fathers. Children in ancient Kemet stayed with their mothers until the age of five. During these years, a strong respect for their mothers was instilled in the children. Parents would instill into their children various educational principles, moral attitudes, and views of life. From an early age, they would be going out to the fields, boys and girls alike, to lend a hand in simple tasks, like gathering and winnowing the corn; tending poultry; in time, cattle; and so forth. Fishermen, boatmen, and others would also take their young folks along with them for practical experience.

Thus, from a tender age, they would receive their basic education in the bosom of the family. During the first golden age, this was usually all the schooling most girls would get, unless they belonged to the royal family or the nobility. But during the second golden age, under Nswt Bety Neb Khrw-Ra Sa Ra Mentchu-hotep, most of the young girls had the same opportunity as boys. At the age of five, education of the boys was taken over by their fathers. Parents instilled their ideas about the world, about folk rituals, their spiritual outlook, and their viewpoints on correct behavior toward others and toward the Ntchru.

However, for boys, it would be supplemented by proper training in whatever line they chose or was chosen for them.

Many careers were determined by the status of the parents. The educational track that a student followed was typically determined by the position that the father held in society, yet students who showed ability was able to receive training for higher-status jobs. An official took on his son as an assistant so that the son would have on-the-job training, and the succession became almost automatic.

The best students, male and female, could train to become scholars for nine years when they turned nine, depending on their field. Education covered both general upbringing of a child and training for a particular occupation.

Even during the first golden age of Kemet, the Nswt Bety had set up the prince's schools. The prince's school was the most respected of all the schools and provided the very best ancient Kemety education. The prince's school would have educated the sons of the Nswt Bety, members of the royal family, nobles, and high officials. Mentchu-hotep and his sister, Neferu, attended a prince's school in Waset. There was also a process that allowed recommendations when young boys who showed great promise were also allowed in a prince's school even though they may belong to the farmer, soldier, or craftsmen class. However, all the educational centers gave a solid, well-rounded education during the second golden age.

The lessons undertaken by the younger schoolchildren in Kemet consisted of basic mathematics and reciting sums. They all practiced writing by copying from existing documents. The youngest schoolchildren would practice writing on wooden tablets that were coated with a smooth white plaster that could be wiped clean. Only older students would be allowed to use *mehyt* (papyrus) paper. The students sat with their legs folded, holding their writing boards on their laps. Older students were given a good, well-rounded education. Their lessons included

Mdw Ntchr, reading and writing, ourstory and history, math using a decimal system based on the ten fingers, and also arithmetic, science, astrology, geometry, astronomy, music, geography, spiritual science, biology, art, and medicine. Any misdemeanors were treated seriously, and punishments for pupils ranged from beatings to writing out lines and even being removed from the *pr ankh* (school).

Shemsu Heru Sa Ra Mentchu-hotep imposed many of the techniques that he learned as a Medjay into the learning system of Kemet. Much of the learning was structured around recitation, but he made sure that symptomatic thought and the scientific process of learning was at the core. Students did their arithmetic silently, but they recited their texts aloud until they knew the texts by heart. Then they attempted to write it down, either from a teacher's model or from memory. Good speech was called *Mdw Nefer.*

Heti, scribe from the first golden age

Mentchu-hotep offered free tuition to top universities, where learning never stopped. Tuition at the top schools was and is free of all charge to gifted students. Moreover, it was accompanied in most cases by a grant that paid for food and lodging. No time limit was set for the students. For most of them, the course of study lasted twelve or fourteen years, but cases were not unknown of a student growing gray within the precincts of the ancient university.

Scribes and priests imparted education in these institutions and also trained colleges for future officials attached to the principal departments of state, such as the public granaries, the treasury, and the administration of royal lands.

Scribes of Kemet during Sa Ra Mentchu-hotep's rulership

Mentchu-hotep believed that a good example was the best teacher, so many copies were made of these books of instruction since they also served as teaching texts in the pru ankh (schools) for scribes. The one that appeared to be the oldest was by the celebrated vizier, architect, and physician Imhotep from the first golden age under Shemsu Heru Djoser. Another was the instruction compiled by the noble and royal prince Heru-Djed-ef for his son. The two authors of these very ancient books were held in such esteem as to be deified.

Of other educational treatises, perhaps the most important was the instruction of Hotep-Ptah, city administrator and first minister during the reign of His Majesty Djedkare Isesi, ruler of Upper and Lower Kemet during the first golden age. The following passages dealt with the art of "elegant and effective speech." Nevertheless, Hotep-Ptah (Ptah-hotep) rated fair in dealing in higher learning.

> You may tell a wise man from the extent of his knowledge, a noble man by his good deeds.

> Do not boast of your knowledge, but seek the advice of the untutored as much as the well educated.

> Wise words are divine like precious stones and may come even from common-girls grinding the corn.

Hotep-Ptah urged his readers to exercise justice and warned against intriguing for self-aggrandizement, bribery, extortion of debts from those unable to pay, and insatiable accumulation of property. His manual abounded in concrete advice on how to behave in various situations—at banquets, in the exercise of high office, or toward friends, wives, petitioners, poor people, and so on.

> Do not over the boundary-stone in the field nor shift the surveyor's rope; do not covet a cubit of your neighbor's land nor tamper with the widow's land-bounds.

> Covet not the poor farmer's property or hunger after his bread; the peasant's morsel will surely gag in the throat and revolt the gullet.

If the poor man is found to owe you a great debt, divide it three ways; remit two parts and let the third stand. That, you will see, is the best way in this life; thereafter you will sleep sound and in the morning it will seem like good tidings; for it is better to be praised for neighborly love than to have riches in your storeroom; better to enjoy your bread with a good conscience than to have wealth weighed down by reproaches.

Never let a powerful man bribe you to oppress a weak one for his own benefit.

The ancient Kemetyu, nevertheless, held education in high regard and saw it as a privilege. A few talented individuals without formal schooling still managed to acquire sufficient knowledge to shine in their own field.

Jhuty and his mate, Seshat, before the tree of wisdom, with the Nswt kneeling before knowledge and wisdom

Wisdom was regarded as something some people grew into. As nobody was born wise, we see wisdom appear in the so-called didactical literature of the instructions as an exponent of the process of acquiring a just perspective on life (i.e., the time of "follow the heart"). Rectitude led to the state of veneration as a "noble deed" in the "beautiful west," the hereafter. One survived and could be immortalized, like the Nswt Bety. Only Nswt Bety took the next step—namely, that of a deification beyond the limitations of wisdom (the canon of Ma'at) and this by being a Ntchr (like Ma'at) and the sole mediator of order, justice, and truth (without the Nswt Bety, the only Ntchr on earth, justice could not be offered to the Creator Ntchru, only conversed with Ntchru, causing the righteous order to collapse). When the Nswt Bety died, he rose up as *Maa Kheru* to the imperishable stars. Indeed, wisdom was the best a nonroyal aristocrat or a common intellectual (priest, scribe) could hope for during the first golden age, but now they, too, could be true of voice and become one with the Ntchru. In the instructions, we could see it at work as the law of existence itself.

Insofar as we relate deep thought to the overall metaphysical question of the nature of the universe and the Remtch, ancient Kemety literature revealed itself to be a fertile ground. Besides the explicit presence of wisdom in moral teachings, such as our *maxims*, we found philosophical strands, elements, and perspectives in creation texts, resurrection texts, songs of praise (hymns), funerary texts, tales, poetry, literature of despair, and scientific texts (medical, astronomical, and mathematical papyri). These considerations were always intermingled with the context at hand, but as soon as a broad, comparative horizon emerged, one could not deny that the ancient Kemetyu had a philosophical inclination: that this "wisdom" was not the result of a free, rational dialogue triggering our interest to find out the silhouette of the ancient Kemety sage. He was not a disputant but one who listened and acted out truth and justice.

Nevertheless, it was true that the wisdom teachings (i.e., knowledge that makes one wise) appeared in a narrative format of their own and enjoyed a considerable popularity and historical continuity. Although the extant record of the wisdom teachings was slightly more extended than the usual instructions on papyri, the teachings of Nswt Bety Neb Khrw-Ra Sa Ra Mentchu-hotep during his lifetime covered the translation and spiritual study of the following major native wisdom teachings:

- The *Instruction of Hardjedef* (OK, first golden age, ca. 2487–2348 BCE)

- The *Instruction of Kagemni* (OK, late, first golden age, ca. 2348–2205 BCE)

- The *Maxims of Ptahhotep* (OK, late, first golden age)

- The *Instruction of MerykaRa* (second golden age, ca. 2160–1980 BCE)

Clearly, the Kemety sage was an intellectual and a thinker but was always within the form of the balance of truth, which was Ma'at and the judgment of *esfet*. The term *follow the heart* was the fulfillment of what existed, the act of Ma'at—namely, order, truth, and justice. So the wise was always a priest of Ma'at, a judge administering the living truth by the grace of his Nswt Bety, lord, and Ntchr person, the Nswt Bety, the archetypal teacher, now with the aid of the priest and priestess. However, both as a keen observer of people's errors and their consequences, as well as a good example to be followed by others, the Kemety sage surpassed the conceptuality of Kemet itself, and then his wisdom was indeed for all ages.

A "staff of old age" was usually taken as a metaphor for a son or a successor in the context of an instruction. The latter seemed indeed more to the point, although in ancient Kemet knowledge was primarily transmitted from father to son or from mother to daughter. Wisdom too? It was Sa Ra Mentchu-hotep who set up the foundation of wisdom instructions to become part of the upper class, middle class, and commoners. The setting of the *maxims* was therefore aristocratic at birth. The command was given by the Nswt Bety and executed by his servant, the vizier Hotep-Ptah (Ptahhotep). The "staff" might also refer to the teaching itself, the good discourse that was about to start. When old age had arrived, wisdom was what kept one upright.

Wisdom was the comforter, the aide, and the "third" leg. The determinative was a man leaning on a stick, which also occurred in words like *old*, *eldest*, *great one*, *chief*, *lean*, and *support oneself*. Wisdom was the youth of old age. Wisdom was the command of elders and the proof of a true and just life. No one was born wise; wisdom was acquired, not given. At least three stages were given: the master hearer, the master of what is good, and the state of veneration—the maxims of good discourse. This also meant beautiful, accomplished, perfect discourse.

To speak well was more than convincing an audience; it was the manifestation (or transformation) of balanced thought as (into) sound. This balance was nothing less than truth and justice (Ma'at), and hence, good discourse inspired respect, awe, and admiration. Moreover, it was authoritative speech (*Hw*) that brought into material manifestation that which it vocalized the good deed, profitting the child of man. The child of man was wellborn (i.e., of good stock). This wellborn was advised to do good deeds. The lesson being that goodness could be multiplied. If nobody was greedy, understood that belongings were relative and temporal, and so shared with his neighbor, a larger good would be attained—a master hearer. Before wisdom emerged, the pupil must be able to entirely concentrate on the teaching.

The Remtch (the original people) then worked on what was heard, like the artisan with his artifact. The master hearer heard his father or teacher speak to his posterity. Wisdom would be for all time. The examples of wisdom were perennial, and they endured. As long as existence lasted, he who knew, he who attained the pyramidion of knowledge known by his wisdom. Wisdom was based on knowledge—master of what was good, master of listening. After one had mastered hearing, one had to be able to grasp the inner meaning of what was said, pierce through the framework of the example, and see the hidden universal truth, which was the final ground of wisdom.

The knower wakes early to his lasting form; the knower is here, the wise who is always aware of his essential, enduring being. Every moment, he awakes in this being and realizes who he truly is. The fool is hard-pressed; the fool does not listen. Hurrying to grasp nothing is the way of the fool, the opposite of when the sage reached veneration. The ultimate realization attainable for the nonroyal, aristocratic Kemetyu (i.e., one who lived near the Nswt Bety) was the venerated state in the "beautiful west," the place of the deceased in the kingdom of Ausar. In the *maxims*, the wise old man "reached veneration," meaning that he was so near that the state was already reflected in his consciousness. However, he had not yet attained the venerated place, his final station in the afterlife, or mastered the craft.

Again, we read that wisdom was not automatic but the result of a long training in hearing and listening. These two made one speak the "good discourse" exceedingly well and rise above the accomplishments of the ancestors. This alone made the "staff of old age"—one's rejuvenation as an elder and one's long-awaited death here and joyful rebirth there in the afterlife. Wisdom saves. The venerated place in the afterlife, the "noble death," reached the heaven of Ausar.

The Nswt Bety Neb Khrw-Ra Sa Ra Mentchu-hotep made sure his son knew this knowledge like the back of his hand, just like he knew them. "Help your friends with things that you have, for you have these things by the grace of the Ntchru.

"Hotep-Ptah [Ptah-hotep] had a son named Akhet hotep, who was also a vizier. He and his descendants were buried at Saqqara. Hotep-Ptah's tomb is located in an ancient tomb in North Saqqara, where he was laid to rest by himself. His grandson, Hotep-Ptah Tshefi, who lived during the reign of Unas, was buried in the ancient tomb of his father. Their tomb is famous for its outstanding depiction." Nswt Bety Neb Khrw-Ra Sa Ra Mentchu-hotep wanted the same respect and to leave this type of knowledge and wisdom behind for future generations to come.

Sa Ra Mentchu-hotep sat down with his wives and son as they were gathering for an evening prayer. "Peace is a quality of the Spirit that is everywhere present. Peace is what you are called to reveal first within your own consciousness and then in your world. Thoughts and actions borne of the inner peace of your soul are in alignment with the laws of the universe. All the peace that you could ever desire is already within you. It saturates the universe and everything in it. You contact this peace through meditation and affirmative prayer." The family closed their eyes. Amen Ra.

CHAPTER 9

THE TEMPLES OF ETERNITY

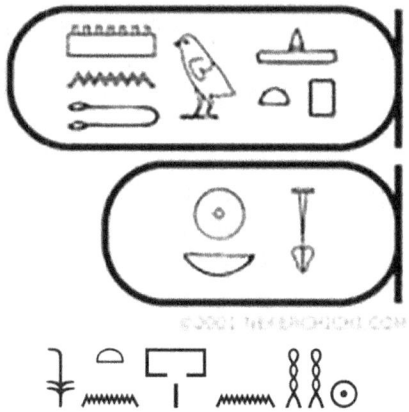

Irtysen, overseer of craftsmen, was trained by Hem Sem Tepy Kha-ef-Ptah as an artisan, and he was a scribe and a sculptor. He knew how to calculate, count, and do the mixing/dissolving of certain substances in water with exact proportions, a secret formula to create stone. He had the knowledge to make some sort of paste and to make relief sculptures not by carving but by casting. He could make blocks, like Geb and Khnum, from a mixture of limestone, clay, natron, lime, and water.

Nswt Bety Neb Khrw-Ra Sa Ra Mentchu-hotep had ordained Irtysen to hand down his professional knowledge to his son— all his wisdom concerning the creation of all kinds of precious stones and minerals. This way, Nswt Bety Neb Khru-Ra Sa Ra Mentchu-hotep knew that the knowledge would not be lost from generation to generation. Their names would be immortalized, like Imhotep in the first golden age and now Hem Sem Tepy Kha-ef-Ptah in the second golden age.

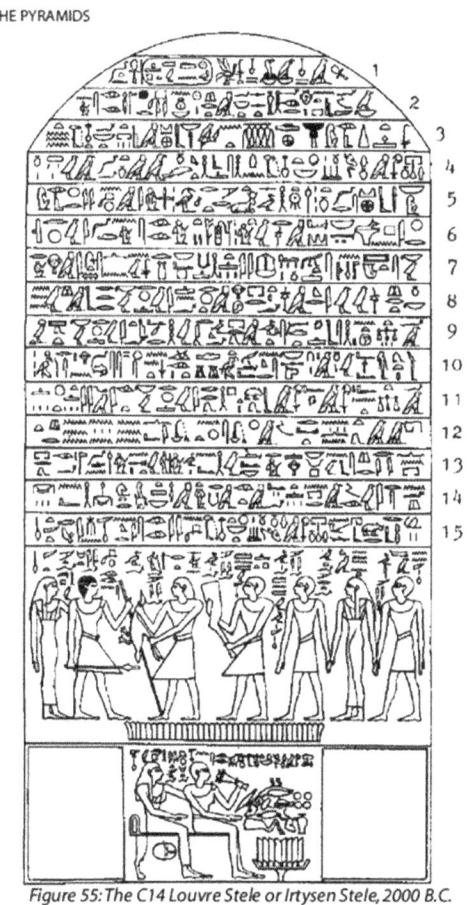

Figure 55: The C14 Louvre Stele or Irtysen Stele, 2000 B.C.

This large limestone stela was placed in Abju, a sacred city that became an important pilgrimage site (dedicated to Asar) during the second golden age, under Nswt Bety Neb Khrw-Ra Sa Ra Mentchu-hotep. Pilgrims who visited Abydos had at least one Wadj erected there.

A *Wadj* at a Pilgrimage Site

This large arched limestone *wadj* was covered in a Mdw Ntchr text fifteen lines long. It was located in Abju, the holy city of Asar. The image beneath the text showed Irtysen (rod and scepter in hand) and his wife, Hepu, receiving the funerary offerings provided by their sons, daughter, and grandson.

On the lower register, an open window framed Irtysen, who was smelling a bottle of perfumed unguent, with his wife sitting nearby. On a pedestal table in front of them was a meal consisting of the offerings that were listed above. Beneath the seat was a basket containing a mirror.

The *Wadj* of Irtysen

[1] The living Heru, the uniter of the two lands, the Lord of Udjat and Nekhbet (Upper and Lower Kemet), who unites both lands, The ruler of Upper and Lower kemet, Son of Ra, Mentuhotep, living forever; [2] his true servant, who is in the inmost recess of his heart, and makes his pleasure all the day long, Is worthy of the respect of the great Ntchr,(signed) Irtysen.

[3] As an offering to the Nswt given to Asr, leader of the west, Lord of Abju, in all his temples, that he may give a [4] voice offering (funereal meal) of bread and beer, thousands of loaves, beer, oxen, geese, linen, clothes, all good and pure things, loaves without number, beer, spirits, cakes o [5] the Lord of Abju (Asar), white cream of the sacred cow on which the manes like to feed, for the devout unto Asr [6] and Enpu, Lord of the Burying Grounds, the Chief of the artists, Irtysen

[7] I know the mystery of the divine Word, the ordinances of the spiritual feasts, every rite of which they are fraught, I never

strayed from them; [8] I, indeed, am an artist, wise in his art, a man standing above (all men) by his learning.

I know what belongs to sinking waters, [9] the weighing's done for the reckoning of accounts, how to produce the form of issuing forth and coming in, so that a member may go to his place.

I know the walking of an image of man, [10] the carriage of a woman, the two arms of Heru, the twelve circles of the blasphemers, the contemplating the eye without a second that affrights the wicked, [11] the poising of arm to bring the hippopotamus low, the coming of the runner.

I know the making of amulets, [12] that we go without any fire giving its flame, or without our being washed away by water!

[13] Lo! there is no man excels by it but I alone and my eldest legitimate son: Ntchr has decreed him [14] to be excellent in it; and I have seen the perfections of his hands in his work of chief-artist in every kind of precious stones, from gold and silver [15] even to ivory and ebony!

Funereal meal of bread and liquors! Thousands of wine, loaves, oxen, geese, linen, clothes, all good and pure things, to the devout Irtysen-the-wise, son of the lady Ad.

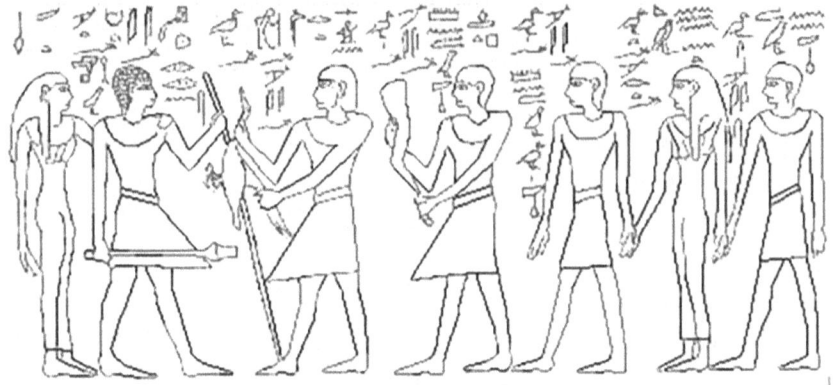

Funereal meal of bread and beer, thousands of loaves,
oxen, geese, all good and pure things to the pious
Irtysen and his pious wife, Hepu, who loves him.

His son, his eldest, who loves him—Usertesen.

His son who loves him—Mentuhotep.

His son who loves him—Si-Mentchu.

His daughter who loves him—Qim.

Her son who loves her—Temnen.

An Artist's Biography

The inscription on this wedge is an extraordinary biographical account in which the scribe and artist Irtysen boasts of his multiple skills:

> I know the secret of the divine word (i.e., of Mdw Ntchr, the composition of ceremonial rituals). I have acquired mastery over all the magical formulas, and there is nothing I don't know about them. Moreover, I am a craftsman who excels in his art and has a superior level of

knowledge; I know how to estimate dimensions, recut, and fit until an element is in place. I know the posture of the male statue and the appearance of the female, the attitude of the eleven birds of prey, the convulsion of the isolated prisoner, how to portray a squint, the enemies' expression of terror, the arm movements of a hippopotamus hunter and the leg movements of a running man.

Manufacturing Secrets

I know how to make pigments and products that will not melt even with fire burning them and are moreover insoluble in water. Nobody will know of this except me and my eldest son, the Ntchr and Nswt Mentchu-hotep having ordered that he become an initiate, as I have noticed his ability to oversee works in all the precious materials from silver and gold to ivory and ebony.

*****

"Mother, come with me to the west bank. I need to show you Father's mortuary temple. We have made many new improvements. It is truly a temple of eternity. It is magnificent. There is nothing like this. It has never been done before, and some of the designs are mine, Mother. Hem Sem Tepy Kha-ef-Ptah and Priest Irtysen allowed me to help them. I want to be the one to take you on the first grand tour. You know how Father is always talking about how our sacred science and knowledge of the universe is hidden in the architectural structure of the temples and monuments. Well, that is exactly what we did, Mother."

As they reached the dock, the royal prince Mentchu-hotep said, "Watch your step, Nebt Wrt. Today we are sailing in my grand royal boat made just for me, the royal prince Mentchu-hotep."

Hmt Nswt Wrt Neferu was very impressed with the style of her son's royal boat. "And you designed this yourself, son?"

"Tiw, yes, Mother, with a little help from Hem Sem Tepy Kha-ef-Ptah of coarse." Four warriors and two Medjay sailed with them. The four warriors rowed the royal boat, while the Medjay stood guard. "And, Mother, on windy days, it also has sails." Djedi Priest-Scientist Ma'at Nefert and two Medjay warriors followed in another smaller royal boat behind them. Djedi Priest-Scientist Ma'at Nefert felt a disruption in the force, that danger was in the air for Prince Mentchu-hotep.

*****

Nswt Mentchu-hotep, while sitting in his royal study in deep meditation, felt this wave of negative energy pass him. He immediately innerstood and recognized this negative energy force was directed toward him and his son, the prince. His eyes opened quickly; he knew his son was in danger. Prince Kaneferre from the north had returned for revenge for his father Nswt Mery-Ka-Ra's death thirty-five years ago. He had been training for thirty-five years for this day.

"I can feel his hate, and now he is here!" Sa Ra Mentchu-hotep strapped his sword around his waist and placed his royal dagger in its holster and picked up his royal spear as he headed for his son's palace. He knew he would need to recall all his Medjay training for the battle ahead of him. When he arrived at his son's palace, he was not to be found. He asked the royal guard about the whereabouts of Prince Mentchu-hotep. The royal guard explained that Prince Mentchu-hotep and Hmt

Nswt Wrt Neferu had traveled to the west bank to view his mortuary temple. *Nen, no,* he thought, *this would be the perfect place for an ambush—secluded on the west bank, almost no witness, right near the mountains and cliffs.* He rushed to the dock to board his royal boat.

*****

Djedi Priest-Scientist Ma'at Nefert followed the prince's royal boat closely because she had felt this same negative energy force filled with hate and revenge directed toward Prince Mentchu-hotep and Nswt Bety Mentchu-hotep, but her major concern was the safety of Prince Mentchu-hotep and Hmt Nswt Wrt Neferu. The Djedi knew that the Nswt Bety Medjay Priest-Scientist Mentchu-hotep could feel what she was feeling and would follow soon. Djedi Priest-Scientist Ma'at Nefert, as she closed her eyes, felt a strong, negative force around the Northern prince.

He had gathered several barbaric, savage warriors from the extreme north, and he was also traveling with an Asiatic wizard. She had encountered their skills before in battle many years ago with her Hee (husband), Djedi Jhutyms Ka-en-Heru, in Sumer. These wizards were masters of illusions, but their illusions did not work on the Medjay priest-scientist who already innerstood that this physical world is not real and that everything we see is created by the ego. The illusions created by the wizard would have a different energy pattern. Djedi Priest-Scientist Ma'at Nefert sank into deep meditation, and she knew that the eyes were useless when the mind was blind! Change your mind and you change your consciousness and then you can change your circumstances.

*****

As the excited prince Mentchu-hotep's royal boat approached the western shore of the sacred land of Asr in Amenta, joy was in his heart as he held his mother's hand. "We are almost there, Mother. Just a short ride and we will witness the greatness of eternity." They mounted several beautiful horses from Yemen. Hmt Nswt Neferu could feel her son's excitement as their horses got within their eyes' view of the grand mortuary temple of Nswt Bety Mentchu-hotep. The white limestone casing of the Mer Khut in the center of the complex was breathtaking.

They dismounted their horses and walked fifty meters on a grand walkway made of pink granite, about fifteen meters wide, with special sycamore and eucalyptus trees five rows wide and fifty meters deep on both sides of the walkway, giving off a heavenly fragrance in the air along with this breathtaking view. About thirty meters from the mortuary temple, they began to walk up a ramp way.

The prince pointed out that the ramp was built on a thirty-three-degree incline so very little pressure would be on the lower back and a carriage could be pulled up with no problem. They arrived on the second level. "My great father selected a site on a rocky hillside, where some of his predecessors of the First Intermediate Period built their row tombs, and these tombs were so named for their row of pillars along their facades. Sa Ra Mentchu-hotep's complex combined architectural elements of both the row tomb and the pyramid complex, a causeway, a stepped terraced mortuary temple that is partially cut into the rock cliff's face, and a subterranean burial chamber. This was a twist of genius, giving it an original appearance of his tomb."

"I see you did your homework, son."

He smiled as he continued the tour. "The main second level was accessed by a broad ramp of limestone blocks with a grove of parallel sycamores and tamarisks planted to either side. This terrace may be divided into three sections. The outer section of this level, like the lower level, consisted of two rows of limestone pillars. It is often referred to as the upper pillared hall. The front of these pillars were decorated with scenes depicting Shemsu Heru Sa Ra Mentchu-hotep and various Ntchru and are inscribed with text in Mdw Ntchr."

Djedi Priest-Scientist Ma'at Nefert walked through the doorway first, with the four royal guards behind Hmt Nswt Wrt Neferu and Prince Mentchu-hotep. She knew that the enemy was not far away. The two Medjay warriors entered the lower level on the ground floor. On the ground floor, the two Medjay encountered several workmen, scribes, and priests carving Mdw Ntchr on several granite karst (caskets). They checked all their names for security.

Back on the second floor, the crown prince Mentchu-hotep pointed out to his mother, Hmt Nswt Neferu, that the Behdet-winged solar disk, a symbol of the victorious Heru, was above every doorway, just like his father's temples on the east bank. All the forty-two columns on the second level were carved out of pink granite from Abu in the south, and they represented the forty-two laws of Ma'at. As they entered the second floor, the prince explained, "Everything here tells the story of the reunification of Kemet after uniting Upper and Lower Kemet, while the first floor starts at birth and takes you through his Medjay training, his initiation, and his herculean victory over Nswt Mery-Ka-Ra and his Asiatic allies.

"There is a third floor underground where all Father's secondary wives would be buried, along with sacred royal women of the family, who will be protected for eternity. But now the real special burial chamber for Mentchu-hotep and for you and Hmt Tem is inside the Mer Khut. In the center will be Nswt Bety Mentchu-hotep in a Nswt chamber, just like Nswt Bety Khufu at Giza, and the Hemet chamber below is where you and Mother Hemet Tem will share a burial chamber.

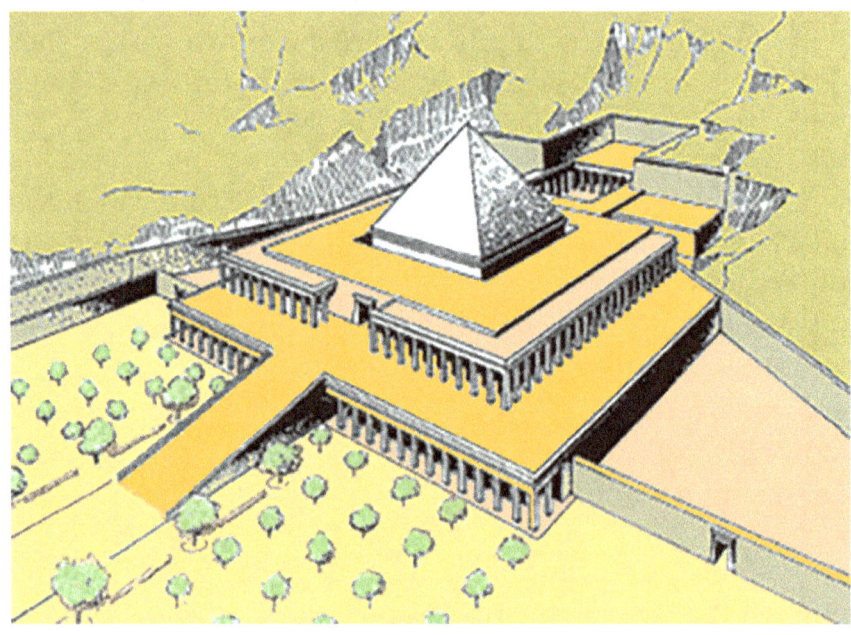

The mortuary complex of NebhetepRa Mentchu-hotep at Deir el-Bahari

"There are two Holy of Holies—one on each floor. The first-floor Holy of Holies is dedicated to Amen-Min and the fertility in the afterlife with the trinity of Asr, Ast, and Heru. The second floor Holy of Holies is dedicated to the trinity of Amen, Mwt, and Khensu. Niches along the corridor walls held some six hundred wooden figurines that were once part of the models of workshops, bakeries, and boats. The burial chamber is located about twelve meters down the entrance corridor. It was made of granite and has a saddle ceiling. Actually, the room is divided into two sections, with an alabaster chapel topped by a single gigantic granite slab, entered by way of a double wooden door, taking up the larger part. This room was for the burial of Mentchu-hotep's Ba or soul.

"On both floors, there are rows of statues of Asr and Nswt Bety Neb Khrw-Ra Mentchu-hotep standing in the Asarian position with his arms crossed, leading to the Holy of Holies— twenty-one statues of Asr and twenty-one statues of Mentchu-hotep. An entrance on the east wing of the pillared portico hall, located on the main axis of the complex as a whole, leads to the inner ambulatory.

"An *ambulatory* can, at least in terms of Kemet architecture, be defined as 'a partial roof that ran around the edges of a structure and was supported by pillars.' Most often, we find ambulatories surrounding an open courtyard, but in this case, it surrounds an inner core. Within this ambulatory stood 140 octagonal pillars arranged in two rows on the west [rear] side and three rows on each of the other sides. The ambulatory was dimly illuminated by shafts in the exterior wall near the outer portico. How am I doing, Mwt?"

"Eqr, my son!"

"Inside of the ambulatory was a central core that was a symbolic version of the primeval mound. On the west side of the second level terrace were discovered a row of six shaft tombs cut into the rock. Their subterranean sections were built of limestone blocks, with spirit doors and statues of the Ntchru. Women of the royal family were buried in these tombs also. This expansion included an open, pillared courtyard, Kemet's first grand hypostyle hall, and a chapel to various Ntchru. Sandstone was used in the construction of the courtyard that was surrounded on the south, east, and north sides by octagonal pillars.

"There were also eighty-two pillars in the hypostyle hall. The hypostyle hall had a limestone floor with walls built of sandstone. Here, the paving is sandstone while the walls are made of limestone. There is a low ramp that leads to a limestone altar at its rear [westernmost part] that sits in front of the niche and the oversized statue of Mentchu-hotep. This altar is the center of the entire temple complex. This room also has a spirit door. There are other Duat objects placed here. A seated statue of the Ntchr Amun is placed here also. However, a small chapel situated off the eastern corner of the western addition's courtyard served the worship of several important Ntchru, including Amen, Mentchu, Asar, and Het Heru."

"This is unbelievable, my son. Your father is so proud of you. We are so proud of you. Has High Priestess Hemet Tem seen this yet?"

"Tiw, I showed her yesterday, my Nebt Wrt. But wait till you see the terrace out back. It will take your breath away. This is the first terraced tomb temple in existence anywhere in the world."

"Are you sure, my son? Have you traveled the world?"

"Nen, no, Mother. But Hem Sem Tepy Kha-ef-Ptah has, and he says it's one of a kind. So, Mother, that is firsthand information. I believe you taught me that the first step in symptomatic thinking is firsthand information, and I verified it with Djedi Priest-Scientist Ma'at Nefert as a second resource."

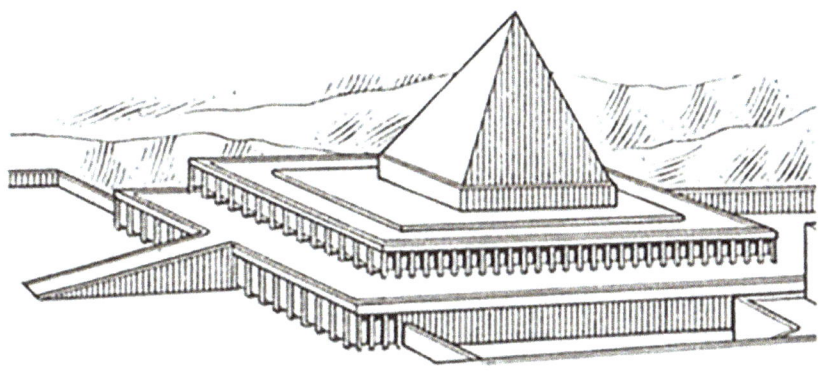

This was the great terraced tomb temple of
Neb Khrw-Ra Mentchu-hotep.

These are a few of the giant statues of Nswt Bety Mentchu-
hotep that lined the inside of the terraced tomb temple.

They all walked out onto the back of the terraced tomb
temple complex. Ra was at high noon, blazing down on them.
A few of the workers—like Irtysen, overseer of craftsmen and
two of his sons—were molding statues of Asr and Mentchu-
hotep in the back courtyard, along with their supervisor and
teacher Hem Tepy Kha-ef-Ptah.

*****

Nswt Bety Mentchu-hotep had reached the west bank, and directly behind him was a Medjay medju unit, along with Medjay Priest-Scientist Akhtoy, head of security for the royal family. They all mounted horses and quickly raced toward Mentchu-hotep's mortuary temple in the rock cliffs of the valley of Amenta without saying a word.

*****

The little baby of one of the workmen's wife, about two years old, wandered over to Hmt Nswt Wrt Neferu. Smiling, she picked up the little baby boy in the air. "My, my, my, you are a cutie," she said in a very high baby-like voice. As she held the little baby in the air, the crown prince immediately felt danger. A flaming arrow was heading directly toward Hmt Nswt Wrt Neferu and the baby. He could see it through her arms, with Ra gleaming in his face as he jumped in front of them, pushing them to the floor.

Djedi Priest-Scientist Ma'at Nefert caught the flaming arrow in her hand only about an inch away from the crown prince Mentchu-hotep's back. "It's an attack!" the Djedi yelled out. The two Medjay placed their shield in front of the crown prince Mentchu-hotep and Hmt Nswt Wrt Neferu, deflecting several arrows. Within seconds, a barrage of arrows rained down on them, killing the four guards instantly. *This looks like the work of the Ta-Sety bowmen,* she thought.

Nine huge Northern savage warriors jumped from the mountain cliffs down onto the terraced floor, maybe twenty meters in front of them. Behind them flew a huge fire dragon with flames coming from his nose and mouth, and on its back was Prince Kaneferre. He dismounted from the dragon and spoke, "You don't know me, but I know you! I am Crown Prince Kaneferre, the real ruling king of Kemet. And today

246

you, Crown Prince Mentchu-hotep, will die, along with your mother! I really came to kill you, so she will just be a bonus. Ha-ha-ha. I have waited thirty-five years for this day, and now it is here!"

The baby's mother ran toward her child, but one of the Northern savages shot an arrow straight through her back, killing her instantly. The husband tried to run toward his wife, but he was killed too by another one of the pink-haired Northern barbarian warrior, with his huge sword. Hem Tepy Kha-ef-Ptah told his workers to run toward the mountains for cover immediately. An arrow was shot at Hem Tepy Kha-ef-Ptah, but he deflected it effortlessly with his hand as he also made sure his other workers were safe.

"None of you will escape. You all will die here today!" shouted Prince Kaneferre. The dragon flew up in the air and circled them, spitting out a ring of fire that circled them like a cage, maybe ten meters in diameter. The flames burned about six feet high all around them.

Djedi Priest-Scientist Ma'at Nefert yelled out, "This is an illusion! There is no dragon, and there is no fire. Just wait for their attack."

Hmt Nswt Wrt Neferu took the extra fabric from around her waist on her dress and wrapped the baby to her back, as she prepared to do battle. The Djedi gave her one of her swords, and then she gave the crown prince Mentchu-hotep her second sword from her double-sword holster on her back. "You know what to do. We have trained for this day."

Crown Prince Mentchu-hotep just nodded his head affirmative as he focused on the Northern barbarians in front of him. The Djedi took her spear and threw it straight through the neck and out the back of the head of one of the barbarians, killing him instantly. He never even saw it coming. That was how much power was behind her throw. The spear stuck in a wall near Hem Tepy Kha-ef-Ptah, and he pulled it out quickly, ready to defend himself.

"Kill them!" yelled Prince Kaneferre to his northern warriors.

Djedi Priest-Scientist Ma'at Nefert leaped onto the back of the fire dragon in the air, wrestling it to the floor of the Nswt Bety Mentchu-hotep's terrace tomb temple. After breaking its neck, she pulled out her lightsword, which glowed and hummed with an unknown power, and cut off part of its wing. Then she cut the dragon's head off, and instantly, it transformed back into a human wizard, very pale and white in complexion. Before it could wave its magical wand, again Hem Tepy Kha-ef-Ptah thrust the Djedi spear through its back, and Djedi Priest-Scientist Ma'at Nefert cut his head off with one quick stroke of her light sword. The flames vanished around them, and the Northern warriors seemed to come out of the trance they were in, making them almost invincible.

Meanwhile, the Medjay warriors had killed three of the Northern barbarians. Now it was even, seven versus seven—six Northern warriors and Prince Kaneferre against Crown Prince Mentchu-hotep; his mother, Hmt Nswt Wrt Neferu; four Medjay warriors; and Djedi Ma'at Nefert.

*****

When the Medjay warriors and Nswt Bety Neb Khrw-Ra Mentchu-hotep reached his royal mortuary temple, they saw workers running for their lives, with a few Ta-Sety bowmen in pursuit. But when the Ta-Sety bowmen saw the Medjay, they threw down their bows and placed their hands in the air.

The workers yelled, "In the back, but beware of monsters!"

Medjay Priest-Scientist Akhtoy sent two Medjay to round up the Ta-Sety bowmen. The rest followed the Nswt up the ramp way to the second floor. *Beware of monsters,* the Nswt Bety thought. *Sounds like the work of wizards.*

*****

"You are mine, Crown Prince Mentchu-hotep." Prince Kaneferre said as he swung his sword toward the crown prince's head. The crown prince Mentchu-hotep blocked and returned the blow.

Djedi Priest-Scientist Ma'at Nefert cut through her barbarian warrior's defense with just three swings of her light sword; the Northern warrior never even saw the third strike that severed his head. Hem Tepy Kha-ef-Ptah thrusted his spear through his Northern warrior so fast it went completely through him out the other side. The Djedi caught it and threw it back through the barbarian from the backside as Kha-ef-Ptah caught it while he was moving out of the way of the dead barbarian's falling body, like a giant redwood tree.

Hmt Nswt Wrt Neferu never backed down from a good fight, not even as a child. She trapped her opponent's large sword with hers as she stepped in close and then stabbed him in the heart with her royal dagger. The two Medjay just outclassed their Northern warriors, killing them both within fifteen strikes of the sword.

Now it was only the crown prince versus the crown prince. The crown prince Mentchu-hotep knew that his opponent was a warrior. He was a scholar, so if he was to win, he had to outthink his opponent. Djedi Priest-Scientist Ma'at Nefert had showed him several trick moves, which would work against this warrior. He ran toward the wall away from everyone so no one could help him, not even the Djedi.

Prince Kaneferre ran behind him. *Yes, this is the one.* When Kaneferre lunged for his back, he would flip over his head, pushing off from the wall, and stab him in the back. He could see it in his head. He had practiced this move over a dozen times. But when Prince Mentchu-hotep almost got to the wall with Kaneferre in the right spot, he set to jump up but slipped and fell on his face. Kaneferre was so close his sword crashed into the wall with Mentchu-hotep under him. He fell on top of Mentchu-hotep. Everyone looking held their breath!

Nswt Bety Neb Khrw-Ra Sa Ra Mentchu-hotep and Medjay Priest-Scientist Akhtoy got to Prince Kaneferre at the same time. They both stabbed Prince Kaneferre in the side with their spears, pulling him off the prince Mentchu-hotep in a diving motion. But they were both a second too late! The crown prince lay in a pool of blood, motionless. Nswt Bety Neb Khrw-Ra Mentchu-hotep fell to his knees as he looked at his motionless son, the crown prince Mentchu-hotep. He lifted his son's head up with tears in his eyes. Everyone was in disbelief and heartbroken. Blood was all over the crown prince's face, neck, and chest.

"My son, my son!" the Nswt screamed. Hmt Nswt Wrt Neferu went to his side and knelt down next to him. Tears filled both their eyes. Everyone knelt down on one knee in prayer. "Amen-Ra, please don't take him away from me! I have done everything you asked of me! Please, not my son. Take me! Take my life. I have lived long and complete, but not my son, not my son!"

The crown prince lay limp in his father's arms for about a minute, then suddenly, he coughed and gasped for air as he opened his eyes. Everyone stood up, except the Nswt Bety and Hmt Nswt Wrt Neferu. He pulled his son into his arms, close to his body. Hmt Nswt Wrt Neferu started checking his body for wounds, but there was none. But when she pulled open his shirt, the crown prince Mentchu-hotep was wearing a beautiful crystal- and gold-plated vest. The mother looked over at Djedi Priest-Scientist Ma'at Nefert.

The Djedi saw the crystal-and-gold vest that she had made for the prince, then the Djedi turned over the dead body of Prince Kaneferre. Prince Mentchu-hotep's royal dagger, just like the one Hmt Nswt Neferu used to kill her Northern warrior (both daggers were royal gifts by the Nswt Bety Mentchu-hotep), was stuck in the heart of his enemy. All that blood that was gushing out of his enemy's heart that was all over the prince was not his. Now everyone knew that Prince Kaneferre was dead before the two Medjay warriors stabbed him.

The crown prince Mentchu-hotep stood up with great confidence, like the spiritual warrior he had become. Everyone rushed to hug him at the same time. Shemsu Heru Nswt Bety Neb Khrw-Ra Sa Ra Mentchu-hotep crossed his arms in front of his chest in the Asarian position and chanted out loud, "*Amen-Ra Nswt Ntchru. Amen-Ra neb n ankh neb!* [Amen-Ra, the unseen and seen manifestation of the Creator, is the ruler of all the principles and laws. Amen-Ra, the seen and unseen creative force of the universe, is the master of all life.] Dua Ntchr! [All praises to divinity!]"

CHAPTER 10

THE FINAL JOURNEY
PASSING THE KNOWLEDGE
ON INTO ETERNITY

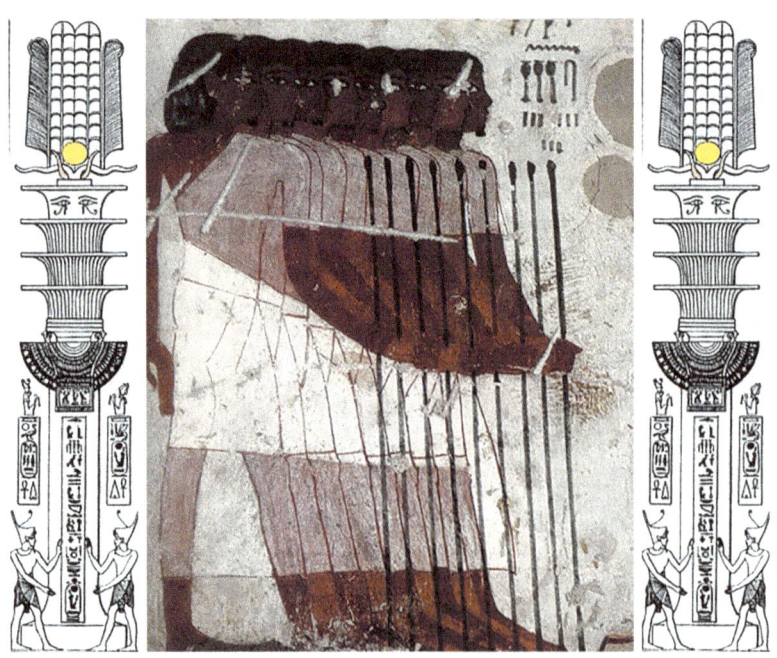

Nswt Bety Neb Khrw-Ra Sa Ra Mentchu-hotep achieved the reestablishment of a single administration for the whole country. The second golden age was a period of revival of the Kemety character. Shemsu Heru Nswt Bety Neb Khrw-Ra Sa Ra Mentchu-hotep established the second golden age and was able to exert control over the two lands, creating Sema Tawy (the united two lands). With many new temples constructed in the north, he still located his capital in Waset, the land of his ancestors. From his southern power base, he promoted and developed economic and political development. Kemety trade flourished, and an elaborate irrigation system was again established.

Sa Ra Mentchu-hotep sat in his royal chair, thinking, *Today my heart tenderly embraces all creation as part of my very own. I open myself and allow the universe to flow through me in loving service to all who cross my path and the path of Kemet. I am not here merely to catch vibrations from things. I, Shemsu Heru Sa Ra Mentchu-hotep, am here to imbue things with my vibration. Everything in the three-dimensional world is made of the Spirit's thought vibrations condensed into form. Its vibration of truth reverberates through me. It radiates outward from me into the world. I am here to anchor the vibration of the divine in the Remtch dimension.*

He looked at the giant statues of the Ntchru of Amen-Ra, Mut, and Khensu. *I kneel at your feet as you stand victorious in your inner dominion because your spiritual practice has anchored me in your identity as a spiritual being.*

Shemsu Heru Sa Ra Mentchu-hotep was challenged by the Medjay priestship to expand and preserve the ancient knowledge through literature, art, and architecture for eternity. He knew that later generations would have gained a distorted view of ancient Kemety literature if we were familiar only with tomb inscriptions concerning the Ntchru and the afterlife. He wanted future generations to know there also existed various forms of poetry, satires, and what were called instructions in wisdom. The latter consisted of sets of maxims directed to the living, and they illustrated some of the humanistic values of ancient Kemety society. The maxims were formed into a connected sequence by inserting them into a letter from a father to his son. The format endured for millennia.

Sa Ra Mentchu-hotep used this same format for his son. It also represented one of the earliest literary formats that carried the author's name. This might not, however, be as personal as one might be thought, for the temptation was to use the name of some famous figures in ourstory as a means of giving the maxims more importance.

The *Instruction of Ptahhotep* (Hotep-Ptah) to his son survived in papyrus copies. It was a collection of maxims (not all are given here) dealing with human relations. The maxims did not cover all aspects of Kemety life. For the most part, they touched on the peaceful virtues of kindness, justice, truthfulness, moderation, and self-control. He was a vizier or high official under Nswt Bety Isesi of the first golden age. If he authored the instruction under this name, then it dated from 350–400 years before Nswt Bety Mentchu-hotep. However, the prominence given to conduct in legal disputes suggested the author's familiarity with the law courts during the Mer Khut period of Khufu, Kha-ef-Ra, and MenkauRa, the period of the first golden age.

Follow Your Heart

[1] Follow your heart as long as you live, do no more than is required . . . Don't waste time on daily cares beyond providing

for your household; When wealth has come, follow your heart, wealth does no good if one is glum!

Conduct

[2] If you want a perfect conduct, to be free from every evil, guard against the vice of greed: A grievous sickness without cure, there is no treatment for it. It embroils fathers, mothers, and the brothers of the mother, it parts wife from husband; It is a compound of all evils, a bundle of all hateful things. That man endures whose rule is rightness, who walks a straight line; He will make a will by it, the greedy has no tomb . . .

[3] Be generous as long as you live, what leaves the storehouse does not return; It is the food to be shared, which is coveted; one whose belly is empty is an accuser; One deprived becomes an opponent; don't have him for a neighbor. Kindness is a man's memorial for the years after the action.

[4] Don't be proud of your knowledge, consult the ignorant and the wise; The limits of art are not reached, no artist's skills are perfect; Good speech is more hidden than greenstone yet may be found among maids at the grindstones.

[5] Do not repeat calumny, nor should you listen to it, it is the spouting of the hot-bellied. Report a thing observed, not heard, if it is negligible, don't say anything, he who is before you recognize worth. If a seizure is ordered and carried out, hatred will arise against him who seizes; Calumny is like a dream against which one covers the face.

[6] Do not plunder a neighbor's house; do not steal the goods of one near you, lest he denounce you before you are heard. A quarreler is a mindless person, if he is known as an aggressor the hostile man will have trouble in the neighborhood.

Trust

[7] If you are among the people, gain supporters through being trusted, the trusted man who does not vent his belly's speech, he will himself become a leader. A man of means—what is he like? Your name is good, you are not maligned, your body is sleek, your face benign, one praises you without your knowing. He whose heart obeys his belly puts contempt of himself in place of love, his heart is bald, his body anointed.

[8] If you are a man of trust, sent by one great man to another, adhere to the nature of him who sent you, give his message as he said it. Guard against reviling speech, which embroils one great with another, keep to the truth, don't exceed it, but an outburst should not be repeated.

[9] Report your commission without faltering, give your advice in your master's council . . . If he is fluent in his speech, it will not be hard for the envoy to report, nor will he be answered, "who is he to know it?" As to the master, his affairs will fail if he plans to punish him for it, he should be silent upon hearing: "I have told. 'In public

[10] He who uses elbows is not helped.

[11] If you are one among guests at the table of one greater than you, take what he gives as it is set before you; Look at what is before you, don't shoot many glances at him.

[12] Don't speak to him until he summons, one does not know what may displease; Speak when he has addressed you, and then your words will please the heart.

[13] If you are in the antechamber, stand and sit as fits your rank.

Which was assigned you the first day. Do not trespass—you will be turned back, keen is the face to him who enters announced, spacious the seat of him who has been called the antechamber has a rule, all behavior is by measure;

Humility

[14] Do not boast at your neighbors' side, one has great respect for the silent man: A man of character is man of wealth. If he robs he is like a crocodile in court. Don't impose on one who is childless, neither decry nor boast of it; There is many a father who has grief, and a mother of children less content than another;

[15] If you are poor, serve a man of worth . . . Do not recall if he once was poor, don't be arrogant toward him for knowing his former state; Respect him for what has accrued to him, for wealth does not come by itself. It is their law for him whom they love, his gain, he gathered it himself.

Friendship

[16] As ill will comes from opposition, so goodwill increases love . . .

[17] Know your helpers, and then you prosper, don't be mean toward your friends, they are one's watered field, and greater then one's riches, for what belongs to one belongs to another. The character of a son of man is profit to him; Good nature is a memorial.

[18] If you probe the character of a friend, don't inquire, but approach him, deal with him alone, so as not to suffer from his manner. Dispute with him after a time, test his heart in conversation; If what he has seen escapes him, if he does a

thing that annoys you, be yet friendly with him, don't attack; Be restrained, don't let fly, don't answer with hostility, neither part from him nor attack him; His time does not fail to come, one does not escape what is fated.

[19] If you want friendship to endure in the house you enter as master, brother, or friend, in whatever place you enter, beware of approaching the women! Unhappy is the place where it is done, unwelcome is he who intrudes on them. A thousand men are turned away from their good: A short moment like a dream, then death comes for having known them . . .

Family

[20] When you prosper and found your house, and love your wife with passion, fill her belly, cloth her back, and give her ointment to soothes her body. Gladden her heart as long as you live; She is a fertile field for her lord. Do not contend with her in court, keep her from power, and restrain her—her eye is her storm when she gazes—thus will you make her stay in your house . . .

[21] If you are a man of worth and produce a son by the grace of god, if he is straight, takes after you, takes good care of your possessions, do for him all that is good, he is your son, your spirit begot him, don't withdraw your heart from him. But an offspring can make trouble: If he strays, neglects your counsel, disobeys all that is said, his mouth spouting evil speech, punish him for all his talk . . .

Leadership

[22] If you are a man who leads, who controls the affairs of the many, seek out every beneficent deed, that your conduct may be blameless? Great is justice, lasting in effect, unchallenged

since the time of Osiris? One punishes the transgressor of laws, though the greedy overlooks this; Baseness may seize riches, yet crime never lands its wares; in the end it is justice that lasts, man says: "It is my father's ground."

[23] If you are mighty, gain respect through knowledge and through gentleness of speech. Don't command except as is fitting, he who provokes gets into trouble. Don't be haughty, lest you be humbled; don't be mute, lest you be chided. When you answer one who is fuming, avert your face, control yourself. The flame of the hot-heart sweeps across, he who steps gently, his path is paved. He who frets all day has no happy moment, he who's gay all day can't keep house.

[24] If you are a man who leads, listen calmly to the speech of one who pleads, don't stop him from purging his body of that which he planned to tell. A man in distress wants to pour out his heart more than that his case be won. About him who stops a plea one says: "Why does he reject it? "Not all one pleads for can be granted, but a good hearing soothes the heart.

[25] Punish firmly, chastise soundly, then repression of crime becomes an example; Punishment except for crime turns the complainer into an enemy.

Superiors

[26] If you are a man of worth who sits in his master's council, concentrate on excellence, your silence is better than chatter. Speak when you know you have a solution, it is the skilled who should speak in council; Speaking is harder than all other work, he who understands it makes it serve.

[27] Don't oppose a great man's action; don't vex the heart of one who is burdened;

[28] Bend your back to your superior, your overseer from the palace; then your house will endure in its wealth, your rewards in their right place. Wretched is he who opposes a superior, one lives as long as he is mild, and baring the arm does not hurt it.

Disputes

[29] If you meet a disputant in action, a powerful man, superior to you, fold your arms, bend your back, to flout him will not make him agree with you. Make little of the evil speech by not opposing him while he's in action; He will be called an ignoramus; your self-control will match his pile of words.

[30] If you meet a disputant in action who is your equal, on your level, you will make your worth exceed his by silence, while he is speaking evilly, there will be much talk by the hearers; your name will be good in the minds of the magistrates.

[31] If you meet a disputant in action, a poor man, not your equal, do not attack him because he is weak, and let him alone, he will confute himself. Do not answer him to relieve your heart, do not vent yourself against your opponent, wretched is he who injures a poor man, one will wish to do what you desire, you will beat him through the magistrates' reproof.

The Worth of Precept

[32] If you listen to my sayings, all your affairs will go forward; in their truth resides their value, their memory goes on in the speech of men, because of the worth of their precepts.

*****

Sa Ra Mentchu-hotep looked into the eyes of his son as he spoke, "Today we must practice intuitive discernment. As I lift my mind into the spirit, the winds of its glory cause me to behold the eternal and reveal its presence in our thoughts, words, and actions. As we meditate and pray, dive below the surface of your three-dimensional being into your nondimensional self to the intuitive consciousness where there is direct perception of truth. As you arrive at that place of alignment with the love and law of the universe, spiritual awareness will permeate your consciousness. You have traded in reliance on your natural human resources for reliance on the Spirit."

Sa Ra Mentchu-hotep walked along the Hapy Eteru with his son, the crown prince Mentchu-hotep. "My son, no matter what obstacles come your way as the Nswt Bety, you must maintain Ma'at!"

"I promise, Father. I will follow Ma'at and all the Ntchru of our homeland."

"Let me share a few words that Medjay Priest-Scientist Ka-en-Jhutyms shared with me from his father, the great Djedi Jhutyms Ka-en-Heru, who taught him, and I agree. Our enemies, the Asiatics of the east and west, including the Libyans and other invaders to our homeland, have taught us [1] that the only way to defeat your enemy's culture is by practicing your own; [2] to always promote your women as the standard of beauty; [3] to view everything from your perspective first; [4] to make a truce if you have a problem with your own kind so that all your attention is focused on the enemy or your problem; [5] to believe that you can end up at the top from any inferior position; and [6] to not forgive and forget if you are attacked by an enemy. A snake is a snake is a snake, and a log can stay in water for *renpt medju* [ten years] and never become a crocodile."

"Thank you, my father," said Prince Mentchu-hotep. "Dua Ntchr. I will remember these things and pass this wisdom down to my sons."

Mentchu-hotep stopped in his tracks and stared at his son for a few seconds, for he loved his son more than even his own life. The emotion was so strong even the prince could feel this love as they both embraced each other with a warm hug. After he regained his composure, he continued his father-son dialogue. "Maa Kheru gives us an innerstanding of the Ntchru and how they can empower our lives today and, in the future, my son.

"First, who and what are the Ntchru of ancient Kemet and Kash? The Ntchru are divine expressions of divinity, cosmic energies, or natural laws, which are powerful aspects of the one Creator's mind. These aspects explain existence as we know it or existence based on our limited perception of the cosmos.

"These Ntchru or natural laws that preside over all forms functions on a multitude of levels of reality. Some are visible and comprehensible. Some are not visible and are incomprehensible, and others are just beyond our comprehension at our present stage of consciousness.

"Because of the mysterious, essentially unknowable nature of the Ntchru, there are multiple layers of meanings attached to each Ntchru, as guided by the deep thought spiritual system of ancient Kemet and Kash. The greater our innerstanding of ourselves and our relationship to nature, the greater our innerstanding of the Ntchru of ancient Kemet and Kash."

"I think I innerstand this, Father. I have watched you my whole life, and I am ready. I am not a Medjay warrior like you, Father, but I am a spiritual warrior, ready to lead our people. Thank you for allowing me to rule the city of Abu. This has been a great experience."

"In the time capsule we call the tomb of my father, Nswt Intef Nakhtnebtepnefer, a host of Ntchru aids in his transformation and protection as a spiritual force traveling through time and space. I will only mention a few at this point: the Mesu Heru, the four sons of Heru—Emst, Hapy, Duamutef, and Gebsenuf. They guard the affairs of Asr-Intef and are the four heavenly spirits of the four Ntchru of the cardinal points of the Heru's vision.

"They define certain organs in the body's temple that if they are functioning on a high level, it will enhance the quality of life on earth and heaven, which is a deep-thought, philosophical concept of everywhere the spiritual mind can perceive. These specific Ntchru will enhance your personal powers, allowing greater harmonious alignment between the soul and the Divine Spirit. Creating Ma'at allows this energy to be true of voice or the vindicated one, representing Heru consciousness and a safe passage for your spiritual soul returning to the source of oneness, which is heaven.

"In this same time capsule of the Nswt Intef Nakhtnebtepnefer, each guardian spirit or Ntchru explains the nature of the healing and the protection and directs spiritual liberation. For example, Ast, Nebt Het, Neith, and Serkhet represent vibrations and numbers, which we call numerology, which can help us build our character, innerstand our weakness, so we can develop greater spiritual strengths. They represent colors called color therapy, which can sooth us and aid in our peace of mind so that healing can take place. These same colors penetrate the physical world and can be found in minerals and compound elements we call gemstones and crystals, and they have an amazing capacity to absorb, reflect, and radiate light in the form of intelligent fields of stable energy that increase the flow of vital life force within the human's physical, mental, and spiritual being. They can be worn for decoration, physical adornment, healing, protection, and spiritual ceremonies.

"This practice of using crystals for health and well-being is called crystal healing. I know you know this, my son. This is just a review. You will be sitting on the throne one day, and I want you to be prepared. I want you to be the captain of your ship! These same Ntchrw represent directions that align with the stars called Heru's vision [astrology], which can give us predictability of events so we can plan for success. These Ntchru represent certain plants and herbs in herbology, which acts as medicine that encourages healing, repairing, rebuilding, and strengthening the life force.

"They represent special smells, which can be duplicated in incense and oils used in aromatherapy. These smells can alter the consciousness of various life forces, creating a harmonious atmosphere, which leads to healing and/or Heru consciousness. These Ntchru also represent sounds through music or prayer. This is the power of the spoken word. This spiritual life force is a unit of physical fluidity, which penetrates everything and can affect everything.

"These are just a few examples of the power that awaits us through the innerstanding of the Ntchru of ancient Kemet and Kash. One of the keys is to know yourself. This is to know the Ntchru. We, as spiritual warriors and divine spiritual beings having a divine human experience, must use these energies and/or natural laws in our lives daily, like the rising and setting sun. The proper knowledge of the ancient Ntchru will bring forward the medicine in our modern lives for healing so that we can empower ourselves to resurrect ourselves, which prepares us to have vindicated souls, *Maa Kheru*."

"Father, you are so wise. I sit at your feet. I kneel before your greatness. If the Ntchru guides me to be one-half as powerful as you, Kemet will remain great. But for now, I promised Hmt Nswt Wrt Neferu I would take her to the market."

"Make sure a Medjay warrior is with you."

"Tiw, yes, Neb aa."

That evening, Sa Ra Mentchu-hotep sat in his favorite chair next to his desk in the royal palace in Waset. He could still remember when Neferu had this wing added to the royal palace. He pulled out a long piece of papyrus paper and a beautiful reed pen wrapped in gold and silver. Normally, a royal scribe would write for him as he dictated his ideas, but tonight, he wanted to write with his own hands. These notes would be for his wives, the healers, and he would dedicate it to the memory of Nswt Mwt Wrt Iah, his own divine mother, one of his greatest teachers. As he began to write, he could hear her voice, like she was standing next to him, dictating this letter.

"By enhancing your seven senses using the ancient Kmt science, you will begin to lay the foundation to awaken and activate your ancestral genetic code that is innately programmed to be in tune with the cosmic and terrestrial energies that are generated from the one creative intelligent source of all that is seen and unseen. Achieving this goal is the core of resurrecting, maintaining, and sustaining our culture based on Ma'at. Ma'at is truth, righteousness, reciprocity, harmonious balance, and unconditional love. We will focus on the seven senses. Although you have more, they are all part of the one consciousness. The seven senses that we are considering are sight, sound, smell, touch, taste, intuition, and will. These senses will be experienced through the five elements of spirit/ether, air, fire, water, and earth.

"Enhancing your seven senses is the key to moving yourself out of the intellectual, scholarly realm of our Kemet legacy and culture into the living light of existing in a higher state toward the way of our ancient Kash-Kemet black ancestors that our Remtch admire and praise in their lives, books, writings, or lectures. By applying this basic science, you can have the means to keep yourself and your elders in a healthy living state so that humanity can benefit from your greatness beyond the average seventy-plus earth years, with no major sickness, high blood pressure, obesity, tumors, cancer, poverty, depression, etc. Too often, the great minds of our country transition prematurely due to diseases. This matter of diseases is equal to disharmony, equal to self-inflicted war from misinformation, plus miseducation, plus ignorance from being a prisoner of one's own mind that was captured by its lower self.

"Like the Heru-em-Akhety, you are now ready to free yourself from your lower self. The *Heru-em-Akhety* means 'Heru in the double horizon.' It represents the principles of Heru, the hero that sustains Ma'at between the double horizons of sunrise and sunset by mastering his/her lower self [physical senses] through the five elements in nature. Daily, Heru rises to battle the density of matter of his/her lower consciousness to restore and maintain Ma'at from sunrise to sunset in all his/her endeavors. By enhancing your seven senses, you realize that it is *not* your so-called oppressor, *not* your hereditary disposition, *not* your traumatic life experiences, *not* your bad relationships. Rather, it's your mind's reality that you planted and nurtured consciously and unconsciously.

"If you are reading these words, then you already made a conscious decision to begin or continue freeing yourself to experience *Ankh* [life], *Udja* [prosperity], *Sneb* [health]—*neb* [all]. As the Great Medjay Djedi Jhutyms Ka-en-Heru would say, 'You are the one you have been waiting for.' The time is *now* to *stop* conversations about 'How our people need to . . .' or 'You know how our people are . . .' The time is *now* to *stop* invoking low vibrational tones that vibrate into the universe and come back to you and us to deal with each time your low vibrational tones are thought, felt, and spoken.

"Today, allow Jhuty, Seshat, and Ma'at [energies of articulate thought, word, and deed and vibrational tones aligning with cosmic and terrestrial energies for foundation of truth, reciprocity, and harmonious balance] to bring forth spiritual victory from the center of yourself, from the center of your consciousness, from the center of your being, which is the ultimate creative intelligence entity that has no name because the entity is *all*. I pray that we all innerstand that the ultimate revolution is within us. No matter how many dynamic leaders, organizations, or movements there may be. To sustain the greatness of anything means that the parts that make up the whole must be self-sustaining. In other words, sustainability 'meets the needs of the present without compromising the ability of future generations to meet their own needs.'

"Now let us begin to enhance your seven senses on a daily basis, from new moon to full moon, from season to season, from the rise of Hapy Eteru to the drop of Hapy Eteru, from year to year . . . then witness yourself and other new beings in the next decade radiating and activating the pulse of the highest organizing intelligence.

"We will apply two activities to assist you in realigning your seven senses within yourself to reflect your surrounding environment of your home, mode of transportation, office, etc. [any abode that one travels to or dwells in]. We will take on the ancient Kash-Kemet proverb 'As above, so below' to a new meaning.

"Hmt Nswt Wrt Iah, the sacred high priestess of Het Heru, would tell you, 'You will design your altar and your holistic medicine bag based on Kemety science—symptomatic thought—that which is fact and proven to work. These applications are foundational steps for those new to this area or are an opportunity to enhance and elevate for those already using these two activities that have become holistic, spiritual rituals in one's life. To begin, Ma'at must be the portal to transmit you. Be true to you. Be kind and take an inventory of yourself or have a trusted colleague, spiritualist, or holistic practitioner to do your reading, wellness assessment, Heru vision—astrology and/or numerology reading.

"'Holistic living was and remains the innate Kash-Kemet culture as taught by the great scribe and healer Imhotep and many of our great contemporary teachers. There was no separation. It was a way of life, and if you are to become the captain of your ship, it must be a part of your life also. Vegetarian meals were the dietary makeup of our Kemet-Kash ancestors before the decline of our high civilizations as influenced by Western and Eastern foreigners or unevolved souls.

"'Kash-Kemet science is a continuance of the universal science that began with the "all in all" Spirit, which is based in natural laws, which translates to one science expressed in different ways yet relates to a common paradigm that makes many the one. Some of these principles will be expounded on within the activities of creating an altar and holistic medicine bag. The altar will represent your five elements as described in the eight-pole star that shows the five elements and their correspondences that modern physical science is based.

"'Your medicine bag will be used to activate, enhance, maintain, and sustain your seven senses that are fused in your five elements. The medicine bag will be based using the Msw Heru [sons of Heru] and their protective mother energies called the Ntchrw Sa Mwtut. In both activities, the practitioner will experience the Kash-Kemet sciences of aromatherapy, astrology, astronomy, colorology, crystallology, herbology, geology, geomancy, numerology, planetology, and more.'"

*****

The path of life isn't a straight line; it's a spiral. You continually come back to things that you thought you understood and see deeper and deeper truths.

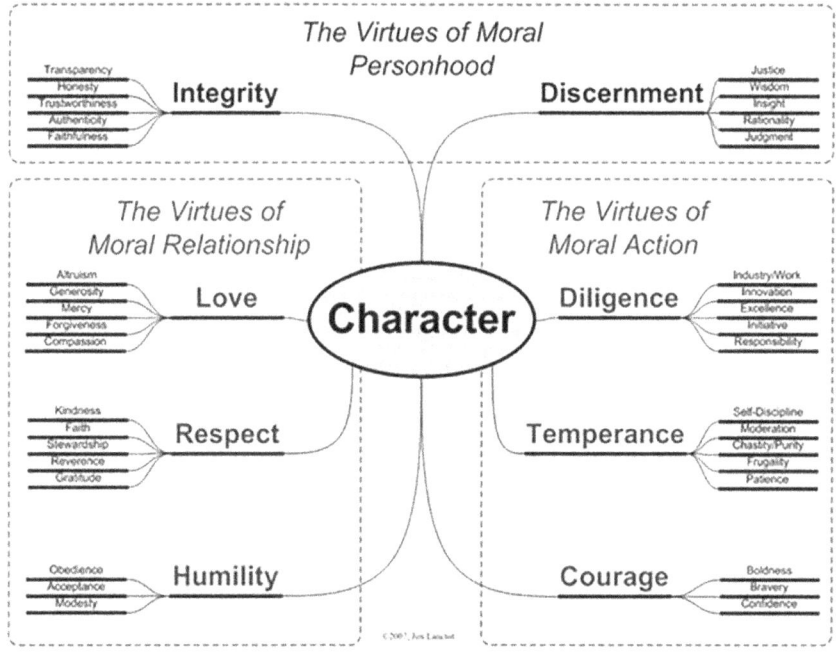

*****

The chief of security Medjay Priest-Scientist Akhtoy received a message from a Libyan messenger that Libyan forces were planning an attack on Kemet at Waset as a retaliation of the killing of Prince Kaneferre, and several of their best Libyan warriors and the Libyan king wanted to challenge Mentchu-hotep personally for killing his nephew Mayor Setyms. When Medjay Priest-Scientist Ka-en-Jhutyms heard this news, he told his brother who was head of security to give him three days before he told the Nswt Bety Mentchu-hotep but to have the troops ready for battle.

Priest-Scientist Ka-en-Jhutyms quickly gathered his Medjay medju unity together with the exception of the Nswt Bety Mentchu-hotep, and by nightfall, they had reached the Libyan borders of their capital city. "We must give them a message they will not forget for centuries, yet we should only kill when necessary. Let's attack their strength! We will enter the front gate and destroy there first unit of defense, then I will let them capture me. The rest of you will vanish and wait for me. When I am taken to the king, you know that is time to attack the king's palace."

They climbed the walls unnoticed in the night, killed all the guards one by one only using a blowgun, bow and arrow, and daggers. Then they waited till sunrise so they could see the lessons they were about to teach them. As the new unit came to replace the night guards, they saw them instead. Their commander yelled, "Sound the—" And he was dead with an arrow through his mouth, killing him instantly.

There were about thirty of them to nine Medjay. The Medjay quickly surrounded them to throw their defense off. Their arrows never missed. Within three minutes, it was nine versus nine. The Medjay backed them into one another, so their shields were useless. They killed eight and took all their heads off. The one remaining soldier was left to live, but he had to promise to let Priest-Scientist Ka-en-Jhutyms see the king with his message. Shaking all over with blood all over his body and face, he took Priest-Scientist Ka-en-Jhutyms in chains to a holding cell, while the Medjay medju vanished in broad daylight.

Once inside the holding cell, another Libyan office came with several dozen soldiers. "Why are you here, Medjay?"

"I have a message for your king from the king of kings, Nswt Bety Neb Khrw-Ra Sa Ra Mentchu-hotep."

"What is your message?" the Libyan asked.

"Why is the cell next to me full of only black men?"

"Is that your question, Medjay?"

"My message—it is only for the ears of your king."

"Very well, die in this holding cell, Medjay, along with your black friends!"

Medjay Ka-en-Jhutyms sat down on the floor and closed his eyes in meditation. When, with sincerity, you say yes to the still small voice speaking within, your soul force takes over and you step into your authentic identity as an individualized expression of the living spirit.

For two days, he did not eat or speak. Finally, on the third day, three dozen guards came. "Get up, Medjay. The king will see you now but only because you are a Medjay. He has never seen one in person. Chain his hands and feet and then tie them together. Pour water on him and clean him up for the king. We have heard about these mysterious powers of the Medjay, but you look like a regular black man to me."

A dozen soldiers surrounded the Medjay, with a dozen in front of him and a dozen behind him as they escorted him to the king's palace.

Six of the Medjay medju moved into position in front of the king's palace. Two Medjay, Medjay Bennu Henenu and Medjay Ni-Sobek, had killed and replaced two of the guards surrounding the Medjay prisoner as they entered the Libyan king's palace. Once inside the king's meeting room chamber, you could see fifty highly trained Libyan soldiers guarding the king.

Medjay Priest-Scientist Ka-en-Jhutyms smiled to himself when he saw how heavily guarded the king was. *The cosmic laughter of the Spirit bathes my soul in joy,* he thought. *I see with clear vision, and all that I do is from the pure joy of being. All these guards are meaningless to the Medjay.* The three dozen guards brought the Medjay before the king. The king's ambassador asked the Medjay to kneel down on his knees when talking or addressing the king. "I am a Medjay. We do not kneel down before any mortal man!"

"Guards, make him kneel down." Two guards on each side tried to pull him down, but Medjay Priest-Scientist Ka-en-Jhutyms did not move. Two more guards with poles tried to hit him behind the knees. The poles broke in half, but the Medjay did not move. They tried to pull the chains from his ankles to buckle his legs, but again, he did not move.

The Libyan general walked up to Medjay Ka-en-Jhutyms and looked him in the eyes. "Is this worth losing your legs and dying for, Medjay?" the general said.

"I have a message for your king from the king of kings, Sa Ra Mentchu-hotep," replied the Medjay, as he stood toe to toe and eye to eye with the general.

The general tried to spit in the Medjay's face, but the quick reflexes of the Medjay moved just in time with the spit, landing on one of his own officer's face. "You talk pretty tough for a man in chains," said the general.

"How about now!" he said as the Medjay broke the chains from his hands and feet and snatched the general's throat out before the general could blink an eye. The king stood up from his chair in shock and amazement, and the three Medjay were in front of him. The king reached for his sword, and Medjay Ka-en-Jhutyms took it out of his hand and pushed the king back down in his chair. "You wanted to see the power of the Medjay king. Well, your wish is about to come true. Watch."

About twenty or more arrows targeted the three Medjay, and they blocked them all. The other two Medjay, Medjay Bennu Henenu and Medjay Ni-Sobek, went to work by destroying the king's guards and soldiers. They have two circles around them with dead bodies on top of one another. The two Medjay were catching arrows in midair and slicing people up at the same time. The two Medjay were sweeping and twirling in the air, untouched, like some kind of invincible fighting machine from another world.

The Libyan king was in shock as he watched two Medjay take out a whole room full of Libyan soldiers. "What kind of fighting is this—spinning and kicking with your feet, flying and swirling in the air?" said the king. When there were only two dozen soldiers left, the palace front door busted open, and six more Medjay came in. The remaining two dozen guards threw down their weapons and surrendered to the Medjay.

"Now, King, you know that the legend of the Medjay is real before you die!" And with one swing with the king's own golden sword, the king's head, crown and all, fell to the floor. The nine Medjay walked through the center of the town, with the king's head and sword visible in their hands. A small group of priests followed them to the front gate. Medjay Priest-Scientist Ka-en-Jhutyms spoke to them, "Free all the black slaves in your cells, men and women, and bring them here now. Also, any black servants in your households!"

One of the high priests of the Tchhnu yelled out, "Go free the black slaves and servants and bring them here quickly!"

Within the hour, maybe two hundred or more black men, women, and children were brought to the front gate. Even a dozen or so blacks who were part of the Tchhnu army took off their armors and joined the Medjay. Medjay Priest-Scientist Ka-en-Jhutyms spoke to them again, "Spend your time and energy rebuilding your country and appointing strong but smart leaders. Do not enter Kemet looking for revenge, or your whole nation will be destroyed and your seeds will be annihilated forever."

*****

Nswt Bety Neb Khrw-Ra Sa Ra Mentchu-hotep had just dressed in his war outfit after hearing about the threat of a Libyan invasion. His three wives and son entered his royal chamber with the Medjay medju. Hmt Nswt Wrt Neferu said, "You look great, my Neb aa."

His proud son came over to hug him, "You are the best father a son could ever wish for, and I kneel at your feet."

His other two wives, Hmt Nswt Tem and Kawit, kissed both his hands as they knelt before him.

Sa Ra Mentchu-hotep looked around the room. "What's going on? Why is everyone so happy when we are about to go to war?"

Medjay Priest-Scientist Ka-en-Jhutyms placed a sack with the Libyan king's head in front of the Nswt's feet, and he also placed his crown next to the sack. And then Medjay Priest-Scientist Akhtoy laid the Libyan king's sword next to Mentchu-hotep's feet also. Medjay Priest-Scientist Medjay Bennu Henenu and Medjay Ni-Sobek stepped forward. "This is how we protect our Nswt Bety of Kemet, Sema Tawy, and Ta Merry. We have liberated over 250 men, women, and children from bondage in Libya."

Sa Ra Mentchu-hotep looked at his family as he spoke, "The supreme awareness, the intimately felt presence bring with it a rapture beyond joy, a knowledge beyond reason, a sensation more intense than that of life itself." Shemsu Heru Sa Ra Mentchu-hotep looked at his divine family, and he thought for a moment before he spoke, "I know and know that I know that the unconditional, divine love of the Spirit is the incomparable grace of my life. I consecrate myself to the purpose of my being and dedicate my thoughts, words, and actions to the Spirit. I am a clear, pure channel of its expression, knowing Kemet is in not good but great leadership.

"I can feel the unconditional mrr [love] in this room, and I know it is a divine gift expressed by mind, speech, and knowledge, the same way we mrr Ntchr. Mind, so that we may approach Ntchr. Speech, so that we may speak to Ntchr. Knowledge, so that we may experience Ntchr. I can see your light, and in your light, there is salvation because we all are sharing in the light of the Ntchr and our mrr fills us with the oneness of Ntchr."

"*Yit e Ntchr aa* [my father, the great Ntchr] Shemsu Heru Nswt Bety Neb Khrw-Ra Sa Ra Mentchu-hotep, let us go downstairs. There are thousands of Kemetyu waiting for you to address them."

When Sa Ra Mentchu-hotep walked on the front stage in front of a crowd of ten-thousand-plus Kemetyu, he was choked for words. His son was asked to lead Qbhw (libation). At first, he was surprised, then he said with pride, *"Tiw sa e."* (Yes, my son.)

After they all gave praise to the Ntchru and greeted one another, the royal prince Mentchu-hotep stood before a sacred altar for Amen-Ra. He was carrying a very fancy bowl of water made of gold and silver with the shape of a ram's head, with a small tree inside a planter with the face of Het Heru on it. He stepped forward with his left leg and his left hand open in the Ma'at posture and then closed his eyes and began the libation. They followed each of his postures.

ROYAL PRINCE MENTCHU-HOTEP: In the name of the Nswt of the Ntchru Amen-Ra, the hidden one, the almighty force, the Ntchr of breath and life. Great Amen-Ra, who was self-produced at the beginning of time, self-existent, almighty, and eternal, which created all the Ntchru and gave form to all things. Amen, you are the unseen and unseeable creative force that is spirit and all thoughts. Ra, you are the Ntchr of light and victory, of protection, and of immeasurable power. You are the seen force of the universe, manifested by the sun. Ra, you are the energy that allows light to shine. You are Kheper in the morning, Ra at noon, and Atum—the complete one—in the evening. As Amen-Ra, you have no equal. You are the sun that keeps us warm and the spirit that offers us life. You mark the cycle of day and night, months and years, centuries and millennia. You are eternal. We ask Amen-Ra to be with us, to strengthen us, and to give us vision for a great Kemet future.

RESPONSE, *as the royal prince poured water into the tree*: Dwa!

ROYAL PRINCE MENTCHU-HOTEP, *his left leg still remaining forward, his hands rising in the Ka posture, and the people following him*: In the name of the great Ntchru, the cosmic and celestial Ntchru, that aid Amen-Ra in the maintenance and general operation of the universe. These Ntchru are laws and principles of creation and act as the managers of all existence for all life known and unknown. In the name of the Duat Ntchru, they represent the intermediate plane. These Ntchru are realms of light that are responsible for transformation between the spiritual and the physical material worlds, and to the terrestrial Ntchru, they represent nature and the natural functions of things on our planet. We ask these Ntchru to be with us, to strengthen us, and to give us vision for a great Kemet future.

RESPONSE, *as the royal prince poured water into the tree*: Dwa!

ROYAL PRINCE MENTCHU-HOTEP, *only his left hand rising in the air, with his right hand across his chest but the left foot still remaining forward, and the people following him*: In the name of the first great Remtch (original humans), who began the march of humanity and civilization; who were guided by Jhuty, Ma'at, and Seshat; and who came out of the womb of the mother of creation—Mwt, Het Heru, Sekhmet. We ask the great mother Ntchru, mistress of the universal feminist energies to be with us, to strengthen us, and to give us vision for a great Kemet future.

RESPONSE, *as the royal prince poured water into the tree*: Dwa!

ROYAL PRINCE MENTCHU-HOTEP, *kneeling down on one knee, his right knee, with his left hand up and right hand across the chest, and the people following him*: In the name of the first great Remtch leaders who began the march of humanity and civilization—Asar, Aset, and Heru—and to the Khemmennu Ntchru.

The Khemmennu Ntchru were eight deities who were the bases of the Kemet's creation myth during our second golden age. They were primarily worshipped in Khemmennu, but their aspects of the creation were combined in other areas with existing stories. Each one is a member of a masculine-feminine pair, and each pair represents an aspect of the primordial chaos out of which the world was created. They all came into being at the same time. Nun and Nanuet represent the primordial seas that which was inert and motion, which is energy. Kuk and Kuket represent the infinite darkness and light. Hu and Huhet represent empty space—infinity and finite. Amen and Amenunet represent quintessence or the secret powers of creation—the hidden and revealed.

The Ntchru Khemmennu at Khemmennu was led by Jhuty. In the name of the great triad of Waset, Amen, Mwt, and Khensu; to the great triad in Kash, Khnum, Anuket, and Satet; to the great triad in the north, Ptah, Sekhmet, and Nefer-Atum; and to the great triad of the south here in Waset, Asr, Ast, and Heru, we ask these Ntchru to be with us, to strengthen us, and to give us vision for a great Kemet future.

RESPONSE, *as the royal prince poured water into the tree*: Dwa!

ROYAL PRINCE MENTCHU-HOTEP, *now kneeling on both knees with his hands crossed like Asr, and the people following him*: In the name of the first great Remtch and Kemetyu leaders who began civilization in the Hapy Valley, establishing their high culture and building their temples, great monuments, pyramids, and tombs to the Ntchru and great human spirits, we ask these great Remtch and Kemetyu, like Imhotep and Ptah-hotep and the best of our ancestors' great spirits, to be with us, to strengthen us, and to give us vision for a great Kemet future.

RESPONSE, *as the royal prince poured water into the tree*: Dwa!

ROYAL PRINCE MENTCHU-HOTEP, *bending his head forward, touching his forehead to the ground, with both knees bending in prayer, and the people following him*: In the name of Shemsu Heru who came from the south to Kemet; from Kash, Ta-Sety, Punt, Ta Khuy, Ta Ntchr; from the three Mountains of the Moon; and from beyond where the Heru Bess dwells, who guided and taught the Shemsu Heru here in Kemet—like Heru Narmer, Heru Aha, Heru Djer, Heru Djet, Heru Den, Heru Anedjib, Heru Semerkhet, Heru Qa'a, Heru Hotepsekhemwy, Heru NebRa, Heru Nynetchr, Heru Set-peribsen, Heru Khasekhemwy, Heru Sanakhte, Heru Netchrikhet, Heru Sekhemkhet, Heru Khaba, Heru Huni, Heru Snefru, Heru Khufu, Heru DjedefRa, Heru KhafRa, Heru MenkauRa, Heru Shepseskaf, Heru Userkaf, Heru SahuRa, Heru NeferifkaRa, Heru ShepseskaRa, Heru NeferefRa, Heru NiuserRa, Heru Menkauheru, Heru DjedkaRa, Heru Unas, Heru Teti, Heru Pepy, Heru MerenRa, Heru Pepy NeferkaRa, Heru WadjkaRa, Heru MeryibRa, Heru MerykaRa, Heru KaneferRa, Heru QakaRa, Heru NebkauRa, and our beloved Heru Sehertawy-Sa Ra Intef—we ask these great Shemsu Heru to be with us, to strengthen us, and to give us vision for a great Kemet future.

R<small>ESPONSE</small>, *as he poured the last of the water from the bowl into the tree*: Dwa! Dwa! Dwaaaaaaaaaa!

The crowd gave out a loud and powerful response of joy as Shemsu Heru Sa Ra Mentchu-hotep hugged his son. He then looked over to Djedi Jhutyms Ka-en-Heru, Vizier Dagi, Vizier Ipi, then his wives, and the Medjay medju. He knew that they felt what he felt at that moment. He turned to the crowd as he cleared his voice. "Dua Ntchr," the royal ruler of Kemet spoke to his people. "My soul honors your souls. I honor a place within you where the whole universe resides. I honor light, love, truth, beauty, and peace within you because they are also within me. In seeing these things, we are united. We are the same. We are one."

The crowd cheered, "Dua Ntchr!"

Shemsu Heru Sa Ra Mentchu-hotep continued, "Authentic gratitude is a way of life for the Medjay, and I offer it to you. When you wake up in the morning, let your first thought be one of thanksgiving that you have another day to walk in the love of Ntchr. As you go through your day, see the giver behind all the gifts freely being given to you. At night, train your last thoughts before sleep to be one of thanksgiving for the miracle of knowing Ntchr, whose pleasure it is to give you Ankh." Shemsu Heru Sa Ra Mentchu-hotep knelt before his divine Kemetyu family. "Dua Ntchr."

Mentchu-hotep, founder of the second golden age of Ancient Kemet

Mentchu-hotep wearing the red crown (*Deshret*) on the
left and the white crown (*Hdjet*) on the right

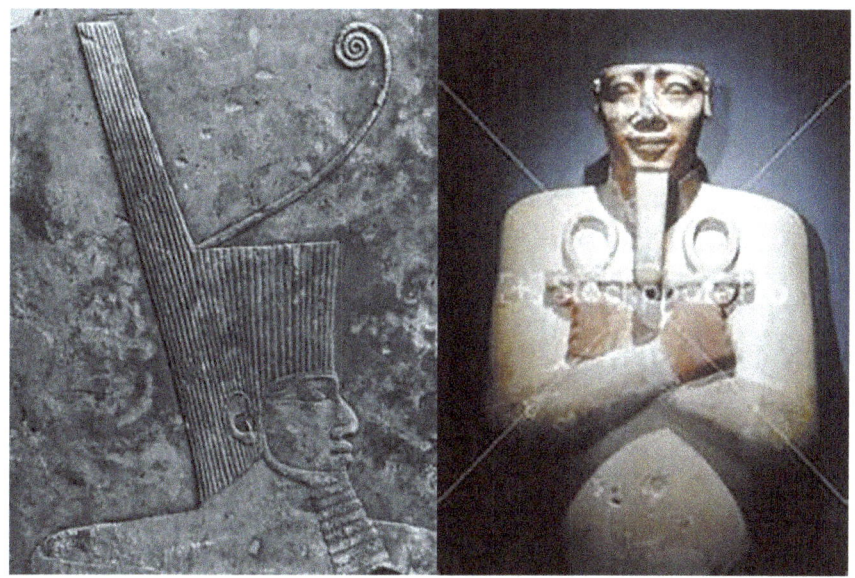

All the *above* images are of Nswt Bety Neb
Khrw-Ra Sa Ra Mentchu-hotep.

The representations around the sarcophagus of Kawit on
the next page were meant to perpetuate activities of a princess

of the palace. Her sarcophagus was one of the most noteworthy in terms of the bas-relief sculpture in the Waset court. Here, we find a new provincial style liberated from the constraints of the old register divisions. On the side of the Sahu's head, there is a palace facade with the central doors decorated with Udjat eyes to permit the deceased to communicate with the world of the living. Kawit is busy with her personal hygiene, seated on a high-back armchair, drinking milk with one hand while the other hand holds a mirror. One of her servants arranges the locks of her mistress's head with dainty fingers. On the other side, Kawit is sniffing a bouquet of blue lotus blossom while her servant offers her an unguent vessel and fans her. The elongated bodies and the beautiful Afrakan facial features reflect the Waset ideal of feminine beauty during the second golden age.

Hmt Nswt Kawit, wife of Mentchu-hotep II, founder of the middle period. The second golden age is the center object in all three friezes.

The End